THE
INNER
MALE

THE INNER MALE

OVERCOMING ROADBLOCKS TO INTIMACY

HERB GOLDBERG, Ph.D.

NAL BOOKS

NEW AMERICAN LIBRARY

NEW YORK AND SCARBOROUGH, ONTARIO

For information address New American Library

Published simultaneously in Canada by The New American Library of
Canada Limited

 NAL BOOKS TRADEMARK REG. U.S. PAT. OFF. AND FOREIGN COUNTRIES
REGISTERED TRADEMARK—MARCA REGISTRADA
HECHO EN HARRISONBURG, VA., U.S.A.

SIGNET, SIGNET CLASSIC, MENTOR, ONYX,
PLUME, MERIDIAN and NAL BOOKS are published
in the United States by NAL PENGUIN INC.,
1633 Broadway New York, New York 10019
in Canada by The New American Library of
Canada Limited,
81 Mack Avenue, Scarborough, Ontario M1L 1M8

Library of Congress Cataloging-in-Publication Data

Goldberg, Herb, 1937-
    The inner male.
    1. Men—United States—Psychology. 2. Men—
United States—Attitudes. 3. Interpersonal relations.
4. Sex role. I. Title.
HQ1090.3.G65   1987   155.6'32   87-15247
ISBN 0-453-00560-8

Designed by Leonard Telesca

First Printing, November, 1987

1   2   3   4   5   6   7   8   9

PRINTED IN THE UNITED STATES OF AMERICA

ACKNOWLEDGMENTS

I would like to express my sincere gratitude to Kevin Mulroy, senior editor at NAL, for his invaluable input and careful attention to this book.

Anita Rosenfield brought a keen sense of thoroughness, intelligence, and unlimited patience to the typing and organizing of the manuscript.

Finally, my appreciation goes to Francis Greenburger, who has been my literary agent for the last ten years and who has placed this book and my three previous ones with sensitivity and wisdom.

CONTENTS

PREFACE

The original *Hazards of Being Male* was a child of the seventies, a relatively innocent period for those of us who believed that opening up about the inner experiences of men and women could significantly improve and transform both the male/female relationship and the separate experiences of both.

Some things were clearly accomplished. For men, the option of behaving in less traditional ways has increased. At the same time, however, new pressures are pushing men to move back into traditional role-playing behavior, and the price for moving too far beyond society's expectations for men is still great. Nevertheless, the men who have the self-awareness, commitment, and capability to be more fully expressive will today find acceptance and support.

The depth and quality of many men's lives have also been improved. Men can now make fathering a priority and can become involved in a relationship with a woman and expect that she will share many of the responsibilities that were traditionally a man's, just as men have learned to share in women's traditional areas of responsibility. The desire and hunger that men have for friendship and closeness with one another can be played out more fully now without the automatic assumption that warmth and caring between men equals homosexuality. Men's sexual behavior also can be more authentic and relaxed today. There is less pressure and apology, although the anxiety around sexual performance for most men is still very great. The expression of emotion by men is something the culture is more supportive of today. Options for men engaging in gentler sorts of sports and physical activities and more self-caring ways of dealing with themselves physically (by paying attention to diet or rejecting alcohol and cigarettes) are also in place. Overall, there is a new social atmosphere that makes it more possible for men to let go of ritualistic macho behavior patterns that are self-destructive.

While these externals have changed, however, many other aspects of the male experience seem to have become more confused, distressing, and hazardous than they were before. Many men, and women as well, are lost in brand-new ways as the boundaries and rules of relationships are less defined and the struggle to connect between men and women is greater. The expectations of fulfillment and depth that were supposed to have become part of the liberated male/female relationship have, by and large, not materialized, and the "joys" of a nonsexist equality have a hollow ring. This is frustrating, particularly for the many who have worked so hard to achieve such an ideal. The current reality is that relationship experiences today often prove to be more brittle, self-conscious, and defensive than the traditional relationships they have replaced. Many who confused attitude change and reaction with growth and real change wound up in a maze of disillusionment regarding the hypocrisy they thought they saw in everybody except themselves.

Many men striving for their personal liberation have discovered that if they bought into the new definitions and expectations of liberation, it backfired. The admiring words they received from many women and men proved to be primarily lip service. At the end they felt more isolated, disillusioned, and disconnected than ever.

Sexual liberation has given way to sexual anxiety over diseases, and the emergence of a new sexual conservatism.

Many of the gurus or "wise men" of the East who were

supposed to create a new enlightenment proved instead to be crafty manipulators and exploiters of Western people's anxiety, confusion, craving for release from pain and isolation, and desire for a higher consciousness that would bring them inner peace. The idealistic religions, communes, and cults that were to model a new way evolved, more often than not, into paranoid, power-oriented, totalitarian environments that made the mainstream corporate world seem benign and innocently humanistic in comparison.

The failures of change have left many painful new questions and distressing dilemmas. Finding the middle zone between traditional rigidities and a new consciousness has become an elusive task for the many people who innocently thought they could blend the best of the old and the new.

In retrospect, defining the nature of relationship problems was simpler before. The issues and the "enemies" were more clearly defined. The solutions and proper direction seemed more clear. Women needed economic, sexual, and personal liberation, while men simply needed to overcome sexist ways and develop their intimate, sensitive side. Then, we thought, everything would start to work out and a new world would be created.

We continue to live with many illusions of progress. The *content* of much of our society, on a surface level, clearly suggests a greater freedom and loosening of role behavior. But the undercurrent in many instances has also become more polarized than ever, as suggested by the continuing tension between the sexes and the desperation for bonding and developing good relationships. Poorly understood elements are producing more suicides earlier in life; serious addictions to drugs; and a general sense of disconnection and confusion about life.

Unfortunately, in an attempt to combat the tensions, there are many signs of regression. Backward trends are emerging everywhere. There are subtle as well as direct pressures on men and women to go back to traditional role playing. A nostalgia for something that never was now pulls at us.

Unconsciously, gender process, I believe, is a missing key ingredient in the understanding and transformation of the experience of life and is the major concern of this book. In the past decades, issues of gender have been unfortunately misunderstood, trivialized, and politicized. Simply changing attitudes and externals, with no attention to the psychological undertow or deeper elements, has put us on the verge of overlooking a powerful tool for understanding and changing the human experience.

This book will attempt, with greater psychological emphasis, to recognize and explore the manifestations of what I call the "gender unconscious," as well as the conscious aspects of gender conditioning that continue to shape our experience.

Where liberation movements have failed us, they have done so because many of their responses, feminism first and then the weaker male liberation movement after, were composed primarily of defensive reactions that were by-products of the gender conditioning. So many of the liberation polemics were surface rumblings, and unconscious expressions and symptoms of deeper gender polarization and the "gender unconscious."

The ramifications of this "gender unconscious," I believe, are enormous. The unconscious defenses of masculinity and femininity create our awareness of ourselves, polarize the life experience of the sexes, and drive us relentlessly in the name of our gender identities into out-of-control, self-destructive behavior. As a result, we continue to be seduced and dazzled by a multitude of illusions that we spend a lifetime pursuing and never reach. These mirages we then pass on to our young, suggesting to them that *they* can achieve something that we never could.

Let this book be a step toward saying that the gender undercurrents by which we are pulled along are powerful, complex, and immense. Great efforts are needed to recognize, analyze, and change them. To understand the gender undertow is to comprehend the powerful defensive nature of our conditioning, and to harness that is equivalent in a sense to the task and potential of harnessing nuclear energy. Gender undertow is the enormous power of our psyches operating invisibly and powerfully, based on the gender conditioning that creates much of the way we see ourselves as men and women.

It is, further, the purpose of this book to deal with matters that are less apparent than those that existed in the recent decades, to attempt to unravel the deeper and more subtle dilemmas, paradoxes, and "blind spots" our conditioning creates. This book seeks to narrow the gap between what seems to be, what we learn to expect, what ought to be, and what I believe actually is going on underneath psychologically.

Herb Goldberg
Los Angeles
April 1987

AUTHOR'S NOTE

In all of the case histories cited, the author has used fictitious names and described traits not identifiable as those of any particular person or persons.

THE
INNER
MALE

PART ONE

WITH WOMEN

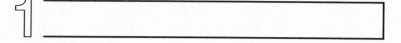

"IF YOU MEET THE MAGIC LADY...": THE SAGA OF THE WOUNDED BIRD

A "Magic Lady" Fantasy

She fixed you with an intimate gaze that cut right down to the deepest layer of your hunger, opening up a floodgate of need and desire that lay masked behind your independent and self-protective facade. The flash you experienced was instant, powerful, and transfixing. There you were, adrenaline racing and your being and vision of life altered dramatically. You felt softer and more open. The world seemed like a warm and hopeful place for the first time in a long time.

For her, you thought, it would be worth returning to a world of people you had been keeping at an emotional arm's length. You could even see yourself giving up some of your coveted freedom for her. You found your "magic lady" and you were ready to rejoin the human race. It felt good to be a person and "alive" again, and *her* magic had made that possible.

Later that evening, you moved toward her, tremblingly touching her body. With no resistance at all, she welcomed you, fully and repeatedly. And while making love, she told you, "It's so wonderful to feel you inside of me. Please stay there forever."

Lovemaking felt like a spiritual experience. She was an altar and you were worshipping her. What was sometimes difficult with other women seemed so easy with her. All of your resistances disappeared. You felt as if you could remain with her forever. Her taste and her smell were beautiful to you. Sex had never been like this, and the words "I love you"—words that had always stuck in your throat before— came pouring out, over and over again. "God, I'm glad I found you," you heard yourself saying.

Lying in each other's arms the next morning, she fantasized what it would be like to have your baby. "What a perfect child it would be," she said. In the past, hearing that would have made you feel suspicious and manipulated, and you would have withdrawn. But from her it was exciting, because you felt she was incapable of ulterior motives. She was fantasizing, *not* making demands or building expectations, and you liked that.

You were living out the great love poems. The music you heard in her voice, the depth, honesty, and sensitivity you believed you saw in her perceptions, and her "untypical" quality excited you.

She told you, "You're wonderful and one of the most beautiful and sensitive men I ever met. Stay yourself—just the way you are. I don't want you to change a thing, because everything about you is perfect."

She said she expected that there were other women in your life but it didn't matter. She envied their good fortune in being involved with you, but felt no jealousy. "You don't have to tell me about any of it, unless you want me to know." Those words made you feel exhilarated and safe at the same time. You realized, though, that you no longer had any interest in those other women.

With no effort she had broken down defenses and barriers you had built up over years and that all the other women you had been with complained and lectured you about. With her, the walls crumbled and she didn't even have to try. It seemed to you she had seen and brought out the "real you" for the very first time. The cynical you melted and the vulnerable man inside that had been waiting in cautious hope for such a perfect woman—the "magic lady"— to appear, seemed to emerge, fully, and fearlessly.

For you to risk becoming "human," it had to be something as magical as this. Other people had been forever telling you that you had been chasing a fantasy, waiting for the "magic lady" to arrive. Your rational mind heard them, but your deeper emotional self never let go of the belief that she did exist. And now, finally, your faith was affirmed.

You wanted to be there for her, strong and protective, giving her everything, though she never asked for anything. It made you a little crazy even, wanting to give to her so badly, when she didn't seem to expect this. No promises, no shoulds, no jealousies. Just you and her enjoying each other fully when you were together was all she said she wanted.

She had laid total claim to your consciousness. The communication between the two of you seemed unbelievable, as if you could read each other's minds and anticipate each other's words and feelings. She seemed to remember everything about you and bombarded you with her love and positive feelings about life.

You could think of little else when she wasn't with you. You carried out your life's business only with the greatest effort. She filled and obsessed your thoughts, crowding everything else out. You, who never allowed yourself to be vulnerable and really "need" anybody, were addicted and very "hungry."

A trouble sign! The first clear one. You were starting to need her "too much." When you first met her, you both discussed loving and letting be. You agreed there would be no possessiveness, no smothering or jealousy. You shared a similar philosophy of relationships and what made them go bad.

You were suddenly haunted by a combination of strange, uncomfortable feelings and a sense of unreality. "This is too good to be true, and it either isn't happening or it will disappear."

You were fighting yourself about your feelings. You found yourself craving her presence *every moment*. You tried to control those growing, insecure cravings. But you couldn't fool yourself about the pain you felt inside, wondering where she was and what she was doing when she wasn't with you.

You wanted to know about other men, a behavior quite unlike you, but you hoped she'd say that there were none—certainly no one important. She didn't say that, however. The first time you asked her in anxious, insecure, and jealous tones about the previous evening when she wasn't with you, you felt the mood between you become strained. You backed off and acted as if that was not what you meant to ask at all. Inwardly, you scolded yourself for being a spoiler of a beautiful experience.

Even though she had told you she loved you, your heart raced with fear each time you'd telephone her and she didn't answer. Where was she? Had she found someone else? Maybe she didn't love you anymore. You dialed every ten minutes. Each hour that passed until you reached her felt like a week.

Perhaps when she met you, she told you there was somebody else, or others, and you said that was fine. Now old-fashioned ideas like commitment and fidelity were entering your thoughts but not hers. You could tell that she felt your "pressure," the little boy hunger coming out, the urgency to be with her and the fear that she was enjoying somebody else, and it clearly bothered her. Her answers to your questions were vague and there were uncomfortable pauses and signs of an impatience and irritation you hadn't seen in her before.

You were off-balance, developing strategies of what to say or do, and when. You were beginning to lose your cherished "spontaneity." In moments of great insecurity, you would talk to her about wanting her to spend more time with you and whether she loved anyone else as much as she loved you. She'd answer coldly, "Nobody owns me. You're going to ruin everything by pressuring me like this."

She reminded you that she had told you that there should be no expectations in love and that she couldn't predict what was going to happen. You tried backing off and detaching, but it seemed impossible. You'd soon find yourself closing in again, pouting, and asking her for commitments, even though you knew it was the worst thing you could do. But you couldn't help yourself. You couldn't seem to get enough distance to gain perspective, because it felt too painful and scary to back away. And at the same time, you couldn't stay this close because it was killing the relationship.

Your insecurity grew. You started expecting her to end it all at any time. You would telephone and sense her voice not being as welcoming as it used to be. She denied that when you asked her and told you it was *you* who was changing, not her.

You constantly wanted her to say "I love you." You craved the reassurance she gave so readily before, when you didn't seem to need it. Now you hungered for it, but it wasn't forthcoming. If you asked her directly, "Do you love me?" her answer seemed evasive and lacking in passion. She spoke of friendship.

When other men were around, you noticed that she sometimes gave them the same kind of intimate look that she gave you when you first met her. You saw other men being drawn to her as you had been. It was making you crazy with jealousy and anxiety, even though she claimed she was not being flirtatious, just being naturally herself.

You would question her, "Do you find him sexually attractive?" She would answer evasively, "I think he's interesting, but that's all." You pushed some more: "Would you sleep with him?" Her answer: "Is that all you ever think about?" That would end the conversation.

Obsessed with trying to understand and clarify, all you wanted to talk about around her was "our relationship," something you had hated doing in past relationships. As your needs and hunger emerged and began to drive her away, you became desperately depressed and panic-stricken. As she backed off, you ran toward her with accelerating speed.

Feeling as if you were pressuring her, occasionally she became cold, hateful, and even vicious in self-protection. The face of the relationship was forever altered and impaired, and the perfect love and communication that launched it were replaced by an atmosphere in which communication now seemed impossible.

By the time the relationship ended, she had become distant and you had become filled with a sense of hopelessness about ever again finding love. The ride down was filled with as much excruciating pain as the trip up was filled with wonderful feelings.

You had started off the relationship feeling strong, beautiful, and loved. At the end, you were behaving like a whining, pathetic dog. You had become everything you hated. You were checking up on her behind her back and talking to everybody and anybody who knew her for "input" to enlighten you about where you stood.

You tried to understand, but she seemed impossible to figure out. She didn't resemble any other woman you had ever met. She had no guilt, no hang-ups, no needs, and no fears of the future, it seemed. There was no way you could move her—or manipulate her. While she had seemed like a fragile bird whom you wanted to protect, she was really much tougher than you.

By now, the power balance had shifted and there were no "right and wrong" things left to say or do. Her exquisite sensitivity to your every response had turned into indifference, a seemingly constant misreading of your motives and an inability to recognize or respond to your pain. She just felt crowded by you and resented it. When you would get angry at her, she never would get angry back. She seemed so much in control, it made you feel that you couldn't affect her at all. The communication that once was so easy and positive had become confusing and ugly. The relationship with the "Magic Lady" ended as suddenly and totally as it had begun.

As relationships between men and women become more fragile and the conscious as well as unconscious resistances between the sexes increase, while the need to bond is still powerful, there is an increasing tendency for men, as well as women, to be vulnerable to the romantic fantasy of a "magical partner."

Romance is a way that men and women give themselves a holiday from their unconscious resistance toward each other—long enough to create a fantasy state that allows for an intense merging. The need for and vulnerability to romance exists in proportion to this underlying resistance to the opposite sex. The experience of "magical" feelings is an extreme expression of counter-reaction to this resistance. Specifically, the greater this resistance and the repressed fear, anger, and conflict toward the opposite sex that constitute it, the greater the need for the magic of romance to create a safety zone for bonding.

The romantic is seeking an intensity of feeling that is not possible in the world of real relationships. He or she is defensively "addicted"—and the mind-altering drug that permits connection to take place is the romantic feeling. Since the need for it is in equal proportion to opposing deeper or unconscious feelings, romantic relationships are characteristically volatile and end with a disappointment and rage that matches the "magical" feelings of loving euphoria that are there at the beginning.

The Dynamics

Extreme romantics often turn out to fear and hate the opposite sex. These feelings are manifested by a need to endow the object of their love with "magical" attributes, such as "She's unlike anybody else of her sex" ("which is why I can allow myself to love her"). A "nonmagical" person of the opposite sex would be too dangerous and flawed.

In moments of casual, spontaneous discussion, romantics often betray their deeper feelings—for example, "Women are manipulators," "Women can't be trusted," or even, "Women are parasites." The female romantic betrays her unconscious fear and resistance to the opposite sex by never initiating conversations with men she doesn't know. She fears men as a sex. She acts aloof and guarded, even at social events. Though she craves a meeting with "Prince Charming," the reality of men overall frightens and angers her. She learned early, "Men just want to use women," "Men are liars," "Men are selfish," and, of course, "Men cannot be trusted."

The powerful unconscious anger and resistance toward men that lie within the feminine woman were manifested full-blown in the beginning of feminism. Men were described with the ugliest epithets imaginable: "Men are rapists," "Men are pigs," and "Men are oppressors of women and want to control and demean them."

Ironically, those who unconsciously resent, manipulate, and use the opposite sex most often masquerade as the great lovers and are able to seduce and "get their way" with the opposite sex the most easily. The "Don Juan" syndrome of the male seducer who is an unconscious hater of women is an example of this.

The female equivalent of "Don Juan" is what I call the

"magic lady." In this time of the breaking down of male/ female bonding, where relationships are fragile and endings are sudden, and where "real women" seem to have become as threatening to many men as "real men" previously have been to women, the "magic lady" has become a powerful and seductive fantasy experience for many men. Indeed, one "magic lady" can wreak havoc in the lives of countless men who are in need of this fantasy for release from their loneliness and for the comfort and reassurance that her "special perfection" temporarily seems to offer.

The "Don Juan" can seduce women away from their husbands and cause them to behave in ways they had never dreamed they would. Likewise, "magic ladies" get men away from their wives, and self-protective bachelors out from behind their barriers, causing them to do things they ordinarily never would. Men and women alike may even become totally immoral, willing to give up their cherished values, beliefs, and ethics when involved with their "magic man" or "magic lady." The "magic lady" brings out the most destructive macho, competitive aspects of the male, just as "Don Juan" brings out the extreme in self-denial, masochism, and desperate yearning in women.

Specifically, for a brief time, the "magic lady" seems to be the ultimate male fantasy, a beautiful woman who adores him, wants nothing from him, and allows him to feel safe and in total control. Her presence reassures him that *he really is* an incredible man and has finally found *his* "incredible woman," who really knows how to love him. The "magic lady" accomplishes this by seemingly giving herself to him, while putting none of the usual female pressures on him for commitment or the proving of anything. She is a magical woman: adoring but unneeding; loving but independent; sexual but with no strings or pressures. In his eyes, she is perfect. To add icing to the cake, she seems also to be a "man's woman," so that a man can be himself around her: say what he wants and feels without monitoring his language or thoughts, because she "truly" understands and loves him for *exactly* who he is. Too good to be true—and indeed, it is.

As a therapist, I have worked for years with many men in the throes of a magic fantasy; the signs and indications are generally the same. The most vulnerable to this fantasy are the men who are the most defensive, closed off, controlling, successfully manipulative and self-protective, when it comes to relating to women. These enclosed men had the most threatening early experiences around women— smothering, guilt-inducing, unconsciously hostile and manipulative mothers. The men had built great walls to protect themselves, tending to hone in instantly on flaws in the women they met, to keep them at a distance.

They have the biggest masculine egos because mother had tied them to her and they were never able to break away. In reaction and denial, there developed a compulsion to prove their manliness and release their anger by seducing and controlling women.

Instead of relating, they learned to manipulate women to get what they wanted while maintaining a safe distance. Theirs was an unconscious strategy of hit and run, and they did so regularly and successfully, turning women over in detached fashion until they met the "magic lady." In her, they met their match, their emotional counterpart.

The "Magic Lady" Is a Wounded Bird

Veronica was a "magic lady," abandoned by her father at age three. She had three more fathers before she was seventeen, one of whom physically abused her mother. During this period of time, Veronica had also been badly beaten by one of the men her mother dated. She was raped soon after moving to Los Angeles on her own from her home in Ohio.

By the time Ron met her, Veronica had become an exquisite manipulator of men, so much so that Ron was convinced that Veronica was a very spiritual person who was not interested in him for material things. This required an extreme suspension of his reality because he was spending a fortune on her to make her happy, all while she protested that he didn't have to.

Furthermore, he saw her as weak and fragile, and yet she totally controlled him and the rhythm of the relationship. Engulfed by his fantasies of Veronica, Ron was unable to see through even her most blatant manipulations. Specifically, one weekend she left for Palm Springs with an old boyfriend of hers, slept in the same bed with him, and insisted to Ron that it was all platonic. He believed her.

When he spoke of her it was in euphoric terms. He described her beautiful almond eyes, her feminine ways, her great sense of humor, and her ability to get any man to do anything for her without trying because she was "so wonderful." He never saw her as the manipulative, angry, calculating, and cold person she actually was until she left him right after he lost his job as the result of an automobile accident that prevented him from driving. First she was simply slow to return his phone calls, but soon after he never heard from her again. Yet he continued to feel that he had lost the best woman he'd ever been with and he mourned his loss for well over a year.

Angela was a "magic lady" also. Though a high school dropout, she could excite even the most highly educated of men. If you were a doctor, she would look at your medical texts with total fascination. If you were an attorney, she would listen in rapt attention as you recounted your legal exploits. She would ask to come to the courtroom to watch you perform and gaze at you adoringly. She would act like a playful child, teasing and making otherwise compulsive, driven, serious, and professional "uptight" men act childlike and uninhibited. She could be the sexy femme fatale or the wise, understanding woman or the compassionate, healing mother.

In pursuing her man, she was full of energy: attentive, wide-awake, and focused. Later on, however, after the chase was successfully completed, she became withdrawn, disinterested, and tired.

In my years of practice, whenever I see a man I suspect is involved with a "magic lady," I ask him if he knows anything about her early experiences with men when she was a child. Consistently they tell me that her background is filled with abuse, rejection, or neglect by the men in her mother's and her early life. She is either the product of a traumatically broken home or she was overtly abused, physically and/or sexually. Like her mother, she needed men for survival but hated and feared them at the same time. This was true of Angela, whose alcoholic father left the family when she was three. She had no memories of him. She had, however, learned at a young age to be the perfect, exquisite manipulator of men, being exactly what they wanted her to be, in order to feel safely in control.

The "magic lady" is a survivor and a jungle fighter. She learns to "tame the beast" by filling the needs of macho men's boundless egos instantly and totally, thereby making herself totally irresistible and powerful, an addictive drug, creating "ego-euphoria." Initially she gives him everything he wants, while seeming to put no pressure on him for commitments or marriage. He believes he has found it all in this woman, and his masculine egocentrism and defensiveness prevent him from seeing that this is impossible.

The "magic lady's" exquisite sensitivities to male needs were unconsciously designed to placate, disarm, and control the feared and hated male: they are coupled with her own search for the "perfect father" to compensate for her early trauma. She can only continue her outpouring of "love" so long as the man maintains the macho image of perfection he initially projected; he cannot betray his hunger, need, or dependency, which will put pressure on her and make him too real.

For the "magic lady," just as for her male counterpart, a safe partner is one you can love from an extreme distance. The guarded, isolated man that "magic ladies" thrive on also appears to her to be "perfect" in the beginning, cloaked behind charming, effective, and smoothly "macho" social skills. In her eyes, he becomes the longed-for "perfect father." She wins him over through complete adoration and love bombardment, which seduces him into believing he can expose his deeper self. However, when he does, and also begins to want to possess and control her, her self-protective mechanisms begin to go into operation. She does not want a "real man" to be close and she starts pushing him away. Her deeper rage toward men begins to emerge and she seeks to hurt and destroy him in retaliation for her early pain.

The "magic lady" is a wounded bird who has learned all the sounds of love without the feelings and is paying men back for all the hurts of her past. Just as the "magic lady" is a wounded bird, the man prone to seek her out has also been wounded or damaged by the opposite sex and has an equivalent terror of a real woman based on his early experiences. There are many such "wounded men" today; thus there are many men vulnerable to the fantasy of the "magic lady." These are men with no tolerance for "real" women.

"Magic ladies" are often also seemingly perfect "earth mothers"; an extreme of traditional women, who learn to manipulate men out of unconscious fear, need, and anger. To accomplish this they submerge their identity and take on the man's style, rhythm, likes, and dislikes. Femininity teaches women to mold themselves to a man's identity. The "magic lady" is an extreme example of that form of behavior.

The "magic lady" fantasy denies the hard work of real

male/female relationships and is a symbol of "macho" men's fear of personal connection. The "magic lady" is the ultimate, exciting, disconnected fantasy—a "relationship" with no relationship and no effort. She is the perfect combination with the "damaged man," who also can handle only the images or fantasy of closeness and not the reality.

Therefore, the "magic lady" has much to teach men about themselves. She does to them what they have so often done to other women. She uses and controls men the way men often do with women. In the "magic lady" a man may find the reflection of his deeper self because she turns out to be a mirror image of who he really is with women.

The "Magic Lady" Fantasy: Progression and Warning Signs

1. The relationship begins with a soulful, penetrating look, and you are instantly galvanized. You feel taken over by a "magical force."
2. You want to take her away and isolate her from others. You talk to her for hours and hours and pour your heart out as you never have before.
3. You seem to read each other's minds. She makes you feel like you've never made love before. You feel renewed and reborn.
4. Intimacy comes in a lightning flash and with no resistance or conflict. Nevertheless you find yourself desperately wanting to please her. Unlike your usual self, you are excessively accommodating to her and want to show off to her.
5. You felt empty before you met her, and you feel even emptier once you've found her when she's not around.
6. She describes her early background as a young girl and it is filled with trauma in regard to men. Perhaps

she's from a divorced home or was abandoned by her father at a very early age or her mother had a series of lovers or husbands.

7. Contrary to your usual style, you become very jealous and protective around her. You lose your usual cynical sense of humor about women and life and relationships. You become "deep," "serious," and "sensitive."

8. She seems extraordinarily independent and unneeding. She never asks for anything and puts no pressure on you.

9. She confirms your best fantasies about yourself—that you're beautiful and brilliant. Yet she is not possessive. You can even talk to her about other women who have been in your life, and she shows no jealousy. She makes you feel you could go to bed with others and it wouldn't matter to her.

10. She seems completely free of "hang-ups"—spontaneous and totally into the present, free of the usual inhibitions, guilt making, and need for reassurance that you associate with women.

11. Sex with her is "fantastic," the best you can ever remember having. She seems totally comfortable and playful with her sexuality, and there is nothing she won't do.

12. She may tell you that there is another man, or men, in her life and secretly you are very jealous, but you deny the feelings.

13. You are constantly trying to prove yourself and perform in front of her, in order to please her.

14. Even though her past history and the realities of her life suggest that you have nothing in common and that this is a mismatch, you "magically" believe that everything that came before in your lives is irrelevant.

15. The "magic lady" melts right into your world. She "loves" your friends and family. She seems to get

along perfectly with your parents. If you're married when you meet, she doesn't expect or pressure you to leave your wife.

16. You rationalize the negatives and you strain to believe her, even when what she is saying defies possibility.

17. She drives you crazy with her freedom. She is often vague about where she's been, what she's been doing, and with whom. Progressively, you realize you can't count on anything. She is totally present-oriented and into expressing her impulses and desires for pleasure spontaneously. At first this is very exciting, but it begins to make you angry and you start to see her as irresponsible.

18. The relationship is an emotional roller coaster ride and your feelings bounce from "She loves me so much and she's never going to leave me" to "It's all over and I'm never going to see her again" over short periods of time.

19. Ordinarily, you are a man who needs distance, yet you find yourself wanting to be with her all the time. It's an unquenchable desire you have, a craving that never gets filled.

20. Other women don't seem to like her very much. When you question why she doesn't have female friends, she tells you that she finds most women boring.

21. While you are ordinarily critical of women, you are unable to hang on to any negative perceptions of her. It seems impossible to remain angry at her, even when she does things that are blatantly hurtful and irresponsible. Readily you believe her explanations about why she failed to return phone calls or showed up hours late. In fact, she has a knack for turning the tables and making *you* feel guilty for confronting her and therefore being "uptight."

22. Other men often are attracted to her. She seems to invite that, even though she denies it. You sense there is something wrong but you can't quite put your finger on it. You believe her when she denies that the looks she gives to other men are seductive, but your gut tells you that she knows full well what she is doing.

23. You seek reassurance of her love. You want to talk to her about the relationship constantly. Contrary to you, she seems very relaxed about it. She is able to go for long periods of time without seeing you, without it bothering her. Whereas you constantly feel you need contact with her, she doesn't. She has taken total control. She is in command and you have become the insecure, "powerless" clinger.

2

WHY MEN AND WOMEN CAN'T TALK TO EACH OTHER: THE HIDDEN UNCONSCIOUS MESSAGES OF GENDER

A Polarized Dialogue

SHE: You're so closed up.

HE: You can't stop. Nothing is ever enough for you.

SHE: I feel like you never really want me around . . .

HE: You're *always* there.

SHE: But we're not close. You're so cold.

HE: I don't know what you mean.

SHE: You're impossible to talk to.

HE: Because you're not rational.

SHE: You don't *really* understand anything, even though you think you do.

HE: Give me specifics.

SHE: If you don't know what I mean, I can't tell you.

HE: If you don't like how it's going, change it.

SHE: I can't change our relationship by myself.

HE: I like my life the way it is.

SHE: You think you like your life, but you don't have friends. Nobody ever calls you.

HE: You never get enough of people. You're *always* on the phone.

SHE: Don't change the subject. You really don't trust anybody.

HE: You're naive. You live in "La La Land."

SHE: You're always on guard; you're always living in the future.

HE: Because of that, *you* can ignore reality.

SHE: You're paranoid about life and about money.

HE: You don't understand money.

SHE: Money isn't everything. What good is it if you can't even relate to your own children.

HE: You never let go of the children. You're a mother hen who doesn't know the eggs have hatched.

SHE: How can you say that? You don't even know who I am.

HE: And you don't understand me.

SHE: I look at you, and I know that you're never happy. Nothing makes you happy.

HE: What's happy?

SHE: Why do you always respond cynically?

HE: That's your perception. I'm not doing that.

SHE: There's never any praise—only criticism.

HE: I feel totally unappreciated by you, too.

SHE: With other people you laugh and joke. With me it's always negative.

HE: Because I can't be myself with you.

SHE: You're never even around; you're always working.

HE: *I'm* always working because *you're* always shopping.

SHE: You always have an answer.

HE: I just do my best. I can't be everything to everybody all the time.

SHE: I'm frustrated.

HE: Go have an affair!

SHE: That's your stock answer. Cut and run!

HE: There *you* go again—always generalizing.

SHE: God, you're like a computer.

HE: What's wrong with being rational and competent?

SHE: I'm every bit as competent as you are, I'm just not a machine.

HE: When will you stop trying to change me?

SHE: When you stop putting me down.

HE: You think it's been easy for me? I've been through hell!

SHE: You don't know how good you have it. You're going to throw away the one good relationship you have. No other woman will put up with you.

HE: What's a good relationship anyway? It sounds to me like psychobabble. If we break up, I don't want another woman.

SHE: Sure, you'd last about two weeks.

The Myth of Communicating

One of the cherished psychological illusions that has emerged powerfully in the last twenty years is that men and women talking to each other about their feelings and "sharing" their inner experience would be the answer to the problems that plague male/female relationships. Taking time to listen and hear each other supposedly would heal the rift between the sexes.

The polarized defensiveness created by the gender unconscious literally nullifies the capacity to accurately hear and nondefensively experience what the opposite sex is saying. The degree and intensity of this impossibility and inevitable breakdown in man/woman communications is directly in proportion to the degree of the masculine/feminine polarization. Thus, the seemingly perfect couple often is the one that will be most tortured by their frustration and repeated failures at communication.

What makes this phenomenon so distressing is that it appears at the beginning of a relationship that the communication between the young romantic couple is total. "We don't even have to talk; we just understand each other perfectly," is often what they think and tell each other.

The problems created by the gender undertow emerge as these two people begin to "hook in" and their deeper defensive selves intertwine. Minor spats become major fights. Working things out becomes increasingly more difficult. Finally, it becomes *impossible.* At the end, all that remains are the many buttons that are continually being pushed in this now poisoned interaction. If the relationship is not rebalanced through the breaking down of the masculine and feminine defenses, the desperate attempts to find a bridge fail, and all that is left is to begin anew elsewhere.

What is this gender undertow that poisons what seemed initially to be an idyllic interaction? Typically, the unconscious messages of feminine defensiveness are as follows:

1. *Talk to me—open yourself up because I want to be close:* But don't expose anything that is weak or needy and threatens my sense of security.
2. *Share your feelings with me:* But don't tell me anything that I don't want to hear, such as that you are angry or bored or want to be with someone else or that you disapprove of something. That would make me feel anxious and attacked.
3. *Be strong and dominant so I can fantasize your perfection and strength and the you I want to believe exists:* But I will feel frustrated, distanced, and insecure when you don't open yourself up to me emotionally and make yourself vulnerable.
4. *Give me your support and reassurance:* But only when and how I want it. Otherwise, I will feel controlled by you and feel I'm being treated like a child.
5. *I want to make you happy and I will do what you want:*

But I'll resent you for being "selfish" and for not caring who I am and what I want when I accommodate you.

6. *I need to be independent of you and assertive:* But this will make me feel frightened you won't like that and will reject me, so I will retreat to my feminine-manipulative approach.

The unconscious messages of masculine defensiveness are as follows:

1. *Leave me alone. Otherwise I feel intruded on and engulfed:* But don't go away. I'm afraid to be alone. I need the contact even if I don't want to interact.

2. *Learn to take care of yourself so I don't have to feel responsible and guilty:* But need me, because it makes me feel secure, reassures me you won't leave, and makes me feel "like a man."

3. *Be real. When you are phony (which I suspect you are much of the time) I see through it and distrust you. You become just one more person whom I don't really trust:* But don't be real about what you're feeling and thinking, because that would threaten the way I need to see myself and this relationship.

4. *Don't talk to me, because I've heard it all before. I already know what you are going to say because you repeat yourself all the time:* But I want to know what you want and what you think, even if I get irritated by your "irrational" communication.

On the surface, overall, her messages *seem to be positive* ("open up and be close"), while his messages *seem to be negative* ("leave me alone"). Below the obvious, however, both are giving off equally alienating messages that are also "crazy-making" because they are seductively inviting and yet rejecting at the same time.

Each begins to feel as if the other is driving them crazy and there is no way to win. He says, "If I open up, she acts wounded and attacked; but if I'm quiet and tactful, she says I'm a closed book, guarded and uncaring." In turn, she responds, "If I leave him alone and go off and do something without him, he gets jealous or moody; but when I stay with him, he just ignores me."

When he gets angry, her feminine fears of anger cause her to feel frightened, as if it's the beginning of the end of the relationship. She rushed in to "heal the wounds" and make everything "right." Then she ends up feeling second-rate and powerless and believes she is unlovable because he could never *really* love a woman who is frightened and allows herself to be controlled. Part of her actually *wants* him to leave so that she can regain her lost power, yet she is frightened of that prospect too.

If she becomes too independent and sure of herself, his defensively isolated self is threatened with loss of its ballast against complete isolation, and he moves closer to her, wooing her back to dependence so that he can back away again.

The sincere and dedicated efforts of many couples to communicate, in recent years, demonstrate that unless the relationship is relatively free of polarization, talking and listening are not enough. Until then it was believed that if men and women could only be open and honest, listen to each other and hear what the other person was saying without being defensive, men and women would finally be able to get close.

"Without being defensive" is often a naive notion. To many, it means that "I'm listening without attacking or getting angry, without putting you down or criticizing you." That doesn't change the fact, however, that the reason men and women "get in trouble" with each other in the first place is that their polarized conditioning literally puts them in different worlds. They have polarized frames of reference and experience the same phenomena in opposing ways.

Consequently their experience of the relationship is different. Each partner gives different meanings to his or her own inner experience and perceptions and to the events of the outer world. They even give different interpretations to the very words they toss back and forth between them. For example, when they are having an argument and he's trying to be rational, she feels he's being cold and rejecting. When she expresses her feelings, he accuses her of being irrational and manipulating him.

When they talk about "intimacy," it means something other to him than it does to her. A good relationship means the freedom to be left alone while they are together, without feeling guilty. To her it means achieving a fantasy of deep, intertwined closeness, a melting together that he couldn't possibly be capable of.

The end result is that she feels herself to be in great pain over being distanced by him; he is tense and raw over feeling pursued and pressured for a closeness he can't give. In his psyche, she is *everywhere* (even when she isn't there) and threatening to engulf him. In hers, he is *never really there.*

She tends to see the world in terms of relating, compassion, and caring. She seems, by her words and thinking, to perceive the world more positively than he; and if she can't always see it as nice, she always knows that it *could* be or *should* be if certain things were done differently or given priority (mainly by him).

He sees the world more in terms of its dangerous side; the place where you have to watch out for yourself in order to survive and not be foolish enough to think someone else is going to do it for you or care if you're okay.

I'm reminded of a couple who sat in my waiting room before a therapy session. When I came to bring them into my office, I noticed he was reading a book called *Winning Through Intimidation,* while she was reading a book by her spiritual guru called *Giggle Your Way Through Life.* Though they were both strong and career-minded people, their consciousness of life was polarized.

Particularly under conditions of stress, when the deeper self emerges most clearly, she has a strong tendency to want to get close, and he tends to withdraw. She will tell him that sex makes her feel too vulnerable. He doesn't understand that, because sex doesn't make him feel vulnerable at all. Commitment and closeness make him feel that way and she can't understand that. To her, the idea of commitment is comforting and necessary, just as successful sex is for him.

Unless this deeper, inner experience of men and women somehow comes together so that they begin to experience life similarly, they really can't hear each other no matter how clearly they speak or how patiently they listen to each other. Because of the gender unconscious, the two sexes, psychologically, live in two entirely different worlds. Therefore, the relationship process creates the problem and that same relationship process stands in the way of resolving problems when they arise.

Milton is a very traditional man. He had a back problem and had to lie in bed and be passive. He started getting angry and attacking Victoria, his wife, because he was feeling unmanly lying there helpless. He was becoming frustrated and started blaming her, finding imperfections in her, accusing her of living off him. He began telling her that if things didn't work out, she could go back and live at home with her parents.

Victoria was getting double messages from him all the time. He was very dependent on her, but didn't really want to make contact with her or be close in the way she needed. He was basically a loner and preferred being by himself, yet he always wanted her around. The unspoken message he gave her was, "Come be with me all the time, but don't be dependent on me. Be here but leave me alone—and let me control you."

He had distrustful feelings about her in terms of his business and his success. He saw her as helpless and incompetent, and therefore he didn't trust her in helping him. Yet he believed that the moment they divorced or he died and she inherited everything, she would be more than capable of taking care of the business. However, she would only get going if he were not around.

He felt she only acted helpless and, indeed, he may have been right. But her "pretending" was unconscious. She "froze" when he was around: partly out of fear of his criticism, partly out of anger over being controlled by him, partly because she knew he didn't really want her to be productive and independent because it would threaten her need and her tie to him, and partly because of her own unconscious anxiety over being independent and powerful and thereby losing her femininity and lovability. He wanted to let go but was afraid to do so, but he blamed *her* for not taking hold and being stronger, even though he would never give up control.

Victoria felt exhausted from what she perceived as him pushing her down. The message she heard was, "You're not doing this right—you're not doing anything right."

She felt she was at her best when she was working apart from him, but then she would begin to feel anxious and fearful of abandonment. She kept checking back to make sure he was not going to reject her if she got too involved in her own activities. "I'm constantly turning back to see if what I'm doing is okay with my husband," she said.

She reacted to him instead of acting on her own. Inevitably she began to feel angry, controlled, and manipulated, which she was partially *allowing* him to do out of her own fear and then blaming him for it. Her *own* process was creating her anger.

She rationalized, "I can't make the decisions because I don't make the money. I don't feel I have the right to spend any money without his approval." Periodically, though, she got angry with him because she felt that he controlled her with money. She went on, "I haven't taken hold of my feelings yet to say, 'This is mine. I can feel free to do what I want.' I don't feel free to do what I want. In my gut, I still don't feel like I can do something that he might not like."

She was afraid of doing *anything* that might lead to his disapproval, but that same craving for reassurance caused her to become enraged at him because she didn't feel that she could express anything that was really her around him. She felt depressed and exhausted by the constant conflict in her—the alternation of clinging to him and hating him.

Her husband exaggerated her unproductivity. His masculine undertow caused him to see her as much less productive than she really was because he was so compulsively do- and goal-oriented. In his eyes, therefore, her opposing style made her seem lazy and unrealistic, which intensified his compulsivity; he felt he had to compensate for her "childlike," "unrealistic" behavior. He blamed her for his compulsions, causing him to be angry at her. Repeatedly he told her, "I'm responsible for everything, and I don't want to be, but I just can't trust you to do anything right when the chips are down."

She would reply, "You're wrong, try me!" But he wouldn't risk it. Instead, he became angry because he "couldn't count on her for anything."

Victoria exaggerated her husband's power over her. Often she would say, "I'm afraid of him for this. I'm afraid of him for that." But the reality was that he had almost no power over her and was actually *very* dependent on her and was terrified of losing her. Her perception of him as powerful and potentially dangerous was largely a distortion. He was more like a little boy with her. He was constantly looking for her approval, but she "refused" to acknowledge that. It served her unconscious purposes to see him as overpowering because it allowed her to blame him and to feel victimized and criticized, which she said was "the cause" that she couldn't get going.

Each had distorted perceptions of the other's messages, yet each was fearful of change. She was the one who undermined her power, not he. She was afraid to take power because her deeper conditioning made it as threatening for her to do so as his conditioning made it fearsome for him to be powerless. But she couldn't acknowledge that, so she blamed him instead. By seeing him as having more power than he really had, she could blame him for her fears and resistance to taking power herself.

By seeing her as irresponsible, he could avoid giving up power, which is what he was really afraid of. He could blame her for being "weak and stupid and incapable," which she wasn't, and which he would find out only after they broke up.

It is the polarized gender unconscious that creates the inability to truly communicate with each other, the same polarization that brought two people so powerfully together initially, in an explosion of romantic bonding. The more this polarization exists, the more unable they are to hear each other no matter how much they try. The process of polarization begins to destroy the "wonderful" content of their relationship as they sink into a morass of mutual blaming and recrimination as extreme as their "perfect communication" at the beginning.

How Communication Can Make Things Worse

Men and women may attempt to bridge this gap with communication techniques and great efforts to "listen" and "communicate." They may have terrific discussions and each might say at the end, "I really understand you now." But when they move back to spontaneous, moment-to-moment interaction and unpremeditated, uncontrolled, deeper responses, they get into difficulty again. Each feels increasingly misunderstood, disappointed, and hopeless about ever *really* communicating. Blaming each other for ill will, hypocrisy, or insincerity, they come to feel betrayed by the other when what was going on was unintentional. The process that created this pain was on temporary hold during their discussion—not transformed, but on hold. When they started interacting spontaneously, the problems reappeared in full force.

A man might say something his partner perceived as critical; though he thought he was trying to be helpful and constructive, they go right back to square one. Or perhaps he was involved in work and she came along wanting to initiate affection. She thought she was being loving and taking responsibility, but he perceived it as deliberately intrusive, a pressure, her not being able to leave him alone for even five minutes.

The couple is in perhaps worse trouble because they thought they had "gotten somewhere" and "made some progress." They had false expectations that caused the disappointments to impact even harder. In some ways, talking about it actually made the problem worse because of the fantasies of change it created. In the past, when couples didn't even bother to try to communicate their deeper feelings, they didn't expect to be understood. With contemporary couples, where one or both have been taught and believe that talking about their problems is the answer, the discussions are open, aware, and caring, and give each of them great hope of things improving significantly. However, because the deeper unconscious process between them remains unchanged, they are repeatedly disillusioned. They feel ground down by constant frustration and often end up saying, "This is hopeless; we've talked about it a million times. I thought you understood me and I find out you don't understand me at all. All of our conversations haven't made any difference."

They are correct. So long as their deeper experience of the same encounter is polarized, talking about it is hopeless. Unfortunately, they began to feel like failures and they blame each other instead of seeing how they are victims of an "invisible" defensive process—the same one that brought them together originally in a romantic explosion.

In polarized relationships, ultimately it is futile, even damaging, to talk about the problem and "share feelings." Talking about it, at best, becomes a consoling ritual that says, "We're trying." The degree to which anger and rage will ignite is directly connected to the unknowing ways in which men and women are polarized.

The "Why" of Defensive Overreaction

Harold and Rebecca are a religious couple in their middle to late thirties. He came in for therapy because he had recurrent fantasies of suicide and had also been partially impotent with her the entire marriage. Eventually she came into therapy with him and it was evident that their interaction was completely polarized. Rebecca felt totally victimized by Harold, accusing him of being egocentric, selfish, hostile, critical, insensitive, and unaffectionate, though she said she loved him very much.

He felt guilty and self-hating. He was always trying to be perfect and had a series of hobbies and part-time preoccupations that were all designed to confirm for both of them his brightness and his brilliance. He had schemes for making money or great inventions. He was trying continually to come up with answers to the great issues of the world, such as pollution, overpopulation, nuclear disarmament.

Rebecca was the classic good girl—"nice" or wanting everything to be "nice." However, barely two minutes into a session they were at each other's throats. She accused, he explained. The rage rapidly escalated to the point where she vacillated between trying to pull out her own hair and wanting to pound on him. Meanwhile, he was retreating from contact or trying continually to calm her down and reassure her.

It didn't matter what issue they talked about, whether it was her feeling he was spending too much money on his hobbies, that he didn't spend enough time at home eating dinner with the family and involving himself with the children, or that he was not making love to her the way he should. They would attempt to talk about the *content* of these issues, but because their process was polarized, there was no way for them to hear each other without a rapid escalation of rage in her and guilty explanations from him.

An additional factor in this case was that he had had a brief affair and Rebecca had found out. She would not let go of her sense of betrayal and victimization over this even though it had happened twelve years before and was, in great measure, an outgrowth of his insecurity about his sexuality because he had not been able to perform well with her. She, however, would use this affair as a weapon to justify her constant outpourings of rage and aggression, while he continually sought to make things up to her. He was fearful of leaving her also because he knew she controlled the children and would turn them against him, and he felt helpless to change that.

She would be constantly disappointed in him. They would go to church and he would hug another man. She would call him a homosexual. She criticized him for the way he talked to the kids. While she was very seductive with other men at parties and at church she was unable to see and acknowledge this. Instead she focused on his infidelity and "flirtatiousness."

Because they were so polarized unconsciously, no matter what the topic and no matter how hard they tried, the rage over feeling victimized in her and the guilt, anger, and tendency to withdraw on his part continued.

Men's and women's oversensitivity to one another, as with Harold and Rebecca, is a major key to understanding the communication impasse between the sexes. Putting the polarized defenses of each sex in perspective is crucial to finding one's way out of the dilemma.

An example is the honeymoon couple holding hands. He lets go of her hand because she won't let go of his. She reacts. "You don't want to hold my hand. You must be angry at me or getting bored and you're not enjoying this anymore. You don't really feel good about being with me anymore, do you?" Consequently he finds himself continually trying to prove to her that that's not so and that he's not rejecting her just because he temporarily stopped holding hands with her.

The tension creates a pressure inside of him to be constantly sensitive to the fact that he might unknowingly do something that might make her feel rejected. The polarization is in progress. Her craving for emotional reassurance that they are close is actually bottomless and causes him to pull inward even more, even as he tries overtly to reassure her. She senses his withdrawal and that causes her to intensify her pursuit of "reassurance" and "love."

He might get upset when she says, "I don't want to have sex tonight. I'm sore and tired and we already had it this morning and three times yesterday." He reacts with hurt feelings and the thought that she must not love him as much as he thought. On matters of sex, he overreacts to *any* negative response on her part.

She winds up feeling she has to accommodate him sexually whether she is in the mood or not, and the stage is set for her growing feeling of anger about being used and exploited as a sex object, particularly because she feels his sexual desire is not connected to an equal feeling of wanting the kind of closeness that she craves. He is drained by what he feels is her pressure on him to prove that he really loves her and wants to be close.

The sexual realm is a good example of one where women often find they don't know how to say to a man what they want because anything they say might be experienced by him as criticism. Inevitably, she explains, "I'm just trying to tell you what I want." However, he retorts defensively, "What you are really saying is that I'm inadequate." He cannot hear her because of his bottomless masculine defensiveness and the resulting need to be perfect.

She reacts defensively to his sexuality because her repressed sexuality ("Sex is only good when you're feeling close") causes her to perceive him as sexually driven even as she indirectly demands him to be sexually driven for the power it gives her over him and the permission it gives her to be sexual herself. At the same time, she fears an absence of sexual desire in him because to her it means rejection and abandonment, since sex is one of her areas of getting the power she can't take directly.

If she doesn't accommodate him sexually, she fears he'll reject her and leave. So she gives in but becomes nonorgasmic because she's angry. She fears sexual abandon in herself because sex is her control over him, and so long as her desires are inhibited, she has a source of great power over him. Sexually, she needs always to monitor and be self-conscious to maintain that control, which prevents her from having the unselfconscious involvement required for orgasm.

If she makes a suggestion and he doesn't go along with it for some reason (e.g., she says, "Let's go eat in *this* restaurant," and he says, "Let's go eat in *that* restaurant") because of her struggle to assert herself, she interprets his response as an attack and his way of discounting her wishes.

She overreacts to decisions by him because of her repressed assertion. Readily, she feels that he is *always* trying to control her whenever he states a belief or desire. At the same time, if *he* doesn't decide, it creates a decision-making vacuum because she won't or "can't." His "taking charge" makes her feel secure and gives her what she needs on one level, even as she comes to hate him for it on another level because it makes her feel like a nobody. At the same time, he overreacts to her lack of assertion ("I don't know where you're coming from. I never know what you want. You don't *ever* take a clear position.") even as his need for control demands her accommodation and compliance. On a deeper level, he comes to feel angry because he is "always made to feel responsible and guilty" when things go wrong. He becomes bored also, because of an absence of separate input.

He avoids any spontaneous personal involvement that doesn't have a goal or purpose or doesn't approach him slowly. He experiences it as a pressure, as loss of control, a demand to be involved. If he withdraws to regain his balance, she perceives this as a rejection. So he feels pressured to have to reassure her constantly that he's not rejecting her.

She feels pressured to have to withhold her desire to talk, be close, to cuddle and to kiss, while he has to hide his desire to withdraw and be by himself. They both have defensive reactions to each other's behavior. *Eventually, she takes the slightest negative comment or behavior as if it were a massive attack and responds in kind while he, in turn, takes the slightest desire on her part to spend time together, to talk, to be close, and experiences it as a demand or pressure on him, or a complaint about his adequacy as a partner.*

Repressed anger causes her to overreact to his displays of anger as if he had destroyed her with the slightest negative comment or irritation, even when it has nothing to do with her. Also, it causes him to perceive *himself* as more powerful and hostile than he really is. Her overreaction to him affirms his tendency to believe the worst about himself.

She overreacts to his autonomy (because of her repressed autonomy) and attacks him for being distant, not needing her, and closing her out. Yet she doesn't want to see his dependency and neediness because it jars her image of him as strong and independent and masterful, which she needs to believe he is to feel secure. At the same time, he overreacts to her dependency (because of his denied and repressed dependency), and therefore any expression of dependence by her makes him feel smothered, pressured, scornful of her weakness, demanded on and clung to, even as he blocks and fears her autonomy because that threatens his control and causes him to fear desertion by her.

She overreacts to his "logical" intellectualized orientation because of her internalization. She accuses him of being cold, insensitive, and unfeeling, even as she fears and blocks his emotions because she doesn't want to see him as weak or "falling apart." She needs him in control of himself to compensate for her "emotionalism."

He overreacts to her emotional displays because of his massive emotional repression and fear of his own feelings. Consequently, any emotional expressiveness on her part is seen as evidence of irrationality or "craziness."

He overreacts to her desires for touch and closeness partially because of his unconscious resistance to sensuality, which causes him to see her desire to be held primarily as frigidity and sex avoidance. It makes him feel invalidated as a man, even as he fears her overt, strong sexuality because of his need to perceive himself as always being able to be sexual upon demand, and great sexual appetite on her part would threaten him enormously.

She sets him up for rejection by overreacting to him in all these areas and blaming him for the problems. It is only a matter of time before she romantically craves someone else whom she won't "fear," and "who will allow her to be herself."

He sets her up for rejection by overreaction to her and feeling responsible and guilty. It is only a matter of time before he craves a new woman "who will not smother him" or "always make him feel guilty" and who will be a "real woman" and not a child.

Often the two of them will try to do something their deeper self is uncomfortable with. He may try to listen to her, but his deeper masculine self desires to disconnect, so he will have a very short attention span, even though he says he's "trying." He will turn away, actually or inwardly, soon after she starts. She will be talking, his attention will wander over to something else, and she will notice this and feel hurt and hopelessly disgusted by his "disinterest." He doesn't see that he is doing this because it is his deeper disconnecting self that causes him to get overloaded quickly when there is personal involvement. He barely has a capacity for any in these polarized relationships. He disconnects unconsciously. She has great capacity for involvement or "connection," which causes her to see him as very rejecting and him to see her as endlessly demanding.

He may therefore become afraid to communicate with her or talk to her spontaneously because he believes that once she starts talking, she won't stop talking. Once she gets a "taste of closeness" she will become insatiable.

Benjamin and Jill are a couple much like that. When they are alone together on Sunday, he is constantly withdrawing. His feeling about this is, "The moment I start getting involved with her, I'm in trouble. She doesn't know how to stop. She doesn't have limits."

He is the opposite extreme, comfortable never talking to anybody. He likes to play with his "toys," his mechanical equipment, go outside and garden, or just sit and stare into space.

Not only do they overreact to each other, she builds up a starvation level such that whenever she sees an opening to talk to him, she admits, "I get so excited; God, he's letting me talk to him! I rush in and try to tell him everything" because she senses that any second he's going to withdraw and break off contact. He experiences the other extreme, and says, "There is no limit to her need to talk. I give her a finger and she takes a hand."

Because Benjamin and Jill as individuals were self-aware and felt good about themselves, and the *way* they interacted was the primary problem, they were able, with the help of several months of marital therapy, to recognize and change their separate contributions to the distressing communication pattern. Their gains were made rapidly because they didn't need to hide from themselves by blaming each other.

The Hidden Power Struggle

I have frequently had men describe the following scenario to me: "If at the beginning of a relationship, I keep the woman at a distance and don't want to get too close, she feels that I am pushing her away and that I am not making a commitment—that I am afraid to be intimate. When I finally let down my guard and try to be intimate and close, when I really make myself vulnerable and give up control, which is uncomfortable for me, then I feel really inadequate. She blames me for things that she never blamed me for when I kept my distance. When I start to get close, that's when I am accused of saying the wrong thing or trying to control her. So I am better off staying at a distance and letting her complain about a lack of intimacy."

Stewart, age thirty-six, described it this way: "Maryann was liberated on the surface, but the undertow was very different. I would find out a couple of evenings after I had been with her that she was very angry and I wouldn't even know that I had done something wrong. She would be angry because she said I wasn't really involved enough. I didn't care enough about her. The irony is that the women in my life whom I've made the greatest effort to get close to are the ones who always wind up saying they are angry because I wasn't getting close. When I made no effort to get close and really kept my distance, I never got any complaints. The moment I felt I was really opening myself up to be intimate, that was when I was found to be failing. That is the double bind for me."

Another such truth was experienced by Alex. He said, "If you keep the control, the distance, then the woman is kept insecure; and so long as she is insecure about the relationship, she will be less inclined to attack. If she's interested in you, but you keep her at a distance, she will be careful about attacking you. She won't criticize you because she's afraid of you. The moment you cross the barrier and actually start to get committed, you find that she begins to feel that you are inadequate as a partner. You know then and there that you are never going to be able to satisfy her.

"I found this to be true sexually. At the times when I personally thought I was the most sensitive and the most involved and caring as a lover, I would find out often that I was a failure. At the times when I allowed myself to be totally selfish, without apology and didn't give one thought to what the woman experienced, I never got any complaints. I was never told I was selfish as a lover. In fact, I was often told that I was wonderful."

An Overall Perspective

Paradoxically, the point is simple, yet frustrating and complex. Relationship difficulties and misunderstandings come out of the polarized and unconscious defensiveness of men and women, not out of lack of communication skills or good will. *Furthermore, the same process that creates the problem prevents its resolution.* So, it is not a "lack of understanding" or "communicating" that is the problem. *Understanding means nothing unless that understanding is undistorted by the gender-polarized defenses. Therefore, communication has little to do with talking. Talking is "content," and while it may calm each person and give a temporary sense of being understood, the moment people start interacting again, the deeper process will destroy the content again and the old feelings of frustration and anger will resurface. The greater the polarization, the more rapidly that occurs.*

Only a breakdown of the polarized defenses will make communication meaningful. Until then, men and women will use a different language and live in different worlds while believing that they are using the same language and living in the same world. They will use words differently. Until then, unconsciously, neither really wants a *relationship;* they want defensive need satisfaction but cannot consciously acknowledge this.

A starting point for communication is not talking, but a balancing, and the creation of this absence of gender defensive polarization. Ironically, when we accomplish this, a minimum of talking about issues, conflicts, and problems will be needed after the early differences are acknowledged and compromised, because distortions, misunderstandings, and frustrations will be minimal and easy to reconcile.

In the meantime, men need to realize that so long as polarization exists, they, more than women, will be seen as failures in the communication process because men are the ones who withdraw and break contact. *It is important, therefore, to realize that this response does not exist in a vacuum. It is part of a cycle. In many ways a man's reaction is a defense against overload, a "survival" response that, although unfortunately unproductive, even tragic, is not solely "his" problem.*

At present, the problems of relationships look and feel as if they are caused by the man, but they aren't. The distortion of gender defenses makes it seem that way, but to fall into the trap of believing that is really to make the prospect of breaking down the communication barriers even more hopeless. Holding the line against that distortion and trying to work out the polarization in goodwill on both sides is where the real challenge lies, rather than in pursuing the fantasy that hearing each other more correctly will finally heal the wounds and produce the desired closeness while men and women leave their own unconscious process unchallenged.

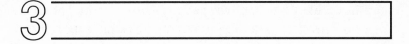

THE COMMITMENT OBSESSION

Much as he hated using stereotypes, Michael couldn't deny a certain reality he was experiencing with the single women he was meeting—"I feel like an object, a piece of meat, with them. By the time I've been with a woman for one or two evenings, I can already feel the pressure: Am I the kind of guy who is ready, willing, and able to commit?"

The pressure was causing him to withdraw and say silly-sounding things to himself, he thought, such as, "All women really want from a man is commitment. They're not really interested in men as people"; and, "They don't *really* want to take the time to get to know me. All women want the same thing."

When he met Jackie, thirty-one, independent and a successful insurance salesperson with a seemingly full and enjoyable life of work, skiing, two dogs she adored, and several good friends, as well as a close relationship with her family, Michael thought he had found someone "different." He let go of his wary style and opened himself up to her as he hadn't done with a woman for a long time. Instead of giving his usual speeches about going slow in terms of establishing a relationship of permanence, he decided that this time he would just let himself be somewhat vulnerable. "I want her to really get to know me—and I want to know her—and maybe we can learn something about what relating can be like between two people who don't have to use the opposite sex for some immediate personal satisfaction since we both have satisfying lives."

However, after a month of dating, during which time Michael had not pressed the issue of going to bed with Jackie ("I don't want to get pulled prematurely into a guilt trip about misleading her about where I was at"), he couldn't believe his ears when she left a message on his telephone answering machine indicating that she couldn't see him anymore. He called her back immediately, confused, angry and hurt, to find out what had happened. What he heard in amazed disbelief was, "I like you a lot—but I sense an immaturity—a desire to play—a lack of seriousness, Michael, and I'm just too drained from false starts and dead end relationships and I have a gut feeling this isn't going anywhere."

"But we were having a great time being together—talking, joking, going places—and we've only had five dates—and I really do like and admire you a lot," Michael responded. "You can't expect me to know what I want or where we're going in that short a time—I'm not that shallow—and you yourself told me you couldn't tolerate being around superficial people. I don't get it."

"Well, I met somebody else this past weekend," Jackie said, "and I just have a stronger feeling that this one will work out. I didn't have that feeling with you. I just don't think your heart is into being serious." Michael hung up dumbfounded. "Whatever happened to women wanting to be people with a man and really getting to know them? Now that I'm ready for that and really want it, I can't seem to find it anywhere. Women are hypocrites. They only say they're interested in getting to know a man as a way of avoiding sex—not as a way of first becoming friends."

The Pressure to Commit

Feminine pressure for commitment from a man in a relationship is the counterpart and equivalent to the traditional masculine pressuring of a woman for sex. Just as the unconscious defensiveness of masculinity produces an obsessive sexual preoccupation vis-à-vis the woman, so does the unconscious feminine defensiveness produce an obsessive relationship compulsion and obsession toward men.

Women choose men on the basis of their eligibility as commitment objects and often reject men who are potentially more compatible as partners in the same way as men choose women who are "sexy" and reject women who are potentially more suitable as partners but are not sexually appealing enough.

In proportion to the strength of their femininity and these compulsions, women are "irrationally" driven by this need and urgency for commitment, and it causes them to be temporarily blinded to objective reality in the same way as a man's sexual hunger impairs and intrudes on his better judgment. That is, it often causes them to make inappropriate, pain-producing, "self-destructive" choices. The preoccupation, soon after meeting a man, with whether or not he has "commitment potential," is as defensive and distorted as the man's premature pressuring for sex when he first meets a woman and hardly knows her as a person.

What a man will share with his friends about a woman—what he will feel good and excited about—will be that she really turns him on sexually; she has a great body and she is beautiful. The things the woman will rush excitedly to tell her friends about an attractive man she has met will be that he says he loves her, he says he can't get along without her, and he wants to make a commitment to live with her or marry her. This will take the man out of the category of being "flaky" or "just like most other men."

The sex-focused male will end or threaten to end a relationship with a woman if she won't go to bed with him because, despite what *she says*, to him no sex clearly means she is not attracted and does not love him. A woman feels the same way about a man who resists commitment. Indeed, for most women to remain in a relationship that "is not going anywhere" is as emotionally impossible as remaining in a relationship with no sex is for most heterosexual men. Suddenly, he is transformed and is no longer attractive to her and she loses interest in him.

Unconsciously they enter into a bartering stance where instead of engaging in genuine loving and spontaneous giving, freely offered as one does with a friend or anyone one truly loves, each party is focused on his or her own defensive need satisfaction, doling out whatever payment is needed to prevent the ending of the "relationship." It may impel her to "give sex" to hold him even though genuine desire is absent, in the same way that he will "make a commitment" he really doesn't want because he knows he will lose her otherwise.

In proportion to the degree of gender polarization (masculine/feminine) in a relationship, the undertow or defensive cravings in a man and a woman respectively masquerade as true love and interest in one another as people. Similarly, a traditional woman with no committed relationship in sight becomes as obsessed with commitment as men do when deprived of sex. She builds up a commitment tension that is just as obsessive, powerful, and unbearable as his sexual tension when he feels deprived. The undertow may push them surreptitiously into an unfortunate, defensive, demanding, and rigid involvement that moves from romantic illusion to mutual intimidation. Because of a deeper sense of being "used" after commitment, she may hold back her true self by becoming sexually "frigid," thereby "punishing" him for not *really* loving her, while he will hold back his true self by becoming emotionally withdrawn and detached, thereby responding similarly.

When a man dates a woman because he wants to have sex and because he considers her a "sure thing," that is considered a low level, dehumanized, and sexist motivation. If, however, a woman dates a man because he is a likely prospect for commitment and marriage, that is considered acceptable—a realistic, even smart motivation. *In both instances, however, there is sexism and dehumanization, the use of the other as an object for the fulfillment of gender defensive needs and compulsions that are beyond conscious awareness* and therefore largely denied. That is, he is an "object" in her eyes and is no more perceived as a person than she is by the macho, object-oriented male. Both are out-of-control and driven by unconscious, irrational, and damaging drives.

The unconscious feminine motives in these relationships, however, are interpreted more positively than the masculine ones because they seem to be more humanized, loving, and acceptable: reflective of society's "values." This falls right into line with the distortions in understanding and interpreting gender motives generally.

It is a subtle, elusive phenomenon, but it is crucial to see beyond these illusions created by gender defenses and to recognize how the sexes are merely polarized, distorting the same phenomena (aggression, assertion, autonomy, and sexuality) in opposite directions, thus mutually reinforcing and perpetuating each other's distortions and defensiveness.

For example, repressed aggression in females makes girls seem "sweet and nice," while defensive overaggression in boys causes them to be seen as dangerous. In fact, both are flip sides of the same coin, acting out the same phenomenon of defensiveness in opposing directions. Indeed, who *is* more aggressive—the violent football player or the cheerleader who finds him attractive and reinforces him with her love because he's a "winner"; the man who fights for the woman's "honor" or the woman who passively and indirectly goads him on by not dealing with a situation she *could* handle herself and who will hold him in contempt if he doesn't fight on her behalf?

The feminine unconscious moves in the inner direction of the personal and creates an obsession with relationship and closeness. It gives the appearance of being positive, loving, and personal. She becomes a symbol of home and family and traditional values. Society supports her orientation and "values" and gives her its stamps of approval. It is hard to see how this can be "bad" or damaging. The feminine unconscious, however, makes women as out of balance and destructive as masculine defensiveness or being macho does to men, only in the opposite direction.

The problems created by the feminine unconscious are much more difficult to deal with and potentially more damaging because they are disguised by a "nice" veneer. Thus it is difficult to see and transform the damage it does.

When a woman breaks off with a man because he is "not marriage material" or "won't commit," however, the dehumanization is evidenced by the fact that this is the very same man that she previously wanted as the central human being in her life and supposedly "loved." Now she won't talk to him and accuses him of being the cause of her great pain.

Kate, a women in her late twenties, had been in an affair with a man she met at a business seminar for three years while he was married. After intense pressuring by her and a fear of losing her, he finally left his wife. Then Kate pushed relentlessly for marriage. However, when she spoke about him to her friends, it was clear that she was full of contempt for him—something that she herself could not really see or acknowledge. She would call him an "egotist," a "con artist," and "immature." She didn't like his choice of friends. She didn't trust him with other women and was looking to discover his secret motives. She called him a baby because he would "whine" when he didn't feel well. Objectively she didn't like this man as a person, yet she was obsessed with her need for him to marry her. Periodically rage would come out when she thought that he was undermining this need and plan. Then she would accuse him of being afraid of commitment or "closeness."

When a woman gets a commitment from a man, she experiences a temporary euphoria and a reduction of anxiety, just as a man does when he first "seduces" a woman to whom he's attracted. But soon an inner pressure builds up because the needs are insatiable and defensive and can never be genuinely satisfied. She can never get enough commitment security to reassure her womanly needs, just as he never has enough sex and other validation to convince himself, once and for all, that he really is an adequate, lovable man.

Inner Intuitive Wisdom

We need to reinterpret the so-called male fear of intimacy and the male fear of commitment and see it instead as a valid response within the context of the defensively polarized relationship where he becomes as much an object as she, and his "frigidity" or withholding is personal, while hers is sexual.

A woman asking a man on or before a first date, or asking another woman, about a prospective man's capacity for intimacy and openness for commitment is setting up a damaging and dehumanizing context for herself and the man. I am reminded of a woman who was involved with a man for a long time, a man she really cared about and loved, and who really cared about her. They were best friends, great lovers, and enjoyed each other's company immensely. He didn't feel ready for marriage, however, though he also didn't rule it out altogether in the future.

She broke up with him to go out with a man she knew wanted to be in a committed marriage relationship with her. Consequently, she entered into a miserable marriage that lasted only a short time, in order to satisfy defensive, "irrational" needs. Any attempt to talk her out of marrying this man would have fallen on deaf ears. She was under the spell of her compulsions, the deeper feminine cravings.

The man she married wanted commitment only because he felt challenged and competitive with the other man in her life. Many men will suddenly be "ready" for commitment when they are threatened, but that does not mean anything in terms of their genuine desire or capacity to be close or their ability to love. They want possession of the woman and validation of their masculinity, or are acting out of fear of losing her, and so they "make a commitment" just as women in challenging situations will use sex to gain control. It took the experience of a painful three-year marriage to allow her to see she had made a mistake. Subsequently, she divorced, and fortunately her real love was still unattached. She resumed her original, intrinsically satisfying relationship and finally married him.

When a woman criticizes a man for being incapable of commitment and intimacy, she is revealing her own defensive unconscious and usually is as out of touch with herself as is the man who accuses the sexually resistant woman of being "frigid" without seeing how his pressure is closing her up. A woman reveals her defensive feminine unconscious when she makes a statement such as, "Men are incapable of intimacy or commitment," or "There are no men around who really know how to be intimate." She is not recognizing how her own unconscious needs are creating a pressure that is an important factor in causing him to be resistant or incapable of "closeness."

Men have been taught to feel guilty about their resistance

to "niceness" and a woman's desire to be close. The guilt prevents men not only from respecting and accepting their feelings of resistance as valid and feeling comfortable, but also from respecting their protective quality. Instead, men are told and come to believe, "You have a problem with closeness and intimacy and *you* had better overcome it." A man learns to see this as his problem solely. His guilt, self-doubt, and lack of self-awareness prevent him from properly translating the meaning of his resistance, and he begins to respond against himself.

Authentic Relating

Commitment and intimacy are terms that are often misused and misunderstood. The prevailing tendency is to give these concepts a life of their own, just as with sex, where people speak of their "sex lives" as if they had little or no relationship to the rest of their involvement. A couple will say, "We are struggling with our intimacy and our efforts to get close to each other." They have to "struggle" because there is unconscious resistance, just as they have to struggle to make defensively motivated, unauthentic sex work. Such couples never seem to get it quite right, because they are unaware of the defensive polarization causing the problem.

In an authentic, loving relationship, the commitment is just there—a by-product, not an entity in itself—as in a best friendship. With a loving friend you *want* to be committed because you care about the person. If friends are in trouble, you are eager to be there for them not *because* you've made a commitment. If they want to talk, you *want* to talk to them or you feel free to let them know without guilt or a threat to the "commitment" that you can't. You don't have to work on it. The trust and the safety are there if it's a friendship built on genuine love and caring. Nondefensive relating, like nondefensive sex, is a process that emerges from two people feeling safe and good with each other. "Working at it" indicates a lack of safety or genuineness.

Thus, when a woman instructs a man to let down his barriers because he can "trust her and feel safe with her," she may actually believe she is trustworthy and means what she says. However, it is much like a man saying to a woman, out of *his* sexual need, "You can trust me—just let go and I know you'll enjoy the sex. I guarantee it." That will do nothing to make her *feel* safe.

Most women feel vulnerable when they have sex without a commitment. A woman will say, "You are pressuring me for sex, and if I have sex with a man, I get very attached to him. It makes me feel very vulnerable." Men feel equally vulnerable when there is early pressure for commitment. They get scared, just as women get scared when they are pressured for sex by a "relative stranger."

When she says, "I love you, but if you don't marry me, I'll leave you, and don't want to see you anymore because it hurts too much," that is obviously not authentic love or friendship she is talking about. It is the fulfillment of her defensive need. She is being driven by a compulsion she must act out, and both she and he are usually beyond seeing that defensive obsession is propelling her.

Society reinforces a woman's sense of being a victim when she is not given what she needs in a relationship. Therefore, rather than dealing with her conflict in a realistic way and working out a mutual, healthy solution with a man she loves who will not give her all she wants, she feels hurt instead, and wants to leave. Her pain and anger and the inner pressure they produce are too great. She is unable to negotiate in a healthy way. Consequently, she does not learn about herself in the experience. Often she ends up with a man who is willing to commit himself because he has a protective "macho" orientation toward women. This means that in return for her commitment he will be relating to her as an object. Thus she pays the price for the fulfillment of her defensive needs. She finds out that she doesn't *really* like the man or enjoy being with him. In fact, she comes to feel he is dangerous to her emotional and physical health.

What she really wanted was the commitment and not the man. This is an important distinction. She didn't want the person; she wanted the fulfillment of her need. Once the commitment was secured and all that remained was the experience of being with him, she became unhappy and angry.

Furthermore, women tell themselves they want commitment and closeness when what they really mean is that they want to be rescued from the tension of externalization. This actually translates into the need to be taken care of, to have reassurance, to fuse and lose themselves because of defensive anxieties. How can one tell that? Simply because she chooses a man who will allow her to lose and fuse herself in him, but who is actually incapable of the closeness *she says she wants*. She cannot get real closeness from him. If she really desired closeness and not defensive fusion, the last person she would be choosing is this "magic man" with whom she has "fallen in love" before she hardly even got to know him. Were she capable of stepping back and taking an objective look at him, she would see that he was incapable of giving her what she is saying she wants. He is too goal-oriented, driven, and self-contained. When she speaks of closeness, therefore, it is a euphemism for defensive needs and has nothing to do with the reality of being close.

Sally was a seemingly liberated woman, an advertising executive for an insurance company. Underneath her independent facade, however, she had powerful feminine cravings for "fusion." She met Ron, an attorney, and he too seemed liberated, but was actually a dominant, rescue- and guilt-oriented male. Their love affair ignited powerfully, and immediately there was pressure on her part to marry, and on his part a need to rescue her and not "hurt her" the way other men had done, even though he knew this "premature commitment" would be a serious mistake.

Soon after committing himself to a marriage date, he began having physical symptoms of dizziness and nausea. After discussing it with a close woman friend, he became aware of his repressed anger over feeling pressured and manipulated. Sally was a woman who was overwhelmed by her responsibility for her children, lack of money, and anxiety over her health. She saw in Ron the perfect man to take care of her, to "rescue" her. He had so much guilt and sense of responsibility that he could not say no.

One evening, shortly after the time he had become aware of his anger over feeling manipulated, he said to her, "I love you very much and really want to marry you, but I just want to postpone our marriage a little while. I need a couple of months just to get comfortable with what is going on with me."

Sally became hysterical. She threatened suicide and ran out of his apartment. After Ron got her to return and tried to tell her that he was not rejecting her but was only asking her for some more time, she refused to discuss it. She just repeated over and over again, "Okay, I don't want to be with you anymore. I want to break this thing off. You don't love me." Unconsciously, or perhaps knowingly, she was manipulating him through playing on his overpowering guilt. She succeeded. He recanted and said he would marry her on the promised day.

Predictably, the marriage soon turned into a nightmare for him. Sally began to turn cold, whereas before the wedding she was completely adoring and sensitive to his every mood. He began to sense, and rightfully so, that she was distracted when she was around him. She could hardly focus on him. She seemed to be bored with him. She blamed him for her "distance," saying she was still traumatized by his "change of heart" over marriage and what he had "put her through." Now *he* became the insecure one, begging for affection. He gave up all his friends and interests to spend his time around her and reassure himself of her devotion.

The idea that he was being manipulated by a woman's defensive need to be rescued, a need that is called "commitment desire," was beyond his capacity to see. His guilt prevented it until a violent encounter with his wife caused him to seek therapy. Then he began the process he should have begun earlier of learning how to translate and understand his responses. Because he had waited so long, the buildup of anger was too intense and the relationship had to be dissolved.

Obsession and Irrationality: In Sex and Commitment

Women will be better able to understand men's obsession with sexuality when they grasp the irrational nature of their own obsession with commitment. This awareness in both men and women would be a major first step to a new humanization between the sexes.

The masculine man and the feminine woman are polarized opposites, neither one better or worse in their defensiveness caused by gender conditioning. Both are organismically repulsed when they sense they are being used as objects, and both potentially know by a sense of safety and comfort, once they are free of defensiveness, when they are really being loved.

Healthy commitment emerges as a natural outcome of a relationship that is comfortable and nurturing; it is not a goal of the relationship. It does not have to be pressured for, worked on, thought about, or deliberated over. It will emerge out of the process, comfortably for both, when the individuals involved are not driven by defensive, polarized needs.

For Men: How to Recognize Defensive Commitment Craving

1. You are made to feel guilty for not getting close enough.
2. You are made to feel that the relationship problems and resistances are primarily due to your "fear of intimacy."
3. Discussion about commitment and closeness and intimacy is ever present, and it is a continued source of pressure.
4. When she talks about men as a whole, it is clear she perceives them to be "damaged" in their relationship or intimacy capacity.
5. You feel guilty whenever you pull back to slow the pace of the relationship.
6. You are afraid to express your resistance to "getting close" for fear it will shatter her or cause her to end the relationship.
7. You see yourself as damaged and hurtful when you compare yourself to her.
8. Both of you agree that the source of the relationship problems is primarily you.

ONE DOES THE DIRTY WORK FOR TWO: UNDERSTANDING YOUR RELATIONSHIP BREAKUP

When Minette and Mark were in the last stages of their deteriorating marriage, it seemed apparent to most people who knew them well that Mark was pushing Minette away. Masochistically, it seemed, Minette hung on in the face of Mark's moody withdrawal and frequent refusals to tell her where he was going and when he'd be back. "Are you my probation officer?" he would ask. She would try to overlook his flirtatious behavior with other women, even married ones, when they were leaving church on Sundays—one of the last activities they did together.

Prompted by their priest and concerned about the possibility of Minette having a breakdown—or, worse, her hiring a "vicious Beverly Hills shark" as a divorce attorney—Mark agreed to join her in marital therapy.

During the first session Minette cried and Mark sat silently. "This all makes me feel like a piece of shit!" he finally remarked. "I couldn't be all that bad—*no one* could be all that bad." Mark acknowledged he wanted out. "This may sound like a big rationalization, but in my heart of hearts I believe that backing out of this marriage will save both our lives. Before we got married Minette was playful, energetic, active, and upbeat. Almost to the day after I married her she became a compulsive housecleaner, always complaining of aches and pains, reading the astrology pages or looking to the latest trendy guru or shrink's kernel of brilliant wisdom to save her and make her happy. No energy, no vitality, no laughs—and I know that's not who she is. I dated her for six years before I married her and believe me, I know what a terrific, relaxed woman she can be."

Jeanette and Nelson had the opposite situation. It was Jeanette who stopped coming home from her evening college extension adult education courses on time. She would blatantly lie about where she was and with whom: "I got into a wonderful discussion with a group of other students. I didn't think you'd mind my being late. You always preach that I should have my own identity, and not just fuse with you. Aren't you happy I'm doing it?"

When a one-night stand blossomed into a passionate affair, it looked as if Jeanette was either being hostile or self-destructive, because the end of a marriage to the affluent Nelson—who was such a "patient, nice guy" in the eyes of most of their friends—was now inevitable. Nelson's pride could not allow him to be cheated on, and it was obvious to him that something was going on.

While Nelson raged and bemoaned the end of his marriage and the "ideal" family life and lifestyle with their two sons that would be lost, in his quiet moments he was inwardly thanking Jeanette, even as he cursed and insulted her to her face. His own guilt would have made it impossible for him to leave a marriage that in his mind and in the eyes of his close friends had made him "an old man" in just six years' time. He was twenty pounds overweight, smoking, constantly exhausted, a work- and television-aholic; and a man whose powerful sex drive had faded into distant memories of the past. Within a month of breaking up, Nelson's smoking ended, his weight came off, his sexuality was back where it was a decade before, and it rarely occurred to him to turn on the television when he walked into the family home that he was now occupying without Jeanette.

The Ending of a Relationship

Typically, when relationships end, there is a tendency to search for causes, to finger-point and blame, to look for the "reasons" it ended or got in trouble. But relationship breakups are always the will of both people, unconsciously mutual whether they seem so or not.

While one person in a relationship traditionally appears to be the "heavy," the other person, the "rejected" party or "leavee," can be shown to have participated equally in the split, even though his or her part in it is not clearly visible or is denied. Relationships are a balance between two people. As they go out of balance in either direction, anger and pain build up in both people, even though one might be repressing, denying, or diffusing the pain and tension through overinvolvement with work, children, illness, etc. When the feelings grow too great to be contained, the relationship splits apart, with one partner being projected into the position of initiator.

Women, in recent decades, have had the tendency to be the ending initiators because men's guilt and dependency paralyzes them, keeping them from acting on *their* anger and pain. However, the fact that most men are "surprised" and bewildered when they are suddenly abandoned—because they thought everything was "fine"—suggests these men were actually pushing the woman away by "tuning out" the reality of her experience. They were not seeing or absorbing *her* experience of the relationship. Unconsciously, the man was probably suffering much as she was, though he may have been denying it out of fear, dependency, or guilt. Or perhaps he avoided reality by drinking too much, watching television endlessly, working constantly, having an affair, preoccupying himself with finances, etc.

In many cases, breakups are a subtle power-play process of trying to end a relationship while making the other person seem responsible, or pushing them into the role of the bad guy. It is not unlike a war situation between nations, where there is a desire to make one party "evil" and the other "good," rather than exploring the deeper mutual causes that are operating in the destructive interaction. To the extent that such an orientation exists and is maintained, there is no growth for either.

Often I find that the person who was the one who was left didn't really like his or her partner as a person, but had been denying it. In fact, he or she may have deeply disliked the other person, or at least didn't see the reality of the other person. He or she was attached to a fantasy, a need fulfillment, and was unable to see who the other person actually was. The one who was left was continually provoking the one who left, through insults, by ignoring, through destructive addictive habits, etc. However, the "leavee" did not see him- or herself as pushing the other away or wanting that person to leave, or acknowledge it once faced with the evidence.

Jim and Tina: He says he wants to leave the relationship. She says she doesn't. Yet the simplest thing that he asks for, she forgets. She forgets to keep salt out of his food—just forgets it. She forgets that he doesn't like her to bring up painful subjects—such as the problems they are having with their daughter—when they are on business trips or vacations. Instead, at first chance, she brings him some kind of bad news that ruins his attempt to relax or enjoy himself.

Frank and Laura: He says he doesn't want her to leave. Yet he controls her, he is very critical of her, and totally unsensual with her, though he knows how she craves touching. He's unhappy too. This can be seen in his sudden rages "over nothing." He can think of little about her as a person that he really likes, yet he says that he doesn't want her to leave.

Jack and Charleen: He feels he married down when he married her. She's very seductive and provocative with other men, and he calls her shallow, unfaithful, and a liar. Yet he desperately pleads with her not to leave him. She keeps pulling away from him, and he is equally responsible for pushing her away because he is so critical of who she is. She tells him plainly that she has a strong need to be independent, but he won't give her any space. Instead, he hovers over her—calls her constantly and suffocates her. In many ways he is totally out of touch with the fact that he is continually rejecting her and unconsciously pushing her to leave him.

So, *one does the dirty work for two*. The relationship gets top-heavy with anger, frustration, and miscommunication to the point that one has to break it up for the good of both. The rage literally builds so high on both sides—overtly or covertly—that either the two people are going to make themselves sick or they are going to damage each other badly. There is no reason, no responsible party. It is the end point of a process that both contributed to and both want out of, though usually one denies that this is true.

The most common course of the polarized relationship is that the woman has repressed aggression, and therefore her part in the cause of the breakup tends to be "invisible." She needs to experience and justify herself as a victim. Furthermore, since the male takes the actor role, because he is externalized by his masculine conditioning, while marriage and relationships are internalized processes that require a focus on "personal" needs, it is almost invariably the male who *appears* to be the cause of the problems that lead to the breakup of the relationship.

In the way that it is constructed, marriage is essentially a feminine institution. Its requirements for success are heavily weighted toward qualities more highly developed in the feminine sphere of consciousness. The man is almost invariably in the role of the heavy when the marriage breaks up because, clearly, he is going to be less capable of the kind of internalized relationship focus and interpersonal sensitivity that marriage demands.

In most cases, he was the one who withdrew and frustrated his wife's attempts to get a flow of communication going between them. He was the one who thought being close meant having sex. He was the one who preferred to spend his day off working on his motorcycle or his car, instead of going on outings with his family. He was the one who "chose" to emphasize his career to the detriment of his personal life while she was not ambitious in that way.

She, however, was lacking too, and her relationship capacity was in part an illusion, because she refused the responsibility for her own life, always skillfully maneuvering him into the position of the responsible one and then complaining that he controlled her or treated her "like a child. " It's true that she was close to the children and gave them lots of attention. Also, she kept the house and did many things for him. She had a good relationship with his family and could always be counted on to remember birthdays, etc., sending cards and letters to friends and family.

Still, she related to him as a person no better than he did to her. She "gave up" her identity and presented a reactive, passive, helpless image that fed on his tendency to feel guilty and responsible. She cried when they argued, instead of "fighting it out" to a healthy resolution free of "victims." She became impatient and critical of him because of his "crude" and "insensitive" ways. She held impossible expectations of him. She unconsciously turned him into a father figure, wanting financial support and backup, and rescue from any difficulty she found herself in, while simultaneously resenting him for the restrictions he and the relationship placed on her. In short, she was unable to relate to him as a person, seeing him for who he really was and understanding and supporting him on that level, and related to him instead out of bottomless need and craving for "closeness" and "intimacy" that was an expression of her unconscious need to give over responsibility. She seemed to do all the right things, but under that, totally abandoned him for anything other than her own deeper purposes.

In discussing their wives, men will often emphasize: She's a very good wife; she's a good mother; she's very kind— wouldn't hurt a fly, etc., etc. But to the perceptive listener, there is a hollow ring, begging to be filled with acknowledgment of the man's emotional pain, his futile, inexpressible alienation and despair—inexpressible because his emotional expressive ability is underdeveloped and thwarted into choices of outbursts of anger and temper or withdrawal; inexpressible because he would feel foolish and childish and "unmanly" doing so; inexpressible because the twisted matrix of the relationship has left him unable even to understand what has happened, let alone express his own deeper, unfulfilled longings.

So both are increasingly unhappy. Both are disappointed and disillusioned in their own ways. They become locked into a process that neither can really see or understand, but both unconsciously feed; hating one another on one level while clinging to each other out of unconscious need, diffusing the tension between them through the characteristic mechanisms of overwork, withdrawal, and so on for him, and overmothering, overconsumption, and so on for her, with intermittent gestures of sentimental rituals that reassure them what a good couple they really are.

Then, when the tension builds to a critical point, when she catches him "screwing around" with another woman, or when his passion for the other woman overwhelms his guilt, or some other blatant "cause" presents itself, they will finally break up.

So in years past, the man almost invariably seemed to be the one who was at fault in s-0he marriage breakup. Sometimes he would do something extreme because of his pain, boredom, and deadness, in an attempt to escape this marriage structure that he wasn't really suited for. He would have an affair with another woman, or he would drink or work compulsively, all of which are manifestations of a build-up of tension and frustration in the male.

Her frustration would be expressed through crying and blaming and through "suffering." However, it was impossible or unconscionable for her to be the heavy. After all, she seemed to have more of what it takes to make the marriage "work" and was supposedly more committed to it.

To say that marriage is a feminine institution and men are doomed to appear inadequate within its structure is not a criticism of marriage or an attempt to blame women. Marriage is an event that requires internalized development—capacity to communicate, to express feelings and needs. None of these are areas of usual strength and competence for the traditional male in the polarized relationship.

Worse still is the fact that the very thing that makes a man a good potential husband for a woman makes him generally an inadequate marriage partner. If he is a good provider, protector, and decision maker, the good Mr. Responsibility to a high degree, then certainly he will probably be lacking in the personal or "intimate" aspects. What invariably happens is that he will look like a hero before he is married to her, then his image will be progressively tarnished to the point where the woman will begin to say and feel he has disappointed her. "He isn't the way I thought he would be. I thought he would be a lot more loving and caring. He turned out to be selfish, a workaholic, and not interested in his family the way he is in his job."

The idea that the good husband is a good relationship partner, then, is a contradiction in terms, particularly in traditional relationships. Many times the man who succeeded in marriage the best was the man who eventually assumed the acquiescent or deferring role. Even though he probably wasn't seen as a great partner, at least he wouldn't be seen as an obvious troublemaker. He would be a "nice guy," a thoughtful guy who would do a lot of symbolic sorts of things to keep his wife "happy." He would bring home flowers, do errands and work around the house, be patient with his wife when she wasn't feeling well, and not be sexually demanding. That would define him as a good husband.

Typically, however, if he was a good provider and protector, he was almost guaranteed to be an inadequate personal relater. There was no way he would be able to relate successfully to his feminine counterpart, because her internalized needs were "bottomless," and his externalized conditioning made him disconnected and therefore personally "inept."

The point is this: In these marital situations and polarized relationships, which almost all marriages become, there is a tremendous buildup of tension on both sides. The woman feels controlled, frustrated, angry, abused, violated, neglected, disappointed; the man feels deadened because he doesn't get the kind of excitement and stimulation and challenge that his externalized self requires, and he feels burdened in his role as actor and provider.

Ruth and Ronald: Ronald was a hardworking businessman, pushing himself to gain an executive position in the computer service company that employed him. Ruth worked part-time as a school aide, but spent the majority of her time at home with their four children.

When they met, Ruth remembered, Ronald could talk of nothing but how much he wanted a family, how much children meant to him, and he wanted lots of them. He thought pregnant women were beautiful. Before long, however, it seemed to Ruth that Ronald was totally focused on work. Even when he was home, the job was uppermost in his mind, and if the telephone rang with a trouble call from some field office, he would soon be out the door to catch a plane.

Once when she was fixing a barbecue on a Saturday afternoon, she had to stop and run to the store for a special sauce. When she came back, he was heading out the door. The lovely day was instantly transformed as she, overwhelmed by disappointment, anger, and need, screamed that he didn't care about her and the kids, all that he was doing was for himself. "It's for you! You! Your own ego! We never have anything—no family time, no vacations together—no nothing!"

While at first she had been rather proud of Ronald's supervisory status and of the importance of his responsibilities to his company, as time went on, she began to feel more and more empty and lonely. When he would go "dashing off on his white horse," as she put it, she would become angry and accusing. "You said you wanted a wife and family and this is how you show it! You're not there for me. You're not there for the children. I do everything for them. When you are home, you sit in the bathroom reading the paper. I even have to do the yard work. You have the television on all the time, and I can only say something to you during the commercials. We can never talk."

He would retort, "I'm doing all this for you and the kids. What do you think I work for?" Ronald saw himself as working very hard for his family. He saw himself as being a good husband and father, though he acknowledged his work did take him away a lot. He was the main support of the family and he felt that not only did he have to provide for *them*, but that it was very important that he build a strong base for future retirement.

He was very hurt by the lack of support he got from Ruth

and felt that she was always jabbing at him, trying to get to him. When he would say this to her, she couldn't understand what he meant.

She did say mean things sometimes, when *he* made her so angry, when she was hurt by *him*. But, if only he would bother to "get to know her," he would know that all she wanted was to be close and loving. If only they could really talk, she thought.

He scoffed at this and called their "talking" simply diatribes by her, as she went on and on about how difficult and miserable he was making her life. He complained that their "talks" went on interminably, and that was the main reason he avoided them.

As their relationship continued to deteriorate over the years, there were countless angry scenes, interspersed with relative calm and, eventually, simply withdrawal from one another. Neither was getting any nourishment from the other.

Ronald began to realize that the end had already come—that the relationship was over even though physically it still existed. Ruth, however, refused to acknowledge or accept this. She cried and promised to try harder, to do better. The more he would try to pull away, the more she would cling to him and deny all the negative feelings she had constantly expressed.

She really wasn't happy with him, any more than he was with her, but she couldn't take the responsibility for saying she wanted out, nor could she accept the fact that he would "abandon" or "reject" her. When he announced, firmly, that he was leaving, she was able to take advantage fully of her position as a martyr.

He knew he couldn't explain himself to her or to his family or to anyone else, really. The price of getting out came down to being the "bad guy," so he didn't even try. He just left town without a goodbye to anyone except his children, and she cried and was felt sorry for by all.

Now, she hadn't consciously tried to set him up in this way. As she adjusted to the new situation, however, she quickly found herself not only accepting it, but being exhilarated with her newfound freedom and power. It was only then that she began to realize that she hadn't really wanted the marriage either, but couldn't see that before. She began to realize that their problems had been a two-way street.

Ronald began to feel less guilty as Ruth gained strength and perspective and the two of them were able to reestablish communication and develop a comfortable environment in which the children could come and go freely between them, with one parent supportive of the other, though not choosing to live together. Ronald and Ruth were therefore able to come out of their situation with enough growth potential to make gains in their self-awareness and understanding of relationships. They became the best of friends, realizing nobody was to blame. Their polarization had done them in.

When relationships break up they do so because the tension builds so high on both sides and the pain is so strong for both that the relationship snaps in proportion to its polarization. It falls under its own weight. At the point at which the tie breaks, unconsciously the race is on. There is a rush and a power struggle—who can leave the relationship with the least amount of guilt—who can blame whom the best— who can walk away feeling justified?

Relationships As Power Struggles

Traditional relationships are power struggles. At the beginning of the relationship the battle is between opposing needs and orientations. The woman is supposedly trying to humanize the man and make him more sensitive. She marries him and she thinks she is going to change him. He's trying to control and dominate the tempo and direction of their relationship. He wants to have both his freedom and the benefits of the relationship. He wants to have space and closeness.

She pretends to give him freedom while she is maneuvering him into more closeness. She doesn't understand his desire for space. She sees it as part of his adolescent behavior, rather than realizing his need comes from a very strong buildup of tension inside him because of his externalization and that when he starts to get close, he becomes uncomfortable, scared, and tense. He's afraid the closeness will weaken him and make him less capable of surviving in the outside world.

At the beginning of the relationship she often wants to marry and he doesn't; not because of a fear of marriage per se, but because of a power struggle—who controls the rhythm and flow of the relationship. Once they marry, the power moves from him to her. As long as he withheld commitment and she wanted it, he had the power.

When they marry, he may act as if he was manipulated into marriage. But in fact he was not manipulated into marriage. Men want marriage just as much as women do, but for different motives. They want the mothering. They want to "secure their property." They want to validate their masculinity and their lovability, but often they don't want to take responsibility for saying, "I really wanted this relationship." He says instead, "I got married for her, to satisfy her needs." In fact, he is really there to satisfy his needs, his own dependency, his isolation, desperation, his own desire for control, his own need to make sure that she doesn't go with any other man. But at the beginning he can feel that he went into the marriage for her (and she lets him). That takes a little bit of the responsibility from his shoulders.

In the beginning of the relationship the man does not want to take the responsibility for saying, "I want in"; and at the end of the relationship the woman doesn't want to take the responsibility for saying, "I want out." She says, "He pushed me out by his behavior."

In all of these instances, the truth of the fact that both of them wanted out can be seen in that neither of them wanted or were able actually to negotiate with the other's reality. This is what I call the "fear of the middle zone." They are either sentimentally making up and promising things that they couldn't possibly fulfill, or they are full of rage and hate and blaming and threatening divorce. If you actually try to get them to listen to what the other person is struggling with and who the other person is, they undermine the effort. After all, it's not *exciting* to be real in a relationship. So they go back and forth between the euphoria of romance and the depression of rage and fighting, and never deal with the reality of each other and the need to rebalance the interaction accordingly.

She wants him to leave because she is constantly in search of the perfect relationship and she never gets it. So when a man starts to get close to her, and turns out, invariably, to be flawed, part of her wants another opportunity to find the perfect man. He, meanwhile, is almost always moving in the direction of disconnection, and so he is programmed, invariably, to pull away from her.

Breaking off a relationship may be a reprieve from psychological death, because relationships get stagnant and unhealthy, as physical beings do. Married couples almost always deny their pain. They say they like being married and are glad they married whom they did. Thus, marriages get top-heavy with blocking and denial, putting the two people out of touch with the reality of their experience. If they don't break up, the anger and pain simply take to the pathways of covert expression. Escape rituals structure the relationship as the two of them indirectly hide from one another any way they can.

One or both people are "dying." The tension and anger are palpable. There is diminishing contact, increasing deadness, overemphasis on the children, psychosomatic and actual illness, depression, weight gain, feelings of being trapped, suffocated, isolated. Both are being poisoned.

When a relationship breaks up, both people have an opportunity to get back in touch with the reality of their feelings. They can see the other—and themselves, too—as they *are*, and not how they needed to see them.

So, one does the dirty work for two, freeing both people to feel again, to be real again, to come out of repression. That is why, when people break up, they often go through a period of discovering and recognizing feelings that had been part of themselves all along, but that they had not been acknowledging.

One woman put it this way: "I didn't want to break up with my husband. I fought it. I struggled against it in every way I could. I cried. I agonized. I felt I was bad for 'failing.' Yet, when the end came anyway, when he insisted on going, I soon began to feel like a butterfly who had been let out of her cage. I began to have a wonderful feeling of power, a wonderful sense of inner congruity and well being. I felt I could be totally real again—that I could act out my most deeply honest self."

Just as we repress our anger when someone dies, and we suddenly remember only their "goodness," we tend to forget also how we fantasized and wished to be alone, after we've been "rejected." We only remember how "good" things supposedly were, or how much we "tried," or how much we "loved" him or her. If we succeed in "winning" our partner quickly back, then it becomes clear again what really led to the breakup.

The volatile extremes at the end serve to hide the essential lack of substance and reality of the interaction and its absence of real friendship and goodwill throughout. Unless there is a "mature" perspective and ability that allows for a nondefensive, goodwilled examination of the mutuality of the conflict, it is often healthier for both to cut the cord. It is not a matter of negotiation, but a matter of altering the process. If that can't be done, a breakup is a release. Polarized finger-pointing, blaming, and guilt-making, and the endless discharging of rage while refusing to "let go," are draining and damaging.

Possibilities of growth occur only after the romantic fog lifts and a crisis sets in—the earlier the better. Motivations and capacity to change are greater in the beginning, when there is more likely energy for that.

There is nothing you "could have done" to keep her or keep him. The origins of relationships doom them—one object marrying another object—two people using each other for defensive escapes, people who don't even really know and like each other as people making a lifelong commitment.

Breakups, when properly understood, are life-preserving, as are all phases and stages of experience when interpreted accurately and integrated in a healthy way.

"Thank" the person who leaves you. *One leaves because the other never will. The one is doing the dirty work for both. The poisoned fruit must drop. "Thank" the woman who takes your man away, "thank" the man who takes your woman away, because the one who leaves has to carry the responsibility and the guilt. The one who gets the other to leave gets to play victim.*

If endings can be accepted and worked through, they continually set the stage and prepare one for something better and healthier. Remember, when you marry you are choosing someone to be the central person in your life. You have to really like and know someone to do that accurately—and you first have to become nondefensive so that your judgment is not flawed.

5

PREDICTING THE FUTURE OF YOUR RELATIONSHIP: "HOW TO CHOOSE A PARTNER"

Hal was a veteran single who'd been through the gamut—from heavy romances to "working at having mature relationships" ("DMRs" he jokingly termed them: "deep, meaningful relationships"); one-night stands and "3- or 4-daters."

"All of my relationships with women seem to fall into one of two categories," he commented. "There are those where I pursue my fantasies of perfection and beauty—and then after I get clobbered by my own illusions. I get into the other kind where I am trying to talk myself into being an adult. Instead of going with my gut feelings, which—pop psychology aside—I frankly have learned to distrust, I get into a relationship that my brain or head tells me is "good for me," even though something inside is screaming that "I'm bored," or "This feels totally dead or phony."

"The upshot is that after all these years of being with different women, I feel as alone as ever and more frightened, and maybe wary is a better word for it, of my choices for a partner. I've been wrong so many times and I've put so many women on pedestals only to watch euphoria and adoration turn into pain and anger.

73

"With the 'right' or 'appropriate' women I found myself overlooking other important things because they had the socially approved symbols of career, independence, and an appearance of being 'together.' I wanted so badly to be able to bond, but finally I had to acknowledge what I was overlooking, namely, my real feelings. Then I know a lot of it is just me—and believe me, I've worked on myself—therapy, soul searching, the whole bit. Still, it seems to get more confusing, not less so. Instead of experience making me more confident, it's made me more guarded—no, the word is paranoid."

Choosing the "Right One" Through Romantic Attraction

Romantic feelings are powerful, and they obscure one's sense of clarity when in the throes of love. They distort reality and create a strong tendency to deny what everyone else can see. We tend to overlook or not want to acknowledge the obvious things that in the long run will make the fantasies unattainable. Then we despair over the "impossibility" of making a "relationship work" and feel beaten down to a point of embittered negativity, depression, and loss of motivation.

Romantic attraction is motivated by defensive needs that make it impossible to see the other for who he or she is. Often the collusion is mutual. The other "can't" see you either. Because each person's purposes are being temporarily served, there is a resistance and resentment toward input or any objective information that will deter him or her from a goal. The romantic couple relates with great self-consciousness and "sensitivity" in order to prevent the deeper, disturbing responses and feelings from emerging full-blown.

The basis of powerful attraction is irrational. The loss of objective reason and the ensuing delirious wonder is the essence of "falling in love." The romantic process holds the promise, however, of personal and emotional growth for those who can glean the lesson from the experience, because the person who attracts us powerfully is the "guru" who can teach us so much about ourselves, if we are ready to see it.

Looking at Her Objectively

Evaluating one's relationship potential with a particular partner involves seeing that person realistically and understanding their deeper process. Keep in mind always that romantic feelings will inevitably work against objectivity. An effective aid can be to pretend you are someone else, so to speak, a friend *you* are advising about the woman. This can help to move your ego out of the way and clear your perspective to some degree.

Her History with Men

Unless great self-awareness has developed in a person and intense efforts at change have occurred, the best way to predict the future of a relationship with a woman is to take an objective look at her past:

1. Is she very angry about past relationships? Does she blame each man for being the one who ruined the relationship, seeing herself as the victim or the "loving" one; or is she able to acknowledge her patterns as part of the process that led to the "failure" of the relationship? Can she look at the past objectively and take half of the responsibility? Furthermore, can she acknowledge the hurt and confusion a past partner might have endured as well? Or has he sim-

ply become the "bad guy"? *If he has,* it is only a matter of time before you, too, will be examined and found wanting. *A blamer is a blamer is a blamer.*

2. How does she perceive, describe, and talk about men in general? Does she portray most of the men in her past negatively and then does she proceed to lump all men into mainly negative categories of being "selfish," "sexists," "exploiters," "woman haters," etc.? If she does, inevitably you will be put in one of those categories too once the relationship stops going the way that she needs it to.

3. What is the pattern of her past relationships? Have they been long and enduring? Short and erratic? Or have there been none at all? How did her relationships end? Has she cheated on other men she was supposedly exclusively involved with? Looking at these things can give you a sense of the depth of her bonding and caring capacity and potential.

4. Has she always been with a man? Does she seem incapable of going for any period of time on her own without being in a relationship? Furthermore, has she centered her life around whatever man she was with, expecting that man to be all things to her? All men eventually fail to satisfy the "man-centered" woman who craves this relationship fusion and perfection, which is a form of addiction—not much different from the "addicted" male womanizer. He is "addicted" to sexual conquest, she to relationship conquest.

Or has she had a reasonably well-defined life and identity of her own that allowed her to go for periods of time without having to be with a man?

Furthermore, has she been able to maintain her own priorities and her own friendships while emotionally involved with a man?

5. If she is divorced, to what extent is she still supported by her ex-husband? To what extent does she feel that she deserves anything she can get from him in the way of help? If she is working hard instead and providing her own sup-

port, does she deal with it positively and bring a sense of energy to her responsibilities, or does she complain of being exhausted, depleted, and ill; angry and tense about her responsibilities and pressure—and angry at her ex-husband for not taking care of her?

6. What has been her level of self-motivation and self-care? How good has she been at going after and getting the things in life that are important to her? To what degree has she failed to do so or expected someone else to do it for her? If she has continually failed to reach or given up on goals in the past, then in all likelihood she will continue to do so, and she will be an unhappy, demanding person to be around.

Family Memories

Men and women alike are powerfully influenced in their relationship process by the dynamics of their childhood environment and their parents' relationship. Therefore, it can be useful to look at a potential partner's family past in predicting the relationship's future.

1. What are her memories of her father? Was he rejecting, weak, or absent, or perhaps all of these? Did her father abandon her or leave her life early? If he did, she will anticipate abandonment. The fear, pain, and anger toward her father may be unconsciously transferred to you. At a certain level of closeness, therefore, she will begin to back off, and blaming rage will emerge that will make you wonder what you did.

Was her father adoring of her and was she the "light of his life"? If so, she may want to reproduce that same relationship with you and may expect the same kind of adoring, indulgent behavior from you. Fairly soon into the relationship, therefore, she may begin to behave like a spoiled, demanding child.

Or does she simply speak openly and lovingly of her father, and have a relaxed respectful, nonclinging, open communication with and realistic perception of him? If she does, that bodes well for your relationship with her.

2. What was her mother's relationship with her father like? What was modeled by them in their interaction in the family? There will be a tendency to repeat that model or, if it is viewed negatively, to go to the opposite extreme in angry reaction and rebellion that will make her defensive about "your expectations" if they resemble what she saw between her parents and "hated."

She may be aligned with a mother who is hostile to her father, or she may be angry with her mother and overly connected to her father. In case of the former, you will be under pressure to prove yourself "different." In case of the latter, she may be defensively self-punishing, and with low self-esteem.

If she has a balanced and healthy relationship with both parents, and especially if her parents like each other, that suggests a positive, nondefensive orientation within her own emotional makeup.

Her Life in the Present

Her level of self-esteem will be an important factor in assessing your prospects for a positive experience with her.

1. How does she feel about herself? Does she project a negative self-image through a defensive hypersensitive attitude, or is she relaxed and open and able to assert or defend herself appropriately?

If she feels bad about herself, she'll have a tendency to project that on you and see you as disliking her or criticizing her, and you will be continually on the defensive, to prove that it isn't so. She may even invite your criticism, but then respond with hurt, anger, and accusations when you tell her anything "negative" about herself.

If she feels bad about herself, you may be tempted to rescue her and "help her" see that she's a worthwhile person. *Don't fall into that trap! She'll only come to dislike you.* You will never be able to prove it enough or to transform self-hate into positive self-esteem.

It is part of the romantic omnipotence of a lover to think he or she can, by the force and power of love, change or heal a partner. For short periods it may seem to be working. However, the illusion can be maintained just long enough for a troublesome commitment to be made. Your fantasies of "helping" and "changing" her will be revealed as deluded and omnipotent, designed to make *you,* not her, feel special.

2. To what extent is she relationship-obsessed? How much discussion is there early on about seriousness and commitment? How much pressure do you feel about that and how soon? To what extent and how quickly does she threaten to break off the relationship with you, suddenly and in anger, when she feels it is not "going anywhere"? Does she play "relationship terrorism" by continuously threatening to leave because you won't commit?

This is all very revealing of a woman's feminine undertow and her tendency to make a man an object for the fulfillment of her defensive needs. It is comparable to the depersonalized pressuring for sex that men often do. Seeing that one is being used as an object is as important for a man as it is for a woman. It will shape the future and feelings of the relationship and the potential of you ever being yourself, a person and a friend rather than an object, in it.

The degree to which you are being used as an object is the degree to which she is relating to you out of her defensive anxiety. It suggests the degree to which she is "out-of-control" and driven by unconscious needs that she will deny, but that will be obvious to you.

She will cling to you romantically out of need, *not love.* Feminine defensiveness predicts that extent to which anger will build on both sides, on her part because she will come to resent her male partner for not being intimate and loving enough, and for being critical, hostile, controlling, and rejecting. Often you won't know what she means when the accusing starts, because it reflects her defensive perceptions and not objective reality.

3. Is sex considered something special? Do you feel as if you have to treat her particularly "well" for the sex? Does she seem to be doing it for *you?* If so, she will later either complain about the sex or withhold it as an expression of her anger.

4. Is "nice" one of her favorite words? If so, you will find it progressively more difficult to discuss anything negative with her. Furthermore, by seeing herself as "nice," inevitably she is going to feel victimized and you are going to be blamed for being "not nice."

5. Does she want to get really close? Does she talk constantly of her need for intimacy? If so, she will eventually become frustrated and resentful because *you* don't satisfy that need in her. Furthermore, you will come to feel engulfed by the pressure of these deep needs for reassurance and "love," while she is going to feel frustrated over your inability to show "real intimacy."

Does the matter of health and diet come up regularly? Is she preoccupied with these matters? Does she complain of not feeling well much of the time? If so, that pattern will intensify once the relationship is committed and her repressed negative feelings are building. Physical ailments will be one way of controlling, denying, and communicating her feelings.

All of these are typical defensive responses. The more they exist, the more of a reactor she will be, building feelings of being controlled, criticized, and feeling "helpless" and the more you will be blamed for doing these things to her.

5. How well defined is her life and her identity? Does she easily give up her plans and goals to be with you? Are you always the first one to break contact because it seems as if she wants to linger forever and never leave when the two of you are together?

Does it seem as if she had no life of importance to her before she met you? Does she tend to take on your friends, activities, and interests for herself? Does she seem to melt into your life and identity? Does she change her schedule regularly and easily to accommodate yours?

Or does she preserve her own priorities and friendships after becoming emotionally involved with you and not accommodate to fit into your life?

While it may be flattering to you at first that she seems to want to make you the center of her life, it is dangerous and deadening for you. There will be no stimulation from separateness. *A woman with a "dissolving identity" is as lethal to a man as a man with an insatiable ego, unable to "take in" his partner, is to a woman.*

A good sign of probable relationship health is that neither of you is inclined to, in any way, radically change your life as a result of the other person being in it.

6. Is she a feminist? If so, at the beginning you may see that as a positive thing because she seems to be an assertive, independent woman. But if her feminism was born of a rage toward "sexist men" who oppress women, inevitably she will lump you with all other men or you will be drained by having to prove otherwise. The defensively angry feminist is a feminine-blamer in disguise.

The Initial Encounter

How did you meet her? The circumstances and feeling tone of your first meeting are significant in determining the potential of the relationship.

1. Was she married or involved with someone else? Or were you? If she or you were cheating, what does that imply about the relationship? This is very revealing about who she or you are and what your future pattern may be.

What does it mean if she, for example, was married when she met you, but became very quickly and powerfully attached to you? Are you caught in an ego-inflating illusion of feeling you were just too wonderful to resist, or it was a "magical" connection?

Are you being set up as her rescuer? Is she someone who "needs a man" in order to make a change, and clings readily to the best and nearest host object to get out of unhappy circumstances? In other words, does she manage her transitions through attachment to and manipulation of men?

2. Did you meet under conditions of intense neediness? Was she lost in her life? Were you? Was she in a lot of pain, or were you very lonely? During these times of emotional vulnerability, one is most vulnerable to choose an extremely polarized opposite, someone to hide behind or be saved by. Distortion is greatest when the defensive need to be rescued is greatest. The "chemistry" in these instances is powerful but volatile.

Romantic feelings are at their peak for women when their life is in trouble. This is when romantic inclinations are the strongest. When she is unhappy and frightened in her life, she is inclined to be filled with romantic longing. Unconsciously she wants to fuse with a man whom she perceives as a rescuer, or Prince Charming. If you are lonely, that too will trigger a very romantic potential in you.

Her need and "helplessness" may create a sense of omnipotence in you. You will feel as if you can give her a relationship that is different from any she has ever had before and that you'll make everything different for her. The promise that the two of you together will have a relationship that is different from anything either of you have had in the past is a classic case of "famous last words."

3. Is it a "whirlwind" situation? If you feel the need to rush into a relationship, something is surely wrong with it. A genuine relationship progresses slowly and with resistance and conflict initially, along with the good and loving feelings. The rushing into the relationship seems to be a way of unconsciously saying, "Let's commit ourselves before we know what we're doing."

Therefore, beware of relationships that start too fast and too easily and where she is immediately always available to you and you are always available to her. People who do this are making a statement about the quality of their personal life. In effect they are saying that there is nothing really good or significant in it, and they are probably blaming others for that. *You* have been chosen to make everything all right and worthwhile.

If the beginning of the relationship is too easy and if there is no resistance, especially when you are generally on guard and careful about attaching to people because you don't trust easily, there is a great romantic distortion operating. *A favorable sign is that you relate to her with the same degree of caution and resistance that you generally have with new relationships and she does the same with you. That suggests that you and she are being "real," and that's the best basis for a beginning.*

Looking at Yourself

1. *Your own "deeper self" is a major dimension in predicting the future.*

How do you really feel about women? What does your pattern with women show?

How does this particular woman resemble other women you have been in love with in the past? Are you imagining her as being different from all other women you have met in the past? If so, you will probably be a victim of the "illusion of content," meaning the false, defensive belief that it is "who she is" and not how you relate (your process) to a woman that makes the relationship different.

2. Do you really want a relationship, and why? Being honest with yourself as to what place you want a woman to have in your life is important. Do you have room for her and the desire to be involved that will be expected?

Most important, are *you* under the illusion that *you* are going to be significantly different this time in relating, even though you haven't worked to make any changes in yourself? If you have done nothing to change since your last failed relationship, but somehow magically feel this time it is going to be different because of how she "makes you feel," you are kidding yourself.

Your Macho Fallacy Potential

The most common macho fallacies, distortions, and tendencies to be aware of are:

1. *The belief that you can rescue a woman from the distress of her life* (a very romance-inspiring motive on both parts). It is very exciting and ego validating to believe you can "rescue" her—especially from another man—and "make her happy." It is the classic white-knight fantasy, and it is doomed because of its polarized undertow.

2. *The belief that other men in her past have mistreated her,* while you really understand her and know "how to love her." This feeds into the distorted yet romantic macho notion of woman as helpless victim, waiting for *him,* the one man in the world who will understand and love her as she needs to be.

Healthy women with positive self-esteem choose men who treat them well. A woman who has a history of having been "hurt," "mistreated," or abused has participated in creating these interactions. Her choices unconsciously reflect her own self-esteem problems, which you will have to contend with inevitably and be drained by.

3. *The belief that this woman has been misunderstood and that she is not the way other people say she is.* You believe that you see the magic and specialness— the jewel others have missed or misperceive and see negatively.

The macho fallacy is that *you* will help her reach her *true potential.* You will give her the guidance and support that will allow her to become the person only you know her to be.

Be very wary to the degree that any of these "macho distortions" seem to be the case. They are the most negative indications.

How Do You Respond to Her Reality?

1. Do you like her family and friends? If a woman really likes you and is right for you, generally her friends will like you too and you will like them. Friends express the essence and true feelings of a person. She is probably much like them. If they don't like you, it is unlikely that she *really* likes you. The same is true of her family.

What kind of values do the people she surrounds herself with have? How do they reflect her? Determine this based not on what she says her values are, but on how she was living before she met you. How does her prior lifestyle reveal her? How did she live? How did she handle money? What is her connection to family and friends? What is the endurance and quality of her relationships with other people?

An honest evaluation of her personal choices is essential to determine longer-range compatibility.

2. Do you give her the same freedom to be herself that you give women with whom you are not emotionally involved? Or are you more critical of her, and have higher

expectations and thus treat her differently? For example, with other women are you relaxed and casual when they express certain kinds of attitudes and feelings, but with her do you get disturbed by, or cringe, when she expresses the same ideas and feelings you would accept in others? If you are trying to place her on a pedestal of purity, you are inviting her to "hide" from you and to manipulate instead of reveal herself if she wants to "keep you" and eventually this will backfire.

If you see her as greatly different from other women, you are probably going to be disillusioned. Men and women in our society tend to be different in their content, but relationships turn on process—the how, not the what. To set one woman apart rather than accept the fact that the struggle with her will be the same as it is with most other women reflects your fear and resistance to the reality of relationships.

The more you tend to set her on a pedestal, the more you are making a statement that you don't like real women. You are going to become angry at her when you come to feel like you were fooled or manipulated. You thought that she was different and then she turned out to be the same. By blaming *her* you will learn nothing about yourself!

A positive sign for relationship success exists when you see her as being similar or not that different from all other women and she sees you as being similar or not that different from all other men, and yet you still love each other. It is a grandiose delusion that you are different from the other men she has been with and that she has seen your specialness in a way no other woman has, or that you have finally found a woman who rises above all others in a perfect blend of values and behaviors that other women don't have. The more you believe she is different, the more likely that she will emerge as just the same, if not "worse."

3. Are you trying to be a different person when you are with her than you are? Why? By doing so, are you exhibit-

ing self-hate, or sensing rejection if you are yourself? It is only a matter of time before you go back to being who you were before you met her.

Have you made changes in the way you dress to please or impress her? Do you choose the kinds of activities to share with her that you normally don't find enjoyable to impress or please her? Do you hide important things about yourself? Why?

Some new experiences can be expanding, but if you are trying to be much different than you are ordinarily, or she is trying to be much different, that will put a pressure on both of you to fear experiencing or expressing the reality and also suggests either self-hate or a sense that the other person does not like you as you are.

4. What is your physical response to her? Is your body relaxed and comfortable when you are with her? Do you feel safe in the free expression of your ideas, feelings, and concerns, or do you feel yourself getting tense when you are about to discuss something difficult? Are you overly concerned or self-conscious with timing and responses because you sense her rejection of you otherwise? What is your body telling you?

How do you feel when she is *not* with you? Are you anxious and distracted, fearing she might not come back or call or be available?

Or do you find that you are more comfortable and actually more at peace when you are apart from her, in spite of your attraction to her?

These are important feelings to recognize. In the former you may be sensing her lack of genuine caring for you and in the latter you may be aware of not really feeling good being with her. These feelings tend to increase with time.

The most positive feeling, in terms of the future of your relationship with her, would be that you feel comfortable and trusting in the relationship so that your times apart, though you might miss her presence, are about the same in level of energy, activity, and satisfaction, as your times with her. If there is a great sense of release or a great sense of anxiety and tension when you move in either direction, that suggests problems for the future of the relationship.

Process versus Content

Ultimately, relationships get in trouble on a process level. No matter how wonderful the other person is, every relationship "becomes the same" when deeper process takes over. It is easy to control an initial image, but living and being that image over time is impossible.

Don't look strictly at content or the "what" of another person. Observe *how* a woman relates to you. For example, she may talk about independence and a career. You may talk together about separate lives and the importance of keeping one's own friends. But to what extent does she, in actuality, make the relationship the focus of her life right after she meets you?

To what extent does the relationship impact on her life so that when you are having an argument with her, for example, she is not able to work, and will even blame you for that?

To what extent do you feel guilty, now that you've met her, whenever you want to go off and do something by yourself or with a friend?

To what extent do you feel an obligation to tell her where you are going and when you are coming back? Do you feel you need to lie to her when, at the beginning of your relationship, you are dating other women too or doing something she might not approve of?

How often, also, do you feel you have to hide a true feeling such as boredom or wanting to be somewhere else when you are with her? Do you have to censor many "negative" feelings? Do you rationalize that you can't tell her because it would hurt her feelings?

This kind of process will tend to intensify rather than loosen up over time, and it will make the relationship progressively fragile, shallow, and uncomfortable. Manipulation will quickly replace relating.

Power Balance

A critical dimension for predicting the future of the relationship is an examination of its power balance. When the power is significantly out of balance, with one person consistently fearful of the other and accommodating, the relationship will be volatile and fragile, moving between sentimental clinging and outbursts of resentment.

As a man feeling insecure with a woman, and thus giving away your power to her by being always the one who is available and accommodating, while she is pushing away or being evasive, it is actually *exciting* at the beginning because there is a sense of challenge, distance, and uncertainty. However, what does this reality tell you about where she is with you?

The general rule of thumb is that the person with an overbalance of power in the relationship will tend to get bored, while the powerless person stays "hungry" for reassurance and love and is thus "excited." The excitement is something other than love and the end result will be profound hurt and self-dissipation.

Habit Patterns

It is important to look at another person's habit patterns early and be honest with yourself about how you feel about them. Irritating mannerisms and habits can be like water grinding away at a stone.

Some examples of the kinds of things you might want to look at are: Is she always a little late? Does she have a tendency to forget things or to procrastinate? What does she do with her leisure time? Does she do active things or is she quite passive? In general, what is her energy level? How magical is her thinking? Is she "into" psychic healing or astrology, and how does that reflect who she is as a person otherwise and how will that impact on you? Does she "love" people and is she therefore "always" on the phone? When you hear her talking to someone, do you cringe or get otherwise uncomfortable?

How dependable is she? Can you count on her to carry through on a promise or commitment, a responsibility or request? Is it common for her not to show up or do something she said she would? Or do you have a sense of ease around her knowing that she will competently handle what she tells you she will and that she can truly be counted on?

Are there issues around matters such as temperature? Is she cold all the time, while you like the windows open and fresh air blowing through? Does she live on fast foods and frozen entrees while you prefer a more natural, whole-foods diet, or vice versa? Does she spend hours making herself up? Does she take pills regularly and is she "always" suffering from ailments? All of these little things that in a romantic period you have a tendency to overlook or interpret generously can build into greater and greater distractions and irritations if you know that you ordinarily react negatively to them.

A client of mine was involved with a woman who was always on the phone with friends and relatives. At the beginning he tended to interpret this positively, even though emotionally it bothered him. "She has so many loving friends and relatives that she cares about. She is such a loving person." The deeper part of him resented the fact that she was on the phone constantly, and it became a crucial factor in their marriage. After a few years, these phone calls readily brought him to insulting outbursts that severely damaged the relationship.

The Dynamics of the Relationship

1. The management of conflict and anger is a crucial element. To what degree can the two of you fight with each other and then move from that to a feeling that there is a better understanding between you and a renewed sense of harmony and relaxed interchange? To what degree are blaming and guilt a part of each conflict and to what extent does she make it "impossible" for you to express anger or confront her, because she cries immediately, or accuses you of attacking her and being insulting and hurtful?

2. Do you see her as perfect and feel you are flawed compared to her? Does she share that perception? Is she supposedly the "loving" one and the healthy, "caring" one, while you are seen as the "insensitive" one with the "problem"?

Do you feel the majority of the guilt and responsibility when there is a problem? This tendency to feel responsible will intensify over time and create a powerful undertow of anger and self-hate.

3. How volatile is the relationship? Does it go from extreme highs to extreme lows? Are there constant break-ups and reconciliations, misunderstandings and hurt feelings? In other words, how careful do you have to be around her so as to avoid "pushing her buttons"? How much intellectualizing is there about the relationship? Are you always trying to figure it out? These are all signs of the fear of encountering the reality of each other and the relationship,

or living with her in the unromanticized middle zone, reality undistorted by false perceptions.

Probably the best or healthiest relationships begin without intensely romantic feelings, but where there is a genuine basis for being with each other on a friendship level and where there is enjoyment of each other's company without concern over commitment or future. Add to that a balanced flow of power, healthy conflict resolution free of blaming and guilt, a sense of being known for who you are and knowing your partner, and a relaxed desire to be fully present with little need to escape or avoid through distraction, and you have a fine potential for growth in a good relationship.

TO THE WOMEN WHO THINK THEY LOVE TOO MUCH

Marcella saw herself as a "woman who loved too much." Talking to her, it was easy to get the impression that men fell into one of two groups: the psychopathic narcissists who used women and could love nothing and no one except themselves; and the "baby boys," as she called them, who were nice and sweet but really were frightened of the world and looking for a woman to soothe and mother them. She regularly read books and articles by other similarly biased women and female psychologists that categorized men into groupings of varying degrees of being losers and louses, unable to appreciate and fulfill the many loving, caring, giving, and "grown-up" women in the world.

The more Marcella read, and the more this negative perception and evaluation of men was substantiated, the harder it was for her to relate to them. They could sense her anger, her judgments, and her analyzing of them. There was no discussion about it. Marcella was convinced that her beliefs were valid.

Some of her friends told her she expected too much and needed to be less perfectionistic and critical. "Don't expect banjos and bells. There are a lot of nice, sweet guys out there—just don't expect the big, romantic rush. It's self-destructive."

Yet it all seemed to her like short-term pep talks, because in her mind she herself had evolved too far in her loving capacity and was living in a society with many other unlucky women who were trying to relate to and love selfish, woman-hating or immature males who manipulated and played on women's vulnerability and need to love. Periodically she would try to be "forgiving" in order to have a relationship. Unfortunately, it never worked, and although this provided further evidence for Marcella that most men were emotionally crippled, she was unable to see that while she saw herself as "loving too much," her deeper, real feelings toward men were contempt and self-righteous rage and that *these* feelings were being unconsciously and consciously transmitted and were the cause for men backing away from her.

The Women Who Love Too Much

Women who think they love too much are like men who work too hard in the mistaken belief that they are doing it for their partner. In fact, each is doing what they do for their own needs, unconsciously using the other person as a rationalization for their own defensive motives and uncontrollable compulsions. The end point for each is the same: feelings of disappointment, rejection, anger, and a frustrated sense of being unappreciated and misunderstood. All the while, each is unable to hear, absorb, and act on the plea of their partner, clearly telling them *"Don't do that for me, because it doesn't feel good."*

On a television promotion for a program about women who love too much, the woman interviewed was quoted as saying in frustration about the man she "loved too much," "I knew he was a creep. He drank too much and he had an eye for women. But I thought that I could change him." Listening to the women on the television broadcast carefully, even the psychologically unsophisticated could observe that she doesn't really like the man at all. Her description of him is clearly hostile and not loving. What she "loves" is the fantasy of fulfilling her needs through him.

Women who think that they love too much and that they get hurt by insensitive men are loving not the man but a projection of their own needs. They are hurt not by him, but by their own distortions in perception, which cause them to see potentials and capacities for "intimacy" and closeness in him that he cannot have, within the context of their interaction. They are not taking in the reality of the man within the framework of their relationship. In other words, with a woman who "loves too much," the man will inevitably distance and "love too little" in order to protect himself from the engulfment he experiences. *In the context of their polarized romance, he can no more move closer to her than she can back off from him.*

Inevitably and predictably, feminine women caught up in the throes of a polarized relationship that is no longer in the early romantic phase accuse their masculine counterpart (the "macho" male) of being selfish, critical, distant, cold, controlling, insensitive, and unable to be intimate. While there is some truth to what they are saying in that his conditioning to be masculine externalizes him, they are unaware, as they hurl their epithets, of how their own defensive and internalized process causes them to "give him what he doesn't want." They are pressuring him for more of something that he doesn't have, and are angered by the reality of who he is and not what he is withholding. They "fall in love with him" because of his "manliness" and then are frustrated by the limitations imposed by the conditioning that makes him attractive "as a man"; the very qualities that create the initial excitement that drew her to him.

Betty, thirty-four years old and very much wanting to be married because of anxiety over her age, a desire to have children, and fears about her financial security, became involved with Sean, an advertising writer, who spent his weekends doing "macho" things such as racing in the desert or hang gliding in the hills and drinking with his buddies.

Betty saw herself as loving Sean very much, yet could not refrain from telling him how critical, insensitive, egoistic, and boorish he was. At the same time, she described herself as caring, patient, loving, and sensitive—even as she insulted him.

She was totally unaware of the hostility she directed at him almost continuously, in the mistaken belief that she was being "helpful" and constructive. She was quick to remember every slight, every painful incident or hurting remark that he had made, while ignoring, minimizing, or forgetting the good or generous things he'd done, which she tended to diminish as guilt-motivated, or as an attempt to buy her goodwill. She spoke of this derisively, even though it was clear that his worldly success was one of his major attractive features. She would throw past incidents up to him frequently in order to show him how hurtful and sexist he was. She would even tell him that his macho manner terrified her and that she lived in fear of being hurt physically by him when he got angry. Then, after attacking him in this way, she would protest her love and desire to be married to him.

There was no awareness of how her process—the urgent, pressuring, and relentless negative responses caused by her powerful and frustrated cravings and needs—was causing him, in part, to distance and respond in the macho ways that she hated, out of self-protection. She could not see how she triggered in him many of the responses and behaviors she abhorred.

She would alternate between demanding more intimacy and criticizing him for his lack of caring: telling him that she wanted to "be closer," then becoming hurt and angered when he said anything that she didn't like hearing; "giving herself over to him," even when he would clearly indicate that he didn't want her to and then acting pained by his withdrawal and resistance to commitment and his supposed desire to control her.

Cynthia also "loved too much." A very "feminine" woman, she cried readily and felt wounded constantly by the men she saw herself as giving to, who, she felt, were too selfish or "fearful of intimacy" to respond as she wanted them to.

When Cynthia came for counseling with her lover, Nathan, she saw herself as there to "help" him. She spoke of him in his presence as being "damaged" in matters of "love" and relationships. According to her, he was immature, his friends were uncouth, his lovemaking was selfish, and he was too ambitious and preoccupied with his work to give their relationship the attention she felt it needed and warranted.

She called him selfish repeatedly because he didn't seem to appreciate or respond positively to things she saw herself as giving to him, even as he told her emphatically that he didn't want her to make him her focus and didn't want her intensity of involvement and "love." He told her he felt engulfed by her and upset by her tendency always to be inquiring as to what he was doing and whom he was with.

Through all of the sessions it was patently clear that she could not see *who* and *what* Nathan was. She had "fallen in love" with her idea of him and her fantasy of the relationship. Whenever his "reality" would intrude on and conflict with that fantasy, she would respond with pain and anger. She was unable to see how this disappointment caused her to attack and accuse him continuously, which polarized him even further and drove him into self-protective withdrawals.

Sylvia, forty-seven years old and a nutrition consultant, loved her husband Fred, an economics professor at an East Coast university, whom she had been married to for twenty-four years, "too much." While she did not attack him directly, she insisted continuously that he was depressed and in need of psychiatric help and had significant emotional problems because he was withdrawn and insisted on his freedom and right not to spend much leisure time with her if he didn't enjoy it, since their son was now grown and on his own.

When they were together, he was often silent and looked unhappy and, in fact, told her he didn't enjoy himself with her. She "diagnosed" him as suffering from a mid-life crisis, and of fearing closeness because he hated his mother. She urged him to see a psychiatrist, which he adamantly refused to do. "My 'sickness' is that I haven't had the guts to be real," he told her, "and no shrink in the world can change that. Only I can, and that's what I'm doing."

He would tell her that throughout their marriage he did not really enjoy the social evenings with relatives and friends, but that he had been too "responsible" and guilt-ridden to acknowledge and act on his feelings. Further, he indicated that he resented the pressure of being "always responsible" for "everything." He wasn't going to pretend anymore, he told her, since he saw himself as being in the last decades of his life.

While Sylvia saw herself as being very loving, it was clear that she didn't really know or hear Fred, nor could she accept the truth of what he was telling her. She saw herself as loving, in part, because she continually responded to him out of *her need* to instantly accommodate him, out of an unconscious fearfulness, of which she was unaware but which exacerbated Fred's sense of guilt and "self-hate" that made him feel depressed and oppressed. Although a successful person in her own career, she seemed unable to maintain her identity or strength around him. She had an insatiable need for reassurance and hung on in the face of his coldness. She "lived" for his "love" and approval, which he had never genuinely given her in their entire marriage and which he clearly did not feel.

Further, she saw herself as "loving him too much" because she stayed with him, in spite of knowing of an affair he had shortly after their marriage. She never retaliated by having affairs of her own. She saw herself as doing this for him when in fact her religious principles and traditional upbringing, inculcated years before she met him, actually kept her from doing this. In fact, Fred often told her that he would feel less guilty and self-hating and possibly more excited and loving if she had only had an affair of her own. It would show, he said, that she could take care of herself and make him feel less responsible.

What saved and improved their marriage to the point where each was able to love the other freely and genuinely was Sylvia's ability through counseling to see clearly how she had been relating to her fantasy of what she needed Fred to be, and thus had unknowingly been rejecting and critical of him. This had contributed to his withdrawal and produced his coldness. Her change freed Fred to respond to the many wonderful qualities that Sylvia did have.

In their "new relationship," they spent less time with each other than they had in the early years of their marriage, but the quality of their experience together steadily improved. The best of each was now able to surface.

Typically, feminine-defensively-driven women unconsciously "love" their men in the same distorted way that macho men "love" their women: as extensions of their own needs and as objects for need satisfaction.

Neither Sylvia, Betty, nor Cynthia really loved their men at all. You can't love somebody in an authentic way and be afraid of them at the same time. Nor is it love when you are unable to maintain your own strong and separate self around your partner, while being unable to see him for who he is without criticizing and attacking him for his relationship inadequacies. In these instances, even the "loyalty" these women felt was defeating to the relationship because it was experienced as engulfment and pressure, not as caring. More love might have been released by the men had the women been able to demonstrate the separate strength and self-esteem required to take care of themselves, rather than "sacrificing" themselves.

To love somebody is to be strong and at your best around them, to be able to resist and say no and not just accommodate, and to be free of the sense of being a victim who blames the other for his or her own unhappiness. Otherwise strong, independent women who lose their strength and autonomy in a relationship with their man and who respond out of fear and the need to please and to search for the reassurance of being loved are not doing that for the man, nor are they loving at all.

The woman who "loves too much" is being defensive because she is not consciously in control of her behavior, nor is she truly making a choice. Rather, she is being driven by repressed and denied needs and feelings, often acting uncontrollably and against her better sense. She is as unable to let go of her compulsive "loving" style as the workaholic man is unable to slow down his pace as he looks to blame his compulsion to work on the needs and demands of his wife and family. While such letting go might actually produce some of the love she desires, she is emotionally unable to do it.

She is giving something by "loving too much" that not only is inappropriate but actually damaging to the relationship she cherishes. She is much like the woman who spends hours preparing a meal "for her man" that was not desired or asked for and that she then puts pressure on him to eat, even though he is not hungry, consequently causing her to feel hurt and rejected because he did not appreciate her efforts or respond enthusiastically.

Women have complained correctly about men's patronizing protectiveness, allegedly done for them (e.g., "I don't want you to make my decisions or fight my battles," she tells him repeatedly). The feminine counterpart to this masculine tendency is a "giving of herself" to a man who not only doesn't want it but is polarized, engulfed, and "damaged" by it, because it promotes his guilt over not being able to reciprocate, and thereby intensifies his proclivity for "self-hate."

Furthermore, by "loving him too much" she sets the stage for "hating him too much" when she finally begins to get in touch with and express the rage and disappointment that continually build up behind her "loving too much" orientation. To add insult to injury, when she finally gets in touch with the anger, she sees him as causing and deserving it.

All of us would rather be loved in limited ways for the person we know ourselves to be than be showered with love when we realize that the person who is "loving" us is responding to a fantasy of who we are and satisfying their own needs, not ours. Nothing is as satisfying as being seen accurately and still being cared about and loved; little is as frustrating, unsatisfying, numbing, and even distressing as being the object of someone's "love" when we know that we must hide or alter ourselves and our responses so as not to disappoint or disillusion. Inevitably, "love" turns to resentment.

You cannot love anybody "too much." Loving somebody in a way that is not self-serving means loving them as they wish to be loved and for who they are and not as we need to love them and for who we need them to be.

Feminine loving, like macho loving, is self-centered love. Both "fall in love" with their fantasy of the other and are, because of defensive needs, unable and unwilling to recognize, acknowledge, and relate to the reality of who they are "in love" with. This is the reason why relationships so often end "suddenly" and abruptly and with great pain, with one person left feeling shocked, betrayed, or deeply hurt. Had the "injured parties" seen correctly who they were with, there would have been no such unfortunate surprises.

The feminine unconscious, by defensively intensifying women's personal needs, perpetuates an imbalance that promotes polarization and causes in men a sensation of being engulfed, at the same time that women feel rejected, starved, and unloved as a result of the externalization and need for distance produced by men's defenses and the masculine unconscious. Eventually this causes women to resent and then to hate men for being selfish and withholding, when in fact the polarization or psychological undertow paralyzes men and makes them literally unable to give *more,* in the same way as women in these relationships are unable to give *less,* even after being informed by objective observers that to do so would help the relationship and allow her to love him better and with less pain.

The polarization produces a standoff. She is unable to back off and he is unable to get closer, and when neither leaves the relationship, the stage for intimate terrorism is set. He stays but gives her almost nothing, while she stays and gives him "too much." He is "paralyzed" by guilt; she is "paralyzed" by fear.

The woman who believes she "loves too much" is an emotional sister to the women of yesterday who "suffered" and generated guilt in their families by playing the role of martyr and victim, complaining that "nobody appreciates me for all that I'm giving."

The woman who "loves too much" often comes to believe that she chose the "wrong man" to love: a man who is unable to appreciate her. By seeing herself as the victim of a "poor choice," she never gets to learn from the experience. The underlying imbalance is the problem. Unless these defensive imbalances are changed, each new relationship ultimately will be transformed into the same one as the last.

Finally, women should know that when they "love too

much" they promote a man's self-destruction because in self-protective reaction he pulls even farther into himself; begins to "do" more to escape rather than relate; behaves inauthentically out of guilt and self-hatred; disconnects to escape from anxiety, boredom, deadness, and anger, and pursues outlets that allow him to distract himself so that he won't have to leave a relationship he, too, is dependent on because of his defensive needs.

Clearly, men and women do not seek each other out as partners in order to frustrate and hurt each other. Therefore, the starting point for a relationship free of victims, blaming, and guilt is the awareness that what we get in a relationship is created unconsciously by who we are and what we give, and furthermore, seeing how the polarization creates an undertow that blocks the movement of the relationship in the direction we consciously believe we would like it to go. If men are "flawed," then women are too, because both are socialized by the same process.

Growth beyond our polarized defenses that causes us to perceive, respond, and choose in defensive ways is the "answer"; the answer is not the pursuit of someone "better," which is a fantasy that perpetuates the "illusion of the difference" or the false hopes created when we try to create change by altering content rather than our own process.

Guidelines for Women Who "Love Too Much"

You are not loving a man when:

1. You are continually angered by who he is when he is with you.
2. You accommodate him and are unable to define and maintain your own preferences and boundaries around him.

3. You are afraid of him.
4. You constantly seek reassurance of his love.
5. Your "love" causes you to be unhappy and feel like a victim of his insensitivity or lack of "intimacy capacity."
6. You expect that your "love" will change him into the loving person that you feel he isn't.
7. You see him as the cause of the relationship problem, without seeing yourself as an equal ingredient in the overall problem.
8. You see him as "damaged" and "incapable" of love and in need of psychiatric help, while you see yourself as the opposite.
9. You see your role as "helping" him overcome "his" problems.
10. You are in pain because of *his* resistances and problems in getting close.

PART TWO

WITH SEXUALITY

7

SEXUAL EXCITEMENT AND DISTANCE: SEX IS NOT SEX, IS SEX, IS NOT SEX

Carl's sex life was starting to "drive him crazy," unfortunately not from pleasure. " I don't understand myself," he thought. "I meet Ann and she excites me incredibly. I thought that if I could get her into bed, I'd want to make love to her forever. Lo and behold, she wants to go to bed with me too—she even comes on to me directly, we go to bed, I come once, and it's like—what's next? I'm not interested anymore. Then I meet someone else, like Alice, who's not half as sexy and she hardly lets me touch her— and I'm hot for her all the time—even though she's not *really* sexual, doesn't like it at all the way Ann did.

"Sex ruined my marriage that way. I loved my wife, but the closer we got the more she wanted to make love and the less I was interested. It seems almost funny thinking about how I was giving her all these feminine speeches. 'Can't we just hug and see what happens?' That's supposed to be liberated, but actually in all honesty I felt like a eunuch saying it, because I knew what my real motives were—to escape, maybe even fall asleep in her arms—*before* anything got started—and, of course, she sensed it too. She knew me too well. I was the guy who always had a hard-on when we first met and she was still living with Brian, and I thought she'd never leave him."

It particularly bothered Carl when he was married that he began to get interested in picking up women at bars and on out-of-town trips. The bottom fell out for him in terms of his confusion and self-hate when he picked up a young women hitchiker on the way to work and found himself practically begging her to have sex with him. The night before, his wife had begged *him* to make love to her and he had refused. Now he was with an "unattractive" woman whom he didn't know—with whom he was embarrassed even to be in the same car—behaving this way; and he found himself so excited sexually that he couldn't concentrate on his driving.

The business of sex confused and filled him with such guilt and self-hate that he found himself sometimes wishing that sex didn't exist at all. The pleasure hardly seemed worth the price he had paid, in so many ways.

Polarized Sexuality

We can understand sex, with its countless dilemmas, illusions, problems, and misleading aspects by not thinking of sex as sex, but as an expression of the polarized distance needs of men and women.

Consequently, when we feel that we are sexually excited and *really want sex,* something else inside of us is being triggered, and our sexual appetite is a disguise for these needs. This is much like the way in which food is not food, is food, is not food in contemporary society, where eating is only minimally used to satisfy biological, nutritional needs, but is more often used to reduce boredom, tension, and anxiety; structure social interactions; sublimate love and dependency needs; redirect anger; provide "excitement" and distraction; reward ourselves and others; "prove" love; ritualize our time; and avoid conflict and pain. Eating becomes an indirect expression of a host of needs other than biological ones among socialized people, particularly when playfulness, interaction, and spontaneity are absent.

Were sex actually sex, the expression of a biological need, it would be relatively easy to manage and we could deal with it sensibly. It would be used primarily for procreation and not as an expression of a myriad of other needs. Because sexual desire in the world of the gender-polarized unconscious is only incidentally and occasionally related to real sexual appetite, it creates a jungle and a jumble of convoluted intertwining motives, illusions, disappointments, expectations, distortions, ensions, and eventually despair about ever "getting it right.'" It becomes unmanageable to the degree that these gender-related motives are unknown to ourselves, generating our sex drive and shaping our sex lives.

We come to believe we have a sexual problem when we don't. When we keep going in that direction and handle it as such, we come to conclude we have a mechanical problem, or a problem born of "ignorance" or misunderstanding. Then we enter the nightmare world of gadgetry, "educational treatments," therapies or even sexual surgeries that temporarily hold forth a promise of a "cure" by reducing our anxieties and changing our focus. However, since our sexual problems have little or nothing to do with sex, we must eventually pay the price of that temporary relief. It is similar to the way people approach their "eating problems" by moving from one diet or new approach to eating to another (chewing more slowly, changing schedules, etc.).

Distance and Excitement

Feminists have taught us that rape is a manifestation of power, not sexuality. The rapist is looking to control, humiliate, and release rage and seeking relief from feelings of unbearable tension stemming from unconscious resentments toward the opposite sex.

Recently, sexually liberated women, newly in touch with their sexual desires and needs and more direct in their pursuit of satisfaction, came to discover that the so-called sexually driven male, as they once perceived him, is now as likely to withdraw and feel threatened by a woman's sexual urgency even as he tries to satisfy her. Confronted with the reality of his former fantasy of a sexually desirous woman, to his despair he discovers that he cannot perform or that his interest is diminished or gone.

The growing singles world gives us another vantage point from which to see how sexual desire and excitement are a matter of distance elements. A couple goes to bed, perhaps on the first or second date, with seemingly great sexual appetite and desire for each other. The sex was "great," but the man, who believed he really wanted "great sex," never comes back for more; or the woman, who seemed to have been so "turned on" and sexually responsive, is not interested in a repeat performance.

There is an often expressed "singles lament": "The ones I'm really turned on to don't seem to want me; while the people who want me, I can't get excited over." Then, finally, the disturbing conclusion: "The good ones are all taken, only the undesirable or 'sick' ones are left."

The fantasy component that made it seem as though sex was what was really wanted in all of these instances was transformed and exposed to be a distance issue. Perhaps the man sensed that the woman was really "needy" for other things and sex was a trap he instinctively sought to avoid; or she realized he was needy, and she was the object that was supposed to satisfy those underlying nonsexual needs he had for control, contact, or validation, and she quickly ended the liaison because she felt used. One or both never again were interested in repeating the supposedly satisfying sexual encounter unless, perhaps, enough time elapsed to allow the former partner to once again become a symbol or fantasy, far enough away psychologically to become of sexual interest again.

Traditional men are known to get turned on to centerfold pictures or pornography, the distant female sex object. In fact, such men may masturbate to the photo, thought, or fantasy while an attractive, willing wife or girlfriend is lying in bed in the next room.

Then again, when a man who has become sexually disinterested in his wife or girlfriend is informed by her that she is leaving and/or that she has found someone else, at once this woman, who had little to no appeal to him anymore, is suddenly the object of a voracious sexual appetite.

Larry had been secretly plotting ways to get his live-in partner to move out. When they first met, Larry, who had recently emigrated to America from a Middle Eastern country, was beginning a career as a jewelry designer. He met Katrina, a classic Middle American, wholesome-looking blonde woman, at a jewelry convention. They went to dinner on their first date and spent the rest of the evening making love and playing in their poolside hotel room.

Soon thereafter Katrina moved into his apartment and seemed progressively less concerned with her career than with what Larry was doing when he was not with her. Her insecurity drove her to bring up marriage more and more frequently. Their sexual honeymoon turned into cold nights of bickering and only occasional good sex.

Though he told himself he wasnt going to do it, Larry
began to have sex with other women, first only when he
was out of town, but soon began secretly seeing the secretary for one of his clients. The tension and frustration he
was feeling at home because of Katrina's insecurity drove
him away from her and to the beds of other women.

Larry decided it was time to end the relationship with
Katrina. Each time he'd try, she would break down in hys-
terics and he would feel too guilty to make her go. He came
for therapy to find ways to resolve the situation and end
the live-in arrangement in a constructive manner.

During the first few sessions, his entire focus was on "exit
strategies." Then one day a dramatic reversal occurred. He
came into therapy crying because Katrina had recently begun
a job as a buyer in a women's clothing shop and he noticed
that she was becoming distant, vague about her schedule,
and would regularly put him on hold when he telephoned
her at work—something she had never done before. He discovered, after continuous prodding, that she was involved
with another man. When Larry became enraged at her "infidelity," she told him she was moving out.

He became desperate. This confirmed bachelor playboy
was now begging for marriage. While he had been the one
who had "fooled around," suddenly his sexual passion for
Katrina was aroused to the point that he was as obsessed
with making love to her as he had been the first weekend
they were together. He completely lost interest in seeing
other women. When he finally succeeded in persuading her
to end her affair and marry him, within six weeks of being
together again, the old pattern returned. He found himself
losing interest again, at the same time that she clung to him
for reassurance and pressured for romantic lovemaking that
he was "too busy" to give her.

Within three months' time he began calling the women
he had been seeing while he was living with Katrina, before

they had gotten married. His sexual desire for Katrina had all but disappeared once again.

Larry's experience in reverse is seen by, for example, the "frigid wife" or girlfriend who learns that her husband or lover finally is going to leave her as he had threatened to do, perhaps for another woman. Suddenly a craving for sex with him appears in her. "Please make love to me," she may be heard to say, something completely untypical of her.

An Object Is "Sexy": A "Real Person" Isn't

A man is married to a women for twenty years and he still can't get enough of her sexually. He wants sex every night, if not more often. As a psychotherapist, I have seen a number of such couples for counseling. Invariably, when talking with the wife alone, it turns out that during all those years, she *never* remembers really desiring sex herself, though out of fear of rejection or her husband's anger, a sense of duty, or the need to accommodate, she never said no unless she had a "legitimate" reason. He may or may not have known that she basically got little to nothing from the sex. More often, in fact, inwardly she felt irritated and pressured by his demands, and sex was closer to a nightmare than a pleasure for her. While he had been thinking that they had a great sex life, she had been totally shut down.

Conversely, there is the instance of Jim, age fifty and married for twenty-six years to a woman who always wanted sexual intimacy with him. He was her masculine ideal, charming, a driven provider, self-contained, unemotional, and seemingly in control and always responsible. He was very sexy in her eyes.

Inwardly, Jim resented the marriage. He felt trapped by it. Had he been honest and free of guilt, he would have told her he was not interested in sexual contact with her. Indeed, on some level she sensed that, and her urgency to be reassured, her fear of abandonment, the great psychological distance from the "perfect man" she "needed" had created in her an insatiable desire for sex with him. *He was the object and she was always ready*, a reverse of the more common traditional polarization where she is a distant, resistant, and "unavailable" object, a mystery in terms of what she was *really* feeling, a constant one-night stand because the man always had the sense that each time might be the last. Therefore, there was always a challenge to overcome, and he never lost interest in "sex."

With the help of psychotherapy, Jim's wife stopped pursuing her husband for lovemaking after she realized that she was responding to his distancing and the insecurity it produced in her. Jim's sexual interest in his wife rekindled and they experienced better sex than they had ever had.

In times past, when women never believed that sexuality was their "need" or even of any interest to them, this would have been considered a "good sexual relationship": The man always able to perform and the woman pleased to be desired because it reassured her that she still had her man, even as her deeper self was resisting, wishing she didn't have to, and feeling angry over being pressured, controlled, and "used" by him. She may not have consciously acknowledged that, but her body, emotions, and deeper self knew it, as she "suffered" an endless succession of physical ailments and/or "mysterious" mood swings, crying spells, and depressions. As long as she liked her husband and wanted to stay married, she was glad he wanted her even though she got nothing from the sex act itself.

She is hiding her true self. He never really knows who she is, what she feels or what her needs are. She remains a mysterious object. The distance he needs in order to maintain a "sexual desire" is always there, so he is always potent. We hear stories about our "horny" grandfathers who constantly lusted after their wives, women who were aware of no real need for sex in themselves, but were willing to service their partners so long as the men were nice to them. Some women claimed to enjoy it, though most could more or less do without it.

Masculinity is an externalized, disconnected state. Therefore, the greatest unconscious trigger for sexual excitement is a reflection of that need for distance and control. So long as she is an object to be used, distant and resistant, and he is in control and reducing the tensions for contact that build in him, he is hungry for her. She has the symbols he needs to validate his masculinity (pretty face, big breasts, etc.). With him, she is only a reactor with no self. He craves her sexually long after she comes to resent or even hate him and wish for his disappearance or death. Or suddenly, in a burst of rage, she leaves him when she gains the confidence to "be herself." He is surprised, shocked, and terrified by this event.

Now, at the same time, his supposedly frigid former wife meets a man with all the symbols of intimacy. He is the gentle man, the "spiritual" person, the understanding therapist or man who will "rescue" her and give her the understanding and intimacy that she craves. He has what she wants. Now he is the object and he is not really there as a person. He does not expose himself nor is he really interested in commitment and marriage. Now *she* has the great sexual longing because he knows *her* very well, while he remains distant and closed off from her, a fantasy object whom she thinks she knows but really doesn't. He is her fantasy now, just as she was her husband's previously.

She would "go to the ends of the earth for him," have sex with him anytime, make a fool of herself, as she often does to be with him. The fantasy distance is now hers and none of his reality intrudes on her, so she is always "hot" for him. *She* has the optimal distance, and her craving to be reassured and her need to have control over this threatening situation are strong. She thinks of herself as a sexual woman and indeed is, in the way her husband was when he was excited by her distance, challenge, and *"unavailability."*

He is an object, distant and unreal, even though he *seems* to be real, much as she did formerly with her husband. He has no genuine motivation to be involved, even if he uses the language of intimacy and closeness beautifully. He manipulates her with the symbols of intimacy that she craves, much as the beautiful woman manipulates the man with the symbols to validate his masculinity that he craves. He believes he has found true love, while she knows inside herself that he has no idea who she really is. So long as she "needs" him she will allow him to feel loved and his macho needs to be fulfilled. While her reality and sexuality are totally distanced, she remains an object of great desire.

Whoever has the symbols the other craves, and withholds their reality because they are not really involved, creates "excitement" in the other. In the singles world, for example, both may do so on the first date when the lust is mutual. Then, when the *reality* of one or the other intrudes, the sexual excitement immediately goes out of balance and the sexual craving rarely remains mutual.

Traditional women understood or learned that to get and maintain a man's sexual excitement, they needed to create maximal distance — make a "mystery" of themselves, withhold their inner reality, and thus create the man's excitement. Actually, they were detached from their supposedly dominant husbands, whom they manipulated. Inside themselves, they knew their husbands were just boys; perhaps even fools in their eyes, though necessary evils.

Distance and Dysfunction (Absence of Excitement)

If we can understand who has the excitement by looking at the distance factor, we can also understand sexual distress, "symptoms" or dysfunction or the lack of "excitement."

Often, the sexually shut-down or "dysfunctional" male turns out to be a masculine machine who has unconscious needs for distance, but who finds himself in a situation where:

1. He is unable to set boundaries with his wife or partner, whose deeper feminine needs for closeness are unleashed and threaten to engulf him. This angers and threatens him. The guilt, however, prevents him from pushing her away as he would like to, or even saying "no" to her. His masculine compulsions compel him to try to perform.

2. She moves relentlessly toward him in search of "closeness" and "intimacy," and perhaps also, unconsciously, to punish and humiliate him for his control, insensitivity, and lack of "intimacy," with sex as her weapon and "closeness" needs as her cover. She is "insisting" on a closeness and involvement he cannot give. To him, she is "out of control" and pressuring. She is no longer the distant, unavailable, mysterious woman or controllable object that he needs in order to be "turned on."

3. She is sitting on intense (though denied and repressed) anger, which is covered by a veneer of "niceness" and the desire to "help him" with his "closeness problem," which only serves to make him feel more engulfed, guilt-ridden, and trapped. Her presence is "always there," and he becomes totally unable to create the distance he needs to

become excited. Even when she seems to give him distance by not being vocal in her demands for sex, he senses her relentless presence, the unspoken pressure she represents, and persistent movement toward him.

4. He *tries* to be excited out of guilt and a need to prove he can perform, rather than real desire. He becomes obsessed with his performance and things get worse.

5. Unconsciously, he desires distance that he can't get, and he becomes physically numb out of self-defense, protecting himself against the engulfment and her anger, not to mention his own anger, which he does not process consciously, but expresses through his symptoms or "dysfunction."

6. This may cause her to crave sex more in order to be reassured. His failure to perform, for example, creates a shift in the power balance. As his anxiety and self-hate over not performing increase, she goes into the driver's seat.

7. All along, she may be "nice to him" and "understanding," which intensifies his feeling of responsibility and his inability to perceive his situation accurately. He is convinced that she really loves him and that *he* has a problem because *he* is afraid of "closeness" (which in some cases is true, but is only one part of the total picture). He comes to believe and even hope that his "dysfunction" is a mechanical problem, because he cannot make emotional sense of this dilemma and therefore feels increasingly powerless or "impotent."

8. To try to "cure" the situation, he may close his eyes and thereby transform her into someone else, a distant sex object he can get excited by. This may work, but only as long as her movement toward him is not such that it forces him to confront the total reality of her again and lose hold of the distance the fantasy provides.

9. If she does make her reality too known, the beginning of the end of his sexuality with her is near. The distance he needs has been eliminated and he is exposed as being "sexless" with this "real" woman. There is no escape and no resolution, until and unless the undertow can be

exposed and rebalanced. At this point, he becomes intensely anxious, confused, and vulnerable to any promise of a quick "cure" or external, mechanical solution proffered by a "sex expert" pandering to his need and desperation to perform at any cost in order to preserve his masculine self-esteem and thus escape the intensely painful anxiety.

His "dysfunction" is not sexual, nor is it a reflection on his manliness. Rather, it is a distance-imbalance issue, and the dimensions of most sex therapy "cures" or "treatments," which promote greater "intimacy," are the antithesis of his "turn-on," which is the beautiful, nonpressuring, distant object who is basically uninterested in sex and keeps herself a mystery to maintain his excitement.

Distance and Impotence

To understand a dysfunction that results from lack of excitement, simply take the dimensions of the man's most exciting sexual fantasy and reverse them. The distant, unavailable object is now the all-too-real woman, demanding closeness and sex, which has stripped the man of all the control and distance that are the requirements of his maximal excitement.

The "frigid woman," until recently the norm, like the impotent male, was "frigid" because she was feeling engulfed by a man who was constantly pressuring her for sex, who was treating her like an object and was unable to see her as a person. Her defensive needs forced her to accommodate him and to fear telling him no. Much like the guilt-ridden, nonperforming male who pretends that he really does want the sex but that something has gone wrong with the equipment, the "frigid" woman is unable to set the boundaries she needs and therefore has no capacity for a real sexual response. Her "frigidity" and sexual closing off are a statement of self-protection and represent a need to regain boundaries and the psychological reality that is being denied and repressed by her "nice" outward self trying to love her man while she feels controlled and powerless.

In the traditional relationship, therefore, you have a man who is always excited but is using the woman to prove himself and maintain control, and the woman who is never excited. The distance needs are on his terms. His excitement, however, is not over her as a person, and she realizes that. She is being used and pushed away as a person, just as she is using the dysfunctional male whose reality she doesn't recognize, always "wanting him" and therefore blocking his need for distance. He is now an object of reassurance to her, just as she formerly was an object of masculine validation for him.

These dimensions of maximal excitement for the traditional man include:

Psychological distance on his part.

The inherent resistance and lack of sexual interest on her part.

An ever present challenge.

A need to control "his possession" and a sense of having that control.

A need for contact and closeness that can be released only through sexual intercourse.

The absence of her "reality"—he doesn't know who she really is and what goes on inside of her.

A lack of pressure to perform because she never *really* wants "it." In fact, there is always a sense that she is "doing" him a favor.

Her manipulation of him for her purposes, at a distance, by not exposing her true feelings.

The following may occur when these are reversed:

He has no psychological distance.

There is no resistance or lack of sexual desire on her part.

She is not a challenge.

He lacks a sense of control over her and the situation.

He does not need to use sex as a channel for his unexpressed needs for contact or closeness.

She is "all too real."

There is a pressure to perform because she indicates that she *really* wants sex and sex *is* her need.

Her true feelings are expressed.

Then the background elements that create a lack of excitement, dysfunction, impotence, or whatever label one chooses are present.

Distance and Liberation

There is a growing problem among "liberated" men and "liberated couples" who seem to get along perfectly—except that he has no sexual interest in her or there is no interest between them.

His deeper distancing self is talking—all while his liberated attitudes and desire to be "intimate" have created a guilt-motivated attempt at trying to be "close."

He invites an intimacy that his idealistic and abstracted "liberated" self tells him is right and healthy and something that he should want. However, his deeper masculine process or defenses, which demand distance for excitement and are not altered simply by adopting "goodwilled" attitudes, are being sabotaged by his "ideals."

His lover begins to feel defeated, having believed that she had found "the perfect man," liberated yet manly, who is now revealed as having a "fatal flaw" that both now seek to rationalize with philosophies about how men don't have to "perform," etc., etc. This is an often repeated rationalization they both express, but neither *really* believes or can live with it for any degree of time because of the constant underlying tension and obsession that is created in bed every night by the all-too-present undertow, even as it is denied or avoided by excuses over "working too hard," being worried, tired, or not feeling well. He has trapped himself with his liberated pretensions, which have made it a new "sin" to acknowledge his still-existing masculine psychological structure.

Talking about the "sex" itself is essentially futile if the undertow or the polarization remains unchanged. "Talking about it" as a "cure" or an antidote to the problems created by polarization must fail. The guilt and desire to be "nice and understanding" prevent the deeper resistances and imbalance from being made known and honestly acted on.

External solutions are then attempted, such as having sex less often, creating artificial turn-ons, or backing off until the uninterested person "really" starts to want it again. These "solutions" prove to be futile also, much like the alcoholic who tries to "cure" his problem by altering the circumstances under which he drinks.

What becomes the ultimate crazy-maker, the final nail in the coffin of sexuality, is the absence of limits to sex that has been generated over the years—as exists in the animal kingdom, where sex is a response to periods of "heat." Polarized defensiveness creates a sexuality without boundaries. This "artificial heat" is fueled by his endless defensive need for reassurance of his masculinity and her endless need for reassurance of closeness and being "loved."

The dysfunctional couple is faced with the cruel situation of being two people who feel that they "should" make love regularly, even while one or both are experiencing powerful resistance.

The stereotyped mental health notions set forth about maintaining a "healthy sex life" as a vital aspect of the good relationship drive the polarized couple deeper into desperation in their search for the ingredients that will create this supposedly obtainable, wonderful state and make them a "normal" couple.

Sex is not sex, or the same man who lusted uncontrollably at the beginning when sex was not available wouldn't suddenly be uninterested in sex when it is available. He is reacting now to the woman's urgent underlying desire to be close, which turns her on and him off.

If the issue were sex, the interest and desire for sex would not be so volatile—urgent one day, nonexistent the next, present in one always, and the other never. Rather, one would simply seek out a willing, skillful partner and create and maintain a sexual liaison of satisfaction.

Biology for Recreation

We are damaged when biology becomes a tool of underlying defensive need. When food is used for reasons other than nourishment, it becomes our master and controller. Indeed, today we live in a society where food has become as much a curse as a pleasure, as almost everybody has an "eating problem," with cases of anorexia and bulimia at almost epidemic levels, the obsession with being overweight almost universal, and the search for the perfect diet constituting a national preoccupation.

This seems to have become the case with sex, too. First

used for nonsexual motivations and "recreation" (tension reduction, distraction, reassurance, structure), it has now started to "drive us crazy" psychologically, while becoming also a serious threat to our health because of rampant, increasingly serious venereal diseases.

While this is not meant as an argument for fidelity or puritanism, which are also no solution, nowhere are the effects and end points of polarization more powerfully seen than in the dimension of sexuality, where what once promised to be a fountain of endless delight is turning around on us and threatens to become a nightmare, much in the way eating for recreation has become for many.

The deepest truths of our psychological makeup are revealed through our sexual response, what turns us on and off, and distance elements that are an expression of the externalized male and the internalized female and express themselves sexually. He moves relentlessly toward disconnection. She moves relentlessly toward fusion ("closeness"). What "turns us on" and "shuts us down" tells us painful truths about our deepest polarized defenses. And then there is much to be learned from our sexual choices and fantasies and the way that these choices play themselves out in our sexual responses.

Polarized sexuality is a mutual using to satisfy nonsexual motivations, which, while it may temporarily excite one or the other of the partners (depending on whose underlying "needs" are being met, or who is threatened by loss, or who feels controlled, engulfed, or trapped) ultimately creates a breakdown in communication leading to alienation and a desire to flee.

If sex was what had really been wanted, would he leave a willing partner and chase a rejecting, manipulating woman? Or would she leave a loving husband to pursue a psychopathic manipulator who can only pretend closeness?

The Widsom of the Penis Revisited: A Partial Apology

In my book *The Hazards of Being Male*, a chapter entitled "The Wisdom of the Penis" suggests that the penis reveals deeper truths that need to be respected. Were I to rewrite that chapter today, I would add that the penis and our genuine sexual "turn-ons" are the truest indicators of who we really are. However, if it reveals a man to be unconsciously a machine who needs great personal psychological distance and control in order to be excited, the erection, obviously, will not lead one to a partner for a balanced, constructive relationship. A man who is excited by "objects," be they prostitutes, centerfolds, "mysterious madonnas," or other such "nonpersons," has to face the reality that he must make significant personal changes if he is to achieve a lasting, mutually supportive and enhancing relationship.

So long as sex remains polarized, sexual excitement is a dangerous guide to making relationship choices or evaluating the "health" or quality of a relationship. When we are sexually excited, our distance craving, and thus our defensive need, is being temporarily satisfied. We are choosing based on unconscious defensiveness, not rational or objective preference. We are entering volatile territory, bound to throw us around as the underlying distance balance changes and dramatically alters our so-called sexual desire.

Unfortunately, many people, particularly men, have become addicted to the initial excitement of getting distance needs met, and are at a loss as to how to bond without that. When the excitement is not there, we are convinced the relationship is over, when, in fact, it might just be the beginning of a self-learning process.

Our sexual excitement is not the lure of the Devil, but for those who do not grasp the reality of the psychological gender undertow, it could easily be interpreted that way because it all comes to feel like an evil trick when we use our sexual excitement as a guide to relationships and keep being lured into relationships that hold wonderful initial promise and then deteriorate progressively.

"Healthy" Sex

Healthy sexuality would probably be satisfying sex with someone where a friendship bond had first been created and the relationship was not founded on sexual excitement. However, this requires considerable growth in both men and women away from polarized interaction.

Because the underlying defensiveness of men and women is difficult to alter, and big psychological risks seem to be involved in changing the situation, we crave the simple external and mechanical solutions the physicians, scientists, and "how-to" mental health practitioners stand ready to provide us. The price for such escapes from our deeper selves is the price we pay for allowing ourselves to be drugged to avoid understanding our pain. The mills of the gods will grind slowly and the price must inevitably be paid for not coming to grips with the deeper meanings of who we are.

We are entering a quasi-sexual nightmare today because our deeper selves are screaming out to protect themselves— and unless we can properly translate and interpret the messages, we are doomed to repeat mistakes and experience increasing despair and a breakdown of sexual communication between men and women. To make sense of all of this is a major step in freeing ourselves from the illusions and agony of polarization. The problem is not sex, but the defensive imbalances and resulting distortions in the way we choose and relate to each other.

THANK GOD FOR IMPOTENCE!: IT'S THE ONLY THING HE CAN'T CONTROL

When Tom began experiencing lack of sexual desire with his wife Annette, he became panicky. Everything else in his life seemed to be going well, but he was impotent and was aware of a "negative erection"; his penis seemed to him to get even smaller than it was usually in a flaccid state. He told himself he had everything—a loving, very sexual wife who seemed to adore him, two lovely children and a third on the way, and a recent promotion in his job as manager of a twenty-four-hour auto parts franchise.

He sought instant answers because, despite his wife's reassurances, the tension in bed each night was unbearably upsetting. He never imagined a time would come when he would be "afraid" of sex. "Oh, my God," he thought. "Is this what women have been talking about—and that I always thought was an excuse?"

He knew that underneath his wife's sympathetic comments, she felt frustrated and angry, and he was building a growing self-disgust because of the evasions, manipulations, and outright lying he did to avoid coming to bed in the evening at the same time as his wife. He'd either "fall asleep" early or "work late"—that is, until his wife had dozed off. Then he'd sometimes pretend or say to her that he really wanted to make love but didn't want to disturb her sleep. While he heard her speak of "starving for affection and closeness," he avoided responding. Not only did he not want to pretend what he didn't feel, he feared also that any physical contact would lead to sexual involvement and his "impotence" would be exposed.

In the mornings, after a few months of this, he began to feel a great depression—as if his life were over. He didn't mind dying, he thought.

He sought the help of a urologist to reassure himself that there was nothing physiologically wrong. He knew inside himself that there couldn't be, because on two different business trips he wound up in bed with a prostitute and was "unbelievably potent." Nevertheless, he thought he'd check it out anyway. Of course, the tests all came back negative.

Next he went to a sex therapist who specialized in visualization therapy and behavior modification. After a few sessions it became clear to both him and the therapist that the problem was more than simple performance anxiety. Tom was clearly trying too hard because of his illusion of the perfect world he had "created" and was almost totally in control of. He didn't want to explore his deeper feelings or inner life, he said, because he liked everything exactly as it was.

With great reluctance, however, after seeing no solution short of an artificial penile device—which seemed "sick" even to his technical and mechanical mind—since he was only thirty-nine years old, he went to a psychologist who, as an added bonus in Tom's mind, also specialized in hypnotherapy.

The therapist put him in a hypnotic trance. As a result, at the end of only two hours of therapy it became obvious even to Tom's defensive mind that he had been sitting on a torrent of repressed feelings that he had been denying, but that his body, specifically his penis, was registering. What he discovered was that he was in a relationship that, out of his guilt and forced attempts to be "nice," "close," and "caring," had gone completely opposite to what he needed and felt comfortable with. He was living out his wife's idea of a happy family.

His therapist explained to him that it wasn't a question of whether the relationship was a good one or not, but that who Tom really was had been severely repressed in the face of his desire to live out the fantasy of a perfect family life. The intense, repressed emotion he was covering had caused, in the past few years, great gains of weight, increasing passivity while at home ("I feel like a slug sitting and staring at the tube"), and strange injuries and body weaknesses that made him feel like an old man. In fact, he would look in the mirror sometimes and see his father when his father was already an old man. However, he had been more than willing to pay this price for the creation of an ideal family life. Only his penis and the sexual response stood in protest to what was happening to him as a person and was forcing him to look at who he *really* was, not who he wanted to be.

While it took almost two years of intensive psychotherapy to work through his self-hate, guilt, and anxiety, Tom reclaimed his real feelings and began relating in the marriage in ways that were real for him. It surprised him that instead of that creating a worse situation, his sexual functioning returned and his marriage took on new life.

The Deeper Masculine Self

The armor of masculinity is rigid. The more defensively "macho" a man is, the more he is deeply locked into destructive patterns that, for the highly masculine man, unconsciously make self-destruction more "attractive" or less threatening than change.

The one "truth-teller" of his deeper self—the dimension

of himself that can arouse intense anxiety and expose the cracks in his armor and can, in effect, act as his "growth edge" when *it* is not "working" as it "should"—is his sexual response. For many a man it is the only growth edge, because his sexual response may ultimately become the only thing that resists or transcends a man's control and therefore is the sole remaining pathway back toward internalization, or a focus on his process and the personal, connected side of himself, rather than the goal-oriented, performance side. "Impotence" is the way he can potentially "get in touch with himself" and change in a life-preserving direction.

In proportion to a man's masculine unconscious process, there is a defensive and relentless movement in the direction of keeping everything in his life in control. Underneath his masculine veneer is a need to distance and intellectualize in order to avoid the powerful inner core against which he must defend himself.

The blanket defense is control, the way he protects himself in every area. His defenses externalize him and make him goal-oriented and mechanical in his experience of his life, in proportion to his fear and need to avoid deeper, internal realities. Progressively, he surrounds himself with people and situations he can control in personal interaction.

This does not necessarily mean he is always *overtly* or obviously controlling. The control might simply be manifested by confining himself to relationships and situations where he can maintain emotional distance and be "left alone." That is, it might seem that his wife controls him, or that he "lets her" do whatever she wants to do. This does not mean, however, that he is not in control. Rather, it is his way of being "left alone" and keeping her "off his back."

He doesn't want to be personally pressured or bothered. He doesn't want anything to impede his work orientation or goal direction. He doesn't want to be questioned about his feelings or inner experience. He may actually give people around him certain control if unconsciously that serves his purpose of remaining emotionally disconnected.

As a result of this powerful need to control, he marries the feminine woman, with whom he feels initially comfortable, because she accommodates him out of fear and manipulates or "uses" him to get what she needs. She doesn't put pressure on him to get personally involved or to "open up" in a way that will expose his deeper feelings, because she is as afraid of them as he is, her protestations about wanting intimacy notwithstanding. Unconsciously she gives him dominance by *reacting* to him rather than *acting,* giving up her power and self to him even though eventually and inevitably this builds rage and even hatred of him in her. Unconsciously her feminine internalization means she will fear and resist taking overt or direct control and power. She has as much anxiety over taking this control and power as he does over losing it. Because of these mutually reinforcing defenses, they initially feel attracted to each other.

The Preimpotence Cycle

As their relationship progresses, the romantic coupling of the masculine man and the feminine woman creates a polarized standoff. He becomes emotionally distant, goal-focused, mechanical, intellectualized, disconnected, and "controlling," as she becomes more accommodating, needy of reassurance, fearful, and without a self when she is in interaction with him. Her building rage is covered by acting very "nice" and "loving" in her continual efforts to "please him" and supposedly to find ways to get closer to him and be more "intimate."

His unconscious control becomes so automatic and encompassing that he winds up functioning essentially as a tyrant, though he may be unaware of that. Instead, he sees himself as being very loving because he provides and "does" for his wife and children. He is performing his functions and, to a certain extent, he is right. On one level his woman partner wants and loves him for what he is and what he gives which is, consciously or otherwise, to be "taken care of" by him. At the same time another part of her builds up intense anger over feeling controlled and distanced, diminished and treated "like a child" or like "nobody."

Her intimacy needs, she will say, are not being met. Either she expresses the rage over this directly through periodic outbursts or she begins to develop physical and psychological symptoms, for example, overweight, complaints of ailments, depression, or moodiness.

In bed, therefore, there is a man who is, in effect, a controller, relating in a mechanical, emotionally distanced way, uncomfortable with intimate interaction and sensuality and out of touch with the impact of his process on her. *He is easily manipulated because he doesn't want to know what she really feels.* With him is a woman who is building intense anger and frustration, often to the point where she "hates him" for what he is but can't acknowledge this because she needs him at the same time that she is blaming him for her unhappiness. Her underlying anger intensifies over time and grows concurrently, alongside his need for control, and the anger becomes more overt as she becomes more secure.

His masculine externalization, however, prevents him from tuning in to what she is feeling toward him. He is relating to her as an object and attributes her periodic outbursts, unhappiness, and growing hostility either to her chemistry or to her "being a woman." "That's how women are," he thinks and often says.

He is unable to see beneath the surface with her, and so, periodically, if she acts in an affectionate way and is there for him, he assumes everything is all right. He can't see the buildup of anger and rage. He can't interpret her physical or emotional symptoms accurately or relate to her growing need for reassurance and her tension over an absence of "closeness." "It's her imagination," he thinks. Nor can he see the process of the relationship, which includes his disconnection and *her* intimacy frustration.

While his conscious self doesn't know it, however, his deeper self does, and he will find himself losing sexual interest and experiencing decreasing sexual pleasure. He may worry that he is always premature, avoids really touching her, or gets "soft." He doesn't, however, interpret this as a response to the interactions in which he is being manipulated. While tremendous anger is building in her, he may see her tension or resistance and hear her endless psychosomatic complaints, blaming, passive-aggression, moodiness, and insecurity, but he can't put it all together and make sense of it. Rather, he will tend to blame himself, because sex is supposed to be his arena mainly, and he is not making her happy.

If she is the dependent, "nice," earth mother woman, religious or "devoted," and out of touch and denying of her own rage toward him, he is in bed with a woman who is both very angry at him and yet being "very nice"; doing her duty in a devoted, clinging sort of way and out of touch with and denying of her real feeling. She tells him she loves him and sympathizes with him. This only exacerbates his guilt. Indeed, the more rage she feels and the more she is out of touch with that rage, the more she may tend to cling to him and to try and "please him," to deny those feelings in herself. Or she may act in alternately mothering and child-like ways.

Her response is the unconscious counterpart to his, and they are in an increasingly destructive, polarized cycle. *As the relationship reaches its psychological end point, her intense anger and manipulation of him, together with his increasing externalization and urgency to maintain distance and control, are the constant undertow.* This may be overlooked or denied for long periods of time as progressively they ritualize the interaction to avoid unstructured, spontaneous encountering of each other.

When he stops being "potent" it is important to see that it is an outgrowth of the dynamic and interaction and not his problem. His deeper self is withdrawing and protecting itself and seeking liberation from a toxic and dangerous interaction, just as hers is when she is "frigid," as a means for her to push away. His uncontrollable sexual resistance expresses the deepest realities of himself and is the sole response he cannot deny, distance, control, or intellectualize away. It forces him to confront the psychological reality he would otherwise deny and avoid.

An impasse has been reached and his impotence is the end point response to a poisoned interaction. *Therefore, it is potentially a lifesaving and life-giving response if properly understood and if his fragile masculine self-image can tolerate the anxiety over not performing long enough to allow it to lead him through the toxified emotional atmosphere he is in.* His impotence may be the only authentic response he has left to measure the toxicity of the undertow and to give him a warning sign, since the traditional masculine man ordinarily has everything else "under control."

The Deeper Dynamics of Impotence

On the one hand, she has a craving to get closer and closer because her feminine defenses crave fusion or "intimacy" and she fears abandonment and externalization. Unconsciously he senses both the impossibility of filling these needs and the buildup of her underlying anger. He feels cornered or trapped by these needs, which he cannot fulfill, and he feels guilty for frustrating her. Nor are his own needs for stimulation, challenge, and distance being met by her, as the frustration and anger she signals begin to make her all too real.

His fear of being alone, his need to have a reason to justify his compulsiveness and externalization, plus his guilt, prevent him from leaving her. They prevent him also from seeing the meaning of his sexual withdrawal as he tells himself, "She's such a wonderful, loving woman and a great mother," "She sacrifices her happiness for me," etc. Underneath the "devotion" and mothering and "love," however, are her frustration and her defensive, oppressive needfulness, which creates an engulfing presence. It makes him feel cornered, though generally he denies it, except in periodic outbursts of his own. He avoids her in countless indirect ways. He feels the "pressure" and he gets more and more distant and enclosed, and his sexual response is simply an obvious manifestation of his total response.

He is "trapped" in a relationship with a woman who has lost her identity in her relationship with him, while he feels guilty and self-hating because he can't satisfy her needs and standards of closeness. She is "trapped" in a relationship where she feels controlled, frustrated, and "unknown." His dependency on her and his pedestalizing of her as a "madonna" mother promotes the self-hate that prevents him from getting in touch with or acting on what he really feels.

Like her, he is building rage inside himself. He doesn't want to be close to her but can't recognize or acknowledge it. He tells himself he *should* want to be close, that it is his problem because he has a loving wife. *But his body knows that he doesn't want to be close.*

The combination of a masculine man, who is very controlling and who distances and is defensively compulsive about his masculinity, and a woman who is very angry and denying of it, tense, frustrated, and demanding of intimacy and reassurance, is lethal.

Sex is the instrument through which he proves his masculinity, and his potency gives her reassurance that she is loved. They are engaged in a symbolic acting out of bottomless needs at the same time that intense anger has built up on both sides. Neither of them is really feeling genuine sexuality toward the other at this point, but the sex becomes very important because *not doing it,* or not being able to do it, invalidates his sense of himself as a man and makes her feel unloved and uncared about and threatens to expose the undertow. As their sexual interest in each other wanes, she feels endangered and powerless and becomes more urgent about sex even though she may say that it doesn't matter that he can't get an erection. She will, however, feel rejected "as a woman" by his "impotence," even while she acts as if she is his helpmate, because a major expression of reassurance and security is gained through his lusting after her, even if she abhors the sex itself.

As he becomes dysfunctional, his urgency to perform increases—not because he wants to have sex but because he needs to prove to himself that he can and needs to avoid facing the undertow that threatens to be exposed and overwhelm him. An erect penis assures him that all is well.

The man most vulnerable to the agonies of impotence is the man whose sense of traditional morality keeps him from exploring other places with his sexuality. He begins to identify himself sexually based on his response in this situation with his wife in which he is trapped, because he won't experiment sexually elsewhere to discover the true nature of his problem.

He senses her rage, her neediness, the suffocation of her insecurity. She senses his tension, his anxiety about proving himself, his compulsiveness about performance, the fear and anger toward her because he feels trapped and because she is increasingly a threat to his masculinity.

As a consequence of his externalization, he tries to manipulate externals in order to "overcome" the "problem." In many cases, she will "feel sorry for him" and go out of her way to try to "be nice to him," which only increases his sense of guilt and humiliation. The power balance shifts clearly in her favor as he feels "grateful" that she still "loves him" even though he is "impotent" (i.e., "I love you so much that even though you are impotent, I am not going to cheat on you"). Making the problem *his* problem is a form of blaming, even though indirect. What is covertly implied is, "It's *your* problem, and I'm putting up with you because I am a loving person."

Her "helpful," "understanding" response buries him more deeply into his masculine self-consciousness, guilt, sense of responsibility, and self-hate. It increases his desperation to "overcome" the problem. It prevents him from getting in touch with his need for distance and the desire to free himself from a sense of engulfment, but he must in order for him to regain his potency.

Neither see his impotence as part of a dynamic. He sees it as his fault; she sees it as her being rejected. The truly helpful response would be one that sees the resistance of one partner as the potential sign and indicator of the deeper condition of the relationship that exists for both of them. If there is a real bond of caring and mutual liking, the "impotence" can be the beginning of opening up of the relationship and seeing how it has been rigidified and poisoned. There would be no sense of blame and they would understand that the crisis they are dealing with holds the promise of rebalance, revitalization, and humanization for both.

The process of self-exploration and change is resisted, though, because a sexual symptom tends to expose threatening realities that neither is prepared to deal with. They fear exposing the poisoned roots because no other foundation may seem feasible.

His impotence threatens to expose the undertow in the relationship—the deeper repressed feelings, frustrations, and anger that escalate rapidly in polarized relationships. He might drink too much or eat too much in order to avoid the issue. He or she might get tired early in the evening for the same reason. She might complain of physical symptoms, while he might complain of overwork and pressure. They use one rationalization after another. But on some level they both know it isn't really any of those things.

In proportion to his masculine neediness, he is with an equally needy woman. The undercurrents of anger both ways are powerful and the survival instinct of the deeper part of him is screaming out of its anger, fear, and craving for release and growth.

On the one hand, he is protecting himself from her with his "impotence." On the other hand, he is protecting her from him. His own deeper desire to hurt her or push her away or "kill her" is being defended against by his symptom, which renders him harmless to her. Impotent men are vulnerable and often too frightened to be angry. They feel ashamed. They feel certain they are going to be rejected, and it makes them very tame. The impotence renders his rage and his aggression in the relationship harmless. Instead he becomes adoring of her or sentimental, as a way of compensating and also as a way of protecting himself from anticipated rejection and punishment. He may buy her gifts, or give her extra attention as a way of compensating and expressing his "gratitude" that she is "sticking it out" with him.

Thus, just as frigidity in the female can be seen as an unconscious protest and resistance to being treated as an object, controlled, distanced, and used, his impotence is a protest and protection too against being used, engulfed, and manipulated by guilt and prevented from taking any of the distance he craves and needs.

Feminists know how men can be dangerous to the personhood and development of women. The opposite is equally true, though more difficult to see because of the seeming power of the male. It is hard to imagine the "nice," "loving," and "helpless" feminine woman being dangerous to a man. However, she can be just as poisonous to him as he is to her. She is a reinforcer of his macho defensiveness just as he reinforces her feminine internalization or powerlessness.

Indeed, a woman in a relationship is dangerous to a man

(just as a man is dangerous to a woman) when she builds up and harbors intense anger toward him that is denied, but ever present. It impacts continuously behind the manipulative facade of "niceness" and "devotion." Mechanical male externalization prevents most men from recognizing or "feeling" these realities as they create a significant part of the interpersonal atmosphere.

In the years past, in traditional relationships, the woman rarely made any demands of the man sexually. She just remained an "unavailable" object, so impotence was less of an issue. Today, however, the woman has become a person in the most threatening sense. She expresses the deeper polarized nature of herself directly by pressuring for closeness and reassurance, and he does not have his traditional escape provided by her "unavailability."

Because of his masculine conditioning, he cannot see his sexuality as a response to the dynamic of the relationship. He sees impotence as coming from *him*. His consciousness of his sexuality is mechanical, and therefore he perceives his impotence as the malfunction of his equipment and wants to fix *it*. He will use anything to do that: hypnosis, drugs, fantasy, etc.

Mutilating the Male Psyche

The medical orientation, which is masculine in its goal-oriented, mechanical, controlling, detached, and intellectualized orientation, while minimizing the impact and reality of emotions on the body, colludes with the male's need to avoid an encounter with himself and his need to believe that he is a victim of a "sexual problem" caused by a physiological malfunction. Because impotence is a product of his externalization, "solving" the problem externally or mechanically permanently reinforces his defensive pattern of externalization. It gives him what he "wants": an instant answer and control regained. The trade-off, however, is temporary alleviation of anxiety or "relief" for long-term potential of nondefensiveness, growth, and change.

Increasingly, the medical literature is pointing to organic factors "causing" sexual dysfunction, affirming to the man who wants to hear that, that indeed, there is nothing inherent in the relationship with his woman that is producing the response. The industry of penile implants, penile bypass surgery, and hormone-administration approaches therefore is burgeoning. More and more advertisements are being seen for equipment such as "discreet penile implants," in which the advertisements speak of the "millions of chronically impotent men" who could "benefit" from them.

The psychological origins of impotence are difficult to see because they are so layered over and the people involved are often "nice" people who couldn't possibly acknowledge being angry with each other, resistant to closeness, or feeling trapped. The woman is so "helpful" and so considerate. She really cares about him. She doesn't put any pressure on him in bed. At the same time, he "really" loves, even "adores" her. He "really" wants to have sex. She "really" wants him to. She tries to help him in every way possible. The conclusion is that it couldn't be psychological. *The problem has to be physiologically rooted.*

Sex therapies, implants, and behavioral approaches all help partners avoid a confrontation with the undertow of their relationship and themselves that would be threatening indeed. One's sexual response reflects the deepest truths of oneself and the relationship. So much can be learned from it. It is a powerful barometer that is "threatening" to the extent that deeper feelings and realities are being denied. However, so much potential humanization could occur if it was understood and dealt with as a mirror of the deeper interaction, a response that reveals and reflects this undertow instead of being seen as a "symptom" to be overcome or cured.

However, the change that often is required is a transformation of one's defensive self, and that is often more threatening than the sexual symptom. Impotence is frightening because it threatens to expose the deepest lies, repressions, and fake fantasies a man cherishes. *Therefore he needs to see his sexual response as existing by itself in a mechanical way. It allows him to try and "fix it" without "fixing" himself.*

It is to be expected, then, that for most men the medical approach will be the most attractive one. The more defensive he is, the more he will reach for a mechanical solution. Most will therefore prefer a mechanical solution over the prospect of exposing the undercurrents and undertow of their masculine personality. *Mechanical approaches, by emphasizing organic causes and downplaying the emotional, are therefore burying the male psyche, putting the final nail in the male coffin and reinforcing his externalization and tendency to disown his personal self.* Because impotence is, for many men, the one thing they can't control, it arouses sufficient anxiety to create at least a beginning motivation to understand himself. If he can escape that, all chances for growth may be lost.

He is told, "You're afraid of closeness." "You are hostile." "You hate women." "You're punishing your partner." "You hate your mother and you're relating to her like your mother." "You've turned her into a mother figure." "Your impotence is incest anxiety." "You don't trust women." "You don't know how to open up." "You're afraid of being vulnerable." "You're too mechanical." "You always have to prove yourself."

He is given all of these insufficient, shallow, and indirectly blaming explanations. They promote more guilt, self-hate, urgency to "overcome" his symptom, denial of the dynamics of the relationship and his feelings, and resistance to exploring his relationship with an interactional perspective.

Impotence Is the Beginning, Not the End

We are faced with a paradox here. Impotence is probably the most frightening and anxiety-provoking thing a man can experience psychologically, and yet, for most men, it creates and promotes the only potential they have of making significant change and personal growth. For many, impotence is the *only* motivating crack in the armor. It is the last hope for self-awareness, the sole pressure that can stir up a man's anxiety enough to bring forth his defensiveness and repressions. Thus, impotence is a pathway to his deeper feelings because it greatly threatens his ego, makes him vulnerable, and motivates him to reach out for help. Otherwise he may remain totally externalized.

The impotence has the potential to bring him back to the full and lost reality of himself. It can put him in touch with himself and force the "poisonous" issues in his relationship to the surface. It gives to the man and the woman an opportunity to confront their deepest fears, rigidities, and damaging game playing. Of course, there will be tremendous resistance. Neither really wants this confrontation, because change may feel hopeless and overwhelming in the context of their interaction.

If men could only decipher their body signals correctly, if their defensive egos did not get in the way, if their guilt was worked through and they were once again motivated for growth, they could see that the penis is a monitoring device of the relationship flow and reveals the deepest realities about themselves.

In that sense, impotence can be viewed as a psychological heart attack that can either "kill" or cause a reworking of a man and his patterns.

Just as the heart attack may be the only event that forces the Type A personality to look at the patterns that are destroying him, impotence can be seen as the last attempt of the psyche to break through the rigid patterns before a man is buried in his defensiveness. Just as the heart attack is *potentially* a pathway to getting back in touch with the body, so is impotence a potential pathway for getting back in touch with the psychological, emotional, authentic self.

There are some Type A men, however, who are so rigidly caught in their habit patterns and have so much resistance to change that they prefer a mechanical solution such as surgery offers. Likewise, there are many men who would prefer a mechanical solution and "psychological death" to the frightening prospect of opening themselves up. However, for those men who are not yet locked into a totally rigid, self-destructive pattern, impotence, like a heart attack, is a way back to a life better than ever before.

Guidelines for Understanding and Dealing with Sexual Dysfunction

1. A relationship that promotes your guilt and self-hate over "dysfunction" is emotionally toxic to you and to your partner.
2. While a sexual symptom may threaten to expose painful truths about you and/or your relationship, they are truths nevertheless. They must be faced and dealt with if other destructive symptoms and consequences are to be avoided.
3. To the extent that the sexual response is uncontrollable, it is potentially life-preserving and growth-promoting in what it stands to reveal about you and your deeper reality.
4. Apologizing or feeling guilty about your sexual re-

sponse is a form of self-rejection and self-hatred that will promote the same kind of attitude in your partner—contrary to any overtly expressed platitudes and concern.

5. A woman who cares for you and really loves you as a person will neither blame not reject you for your sexual symptom, but will see it as a mutual problem that demands that she too get involved in self-exposure and exploration, and *not* in primarily helping *you* to "recover."

6. If a woman-partner rejects or abandons you because of a "sexual symptom," your penis has facilitated the ending of a destructive and manipulative relationship.

7. If your woman-partner wants to "help you" without confronting her own deeper self in the relationship and how it is inextricably intertwined with you, her "help" is harmful.

8. It is possible to "cure" a sexual problem without ever focusing on it as an issue in itself. Specifically, your sexuality does not have a life of its own. It is a part of your total responsiveness. As you change, "it" will change.

9. The time period for a "cure" for sexual dysfunction is as brief or as long and difficult as the depth of the repressed undertow it is a manifestation of.

Be patient with the change process. You are the one who will pay the price for shortcuts and evasions. You do yourself a disservice, and you reinforce the mechanical defensiveness that denies you your humanness, by seeking out a quick solution.

10. While the rapidly accelerating spiral of sexual dysfunction may make it seem as if there is something physiologically wrong, remember the times you were "horny" yet totally exhausted, depleted, or even sick—and how easy it was to have an erection. Re-

member, when you're genuinely excited, it doesn't take much to be potent.

11. True strength and self-esteem lie in the willingness to confront your deepest feelings patiently and fully, no matter what they threaten to reveal.

12. To hate and fear your dysfunction is to throw away the most powerful guide a man can have to the recesses of his deepest self.

PART THREE

WITH LIBERATION

9

EARTH MOTHERS IN DISGUISE

"Most so-called liberated people that I know are full of it," remarked a caustic, albeit articulate, businessman attending a seminar I gave on emerging male/female relationships. "The feminist leadership is a good example. They have the worst qualities of both men and women. They have all the answers and nothing you can say *ever* changes their mind. Then, from what I read, one turns on and attacks the other—supposedly for ideological reasons, but it's just a variation on the old-fashioned male ritual of ego-tripping—'I'm for real, you're not—I'm the greatest, you're nothing.'

"It's a real cast of characters, these feminist leaders," he continued. "There's the glamor queen one who's trying to be a movie star without copping to what she's doing. It's obvious, though. She's always being seen with celebrities and she's always dating the richest, most successful guys. Then there's the other one who's like a Jewish mother—complaining and telling everybody how to change, and how to live. I'm surprised she doesn't try and tell us what to eat.

"I looked through their magazine recently. It's full of the same kind of ads as the other women's magazines that *Ms.* supposedly abhors. You know, jewelry, deodorants, perfumes—and the articles are mainly old-fashioned victim vari-

ety stuff, an updated variation on the old "poor downtrodden women" theme.

"The 'liberated' guys they hold up as shining examples
of what men should behave like are just as phony as the
feminist women pretending to be so pure. They're workaholics, and they're the worst kind of arrogant—because God
is on their side and unless you imitate *them,* you're a mis-
guided pig. It feels like being at a church social when you
watch them—at least as hypocritical, if not more so—because at least church types don't *pretend* to be open to discussing their beliefs. They're out front in thinking that they
have all the answers.

"When what's-her-name ran for vice-president and lost,
what did she do—she *blamed* the male establishment. God
save us from female leadership! They can't stop blaming—
even at that level. I thought of reminding her that this country has at least ten million more women than men and the
odds were totally on her side and it was women who rejected her, and saw through her act; but I know better than to
argue against that stuff with facts."

Eliminating the angry undertow, what he was saying was
not that different from what so many others of the "uncon-
verted" said shortly after he finished. While most said so
in more genteel terms, a prevailing feeling was that "liberated" people were really hypocrites and arrogant under their
liberated facades.

*The psychological underpinning of this gut-level reaction
has, on a deeper level, a basis in psychological reality.*

Defensive Liberation: Tradition in Disguise

When women become "liberated" via reaction against
their feminine upbringing, the core of deeper feminine needs

remains but gets covered over or disguised by a set of rigidly defensive counterattitudes.

The existence of a feminine core and a liberated layer on
top of that core creates a crazy-making, eventually impossible relationship situation between men and women
because of the contradictory signals created by these two
layers and the sense of frustration and incompleteness the
defensively liberated woman experiences regardless of
what kind of response she gets. Something is always "not
quite right."

What makes the relationship process so difficult is that
the feminine core, which is actually the more powerful of
the two layers, is repressed and defensively denied in proportion to commitment to image. While the traditionally
feminine woman tends to be unable to see herself as anything but a victim, the "earth mother in disguise" (a traditional woman hidden behind a liberation philosophy) will
tell you that she takes responsibility for herself. Yet her
emotional reactions signal blaming rage and frustration that
are bewildering because it is so often unclear what has triggered them.

This seemingly liberated woman, who is still traditionally feminine, may *believe* she is aware and ready to engage in an equal, person-to-person relationship. In reality,
however, she is more likely to involve her partner in an
explosive spiral of confusing messages and impossible
double binds. Inevitably, the complete and total breakdown of a communication that appeared to hold such promise occurs.

The main way to recognize an earth mother in disguise
or a "macho in disguise" (a traditional male with a liberated facade) is by their *process*—how they relate, not what
they say or even do. What they say or do is content, and
content is consciously controllable and easy to manipulate.
Deeper process is not.

The Traditionalist

Paula is a financial planner, age thirty-four. She likes her job and feels it makes a statement about who she is: an objective, reasonable person who functions independently of men, yet enjoys their attention and companionship. She is at the same time very feminine and traditional in her process. She dresses seductively and glamorously and uses cosmetics to make herself look soft and feminine.

Once in a relationship, her traditionalism emerges. She becomes a moralist about sex. She is resentful of her lover because she feels he is too passive and unromantic. This lack of dominance causes her to withhold sex, but she does it indirectly. When her lover touches her breast, she says it tickles, that it gives her a sensation she can't stand, that he's too rough or her body is too sensitive. When he touches her vagina, she says it hurts.

She chooses strong men to involve herself with, then "punishes" them in traditional ways disguised as physical symptoms. She has no energy and complains of being tired, which she says comes from her long hours at work but inwardly represents her resentment and conflict over not being "taken care of," which she denies she wants but is angry she doesn't get. Only when she is afraid she is going to lose her lover does she get really sexual.

These are all protests that express her deeper frustrations and resentments emerging from her "nonliberated" core. Yet at the same time, she would resent any man who asked her to work fewer hours or implied that she was withholding energy or sex to be punishing. So, unconsciously she blocks the communication and sharing of feelings her "liberated" self says she wants, because her feminine core overreacts to criticism or less-than-positive input by construing it as an attack and then "punishing" her man for it.

The Female Macho

Marilyn, age thirty-two, is a college professor and the author of several books on women's issues. She is a militant feminist on the surface, readily enraged by any sign of sexism in a man, vehement in her assertion that women should not depend on men, sexually aggressive and demanding of sexual satisfaction.

She is an earth mother in disguise and reveals her feminine core by her perception of men as the cause of all the world's problems and by her continual denial of her own responsibility in creating the rejection and distressing relationship experiences she has with them. After each relationship breaks up, she says she doesn't want any more involvement with men; but she continues in search of a male to whom she can attach and who will accept her feminist interpretation of everything and her "macho" inability ever to acknowledge that the other person may also be right. She lacks the ability to acknowledge being wrong because she considers that a form of submission.

Periodically, when she gets involved with a "nice," "sensitive" man who accepts her strident style, she finds herself getting bored and frustrated. Her attempts at relationships with stronger men, however, fail as she accuses them of insensitivity and the desire to control her.

No contemporary woman will "drive you crazy" with split messages more than the "female-macho," who has reacted against traditional women's roles by adopting a Type A, driven, autonomous, highly sexual, controlling, and disconnected pattern. On the one hand she pushes away in a relationship and reacts severely against any attempt to "slow her down" or "control her." On the other hand, she builds up anger and rage over the lack of romance and "closeness" that she blames men for.

She reacts negatively to male weakness and passivity and wants a man who is ambitious and energetic like herself, yet reacts with anger at any attempts to "turn her into" a wife. She sees any demand on her time and freedom as pressure. When men back off to give her what she says she wants, she complains that "men are afraid to deal with the problems of a relationship."

Any attempt at real dialogue regarding a conflict with her breaks down because of her aggressively logical, mechanistic style. She turns out to be an aggressive blamer-victim, and breaking through her defensive barriers is impossible. She demonstrates *no* willingness to see her process or her part in creating what happens to her because she is so focused on making sure she will not be controlled or intimidated by a man. Therefore, she needs always to be right, but she denies that. She has to win, and she denies that, too. She won't see or acknowledge the validity of her partner's reality. She is convinced that men are flawed and women are the positive force in the world. *Any* "backing down" on a woman's part she equates with subservience and regression.

She is classically feminine in her complaints over a lack of intimacy and closeness, in her guilt making, in her demand for romance, and in her criticism of men as being "closed off," with no awareness of how she helps to create the response she gets. She demands excellent skill at lovemaking and she accuses her lover of selfishness if he fails to satisfy her. She sees herself as a sexually perfect partner because she is open to doing anything, but she does not recognize the impact of her demanding approach in turning her man off. Any man she is involved with eventually stands accused of being a selfish, limited, or uninteresting lover.

As her partners, men wind up feeling defensive and accused, explaining themselves constantly, walking on eggshells in order to prove that they are not "macho pigs." Men work at trying to prove that they are able to get close, although they never do it "right." They are left exhausted and feeling as if they have been on a roller coaster ride— accepted one minute and attacked the next.

Very much like the male macho, when she gets the "nice," sensitive partner she thinks she wants, she's bored. Then she will go to the "macho man in disguise," by whom she is sure to be enraged and whom she will accuse of sexism and hypocrisy.

The Liberated Ice Queen

Ann, age thirty-four, was a traditional "ice queen" behind her sophisticated articulation of liberation issues. She had a perfect, femininely thin body and flowing blonde hair. She was beautiful, aloof, and compellingly attractive to men, who found her difficult to approach and talk to. She "excited" men by giving them the impression that even talking to her was a conquest and validation.

The ice queen has a liberation philosophy of complete equality between the sexes and could wither a "sexist pig" with one cutting look. Behind the image, however, on a process level she is the traditionally distant, hard-to-get female who never lets men know what she is thinking or feeling. She plays "I am a mystery" to perfection and can make a man feel guilty and "dirty" for his sexual interest in her. Unconsciously she demands to be pursued, making him responsible for the initiation and course of the relationship, and yet she takes total control passively, through her detachment.

At a party, for example, she stands there looking beautiful, and it is impossible to know what she is thinking or how she is reacting. Hers is a *very feminine,* reactive stance vis-à-vis males, yet unconsciously she is power-oriented and tends to attract the same highly macho, success-oriented, powerful, and competitive men she claims are destructive to women and the world.

Men retain a constant sense of excitement with her because of the challenge and vagueness she projects. They never know where they stand. She brings out traditional macho responses because of her passive behavior, yet doesn't see herself doing this.

Men become obsessed with getting her to bed. She brings out the "challenge and conquer" orientation to male/female interaction. Men fall all over themselves trying to figure out how to please her. They find themselves making premature commitments to her in their desire to "own" her, so to speak, because of the insecurity and excitement generated by her aloofness. Then they find themselves feeling they are being driven crazy by her because they are constantly trying to figure her out and can never successfully do so.

On the one hand, her thinking is liberated and she doesn't want to be treated like an object, yet on the other, she acts like an object and brings out the ultimate in "macho" behavior. Then men find themselves accused of treating her like an object even though their attempts at relating to her as a person are thwarted by her refusal or inability to interact freely by giving them input.

With the ice queen, the undertow is her cold, rejecting anger toward men, which manifests itself in distance. Her passivity produces her anger over feeling controlled; then she invariably ends up feeling men are sex-obsessed, dominating, possessive pigs.

The ice queen is an earth mother in disguise in that she has "liberated" herself by becoming economically and emotionally autonomous. Yet in her relationships with men she continues to behave passively, never initiating contact or taking the lead in conversations or decision making. She creates a double aura of excitement through her "independence" and her feminine unavailability. Because she is reactive rather than active, she brings out the extreme macho in men, who must perform, initiate, and take complete responsibility in their interactions with her.

Because of her special characteristics, she very much excites men, but then she builds rage rapidly in relationships because her passive-reactive quality attracts dominant men, whom she then accuses of wanting to possess and control her. She is out of touch with and defensively denies her process, which creates the feelings she has. Instead, she sees herself as "perfect" because she is the ultimate feminine woman who supposedly doesn't want anything from a man. In reality, she is the perfect "blamer" because her responsibility is so hard to see.

She "drives men crazy" as they try to navigate between her independent content and the feminine-defensive, reactive process that "forces" men to be "macho" if they want to be involved with her, and many do. Relationships are doomed to failure because her extreme femininity prevents her from seeing herself as part of the problem, and her "independence" reassures her that, indeed, she is "liberated" and that the problems couldn't be her fault: "I don't want *anything* from men," she says and believes.

Several female celebrities are ice queens and have been highly effective in attracting society's most powerful and wealthy men, who go to desperate extremes trying to please these "exciting" women. Ultimately they fail, and many find themselves having been exploited and devastated. These powerful men have more than met their match. They have been easily "defeated" because they could not see the extremely traditional process behind the liberated veneer that doomed them to making fools of themselves.

The ice queen is left with the "righteous" feeling that there are really no liberated, worthy men around. She concludes inevitably that "all men are the same." Her process, indeed, grinds all the men who are attracted to her down to the same level.

The Liberated Engulfer

Karen, age thirty-six, is a social worker. She is articulate, good at taking care of herself, and comfortable expressing angry feelings. She works hard, is giving and generous, and does a lot for others. A skilled therapist, she has good insight into psychological process and balances this with a pragmatic orientation to the world. She acknowledges openly her fears of surviving as a single mother and her wish to remarry an "old-fashioned" man who likes taking care of women. "I'll take good care of him, too," she says.

The deeper, defensive feminine process of Karen and women like her is revealed by a smothering, engulfing style with her friends and intimates. She concerns herself obsessively with their well being, whether they are "correctly" dressed, fed, doctored, etc. She discusses in great and delineated detail all of her concerns and efforts to take care of her family as a single parent and, despite the sizable child support payment she receives from an ex-husband, she frequently talks of men as being self-centered, repressed, "psychopathic narcissists." Traditional blaming and feelings of being victimized are disguised behind psychological jargon and diagnostic labeling. She sees herself as "very giving," but unconsciously this represents her desire to be given to. She builds up great anger when the other end of the bargain she has struck without negotiation is not maintained.

At home, she takes control of the kitchen and the house. Nary a personal detail or piece of information about anyone in her life escapes her. Under the guise of "helpfulness," she feels sure she really knows everything about what others feel and think all of the time. In fact, she knows you better than you know yourself. In addition, she knows what is best for you, what you should be doing, and in spite of her great personal fears, feels she can give advice on how to handle the world competently. You wind up feeling watched. She takes note of what you are doing all the time, like a hovering, overprotective mother.

Behind the psychologically enlightened, liberated image, mothering is her control. She takes over everything in the personal realm and tries to generate dependency on herself.

You wind up pulling away from her and avoiding closeness with her because hers is an omnipresent, critical, and engulfing style in the traditional way, and then you stand accused of not being able to tolerate love. You feel you should appreciate her, but in reality you resent her and don't understand why. She tells you that she doesn't expect appreciation, nor does she want you to feel guilt or behave toward her out of a sense of duty. Yet your deeper self is telling you that the "love" is really engulfment, which is her indirect way of gaining control and promoting guilt; it is *that* and not her "caring" and "warmth" that you are reacting to negatively.

You are responding to her intrusiveness—the constant underlying message that she wants to be close and is monitoring you. She feeds you when you are not hungry. She worries to the point of irritating you. Her accommodating omnipresence and "devotion," coupled with the sadness and hurt you sense in her when you pull away at all, tug at you and make you feel bad about yourself for being "selfish."

Periodically you feel manipulated, controlled, guilty, and angry at her; at the same time, though, you feel "comforted" by the fact that she's always there. You find yourself unstimulated sexually, and then you stand accused of having a mother transference because you are losing sexual desire.

The liberated engulfer presents a facade of strength and responsibility, but the undertow is a traditional one of intrusion, assumptions of relationship superiority, and smothering that creates the psychological reality of the situation.

When you attempt to make sense of your reaction of wanting to "pull away," she interprets that you're just a man who doesn't know how to accept love, care, and concern and are threatened by any woman who wants to give and be in a loving relationship with you.

Based on content, it seems she is right. In fact, you do back away from her "love." However, your deeper self is reacting in self-protection to the deeper reality. When you begin to withdraw and become resentful around her, she worries that you have emotional problems and should seek help.

The Fusion Sublimater

Sara is a thirty-two-year-old attorney committed to seeing herself as a fair and equal person. She refuses to take anything from a man. She has many male friends and continues her friendship with ex-lovers after the relationship is over.

She has a successful career, owns her own home, is comfortably sexual and playful, and seems completely free of traditional concerns about commitments and being courted.

As a "fusion sublimater," this earth mother in disguise seems closest to the model of genuine feminine independence. Her prime relationship concerns are about freedom, independence, and space. Men find her particularly attractive because she never blames. Initially, it makes her seem perfect. She is very sexual, without any expectations. She is very independent, without resentment that men don't seem to want to take care of her. She is warm, sensitive, and humorous. She loves to laugh. She seems too good to be true, and indeed, there is a fly in the ointment.

No "real" man ever gets close to her, because she is terrified of giving in to her dependency cravings. When men get to a certain point of closeness, she backs away. She sees it as men not wanting her to be herself. "Men are afraid of my strength," she explains.

Her real terror is of identity dissolution and dependency and so she sublimates her powerful fusion craving, by becoming obsessively attached to safe machos in disguise, such as male spiritual gurus and her therapist, whom she has seen regularly, twice a week for seven years. She is also a strong believer in astrology and psychic readings. She doesn't give herself over to "real men" but instead attaches herself to a male figure who is sufficiently distant and safe that he seems to be "perfect"; she does not have to deal with her terror of giving in to her dependency hunger. Her therapist, guru, and psychic sublimate her feminine need to adore, love, and give up her self. She allows others to depend on her, while she depends only on "safe" symbols.

Her feminine process is also seen in that she describes everything as "nice," "beautiful," and "wonderful." There is a denial of the negative and an almost gushingly positive way of seeing life. She talks about how special everyone is that she knows. "I feel so close to her"; "I just adore him"; "We have such a magical connection" are among her favorite descriptions of her many "close" friends. Her craving to be close is handled "safely" by spreading it around to so many people that there is no danger, or by involving herself with men who are sure to try and control her, whereupon she always ends the relationships. She makes "friends" out of them instead.

She is an extreme of the feminine woman who has become controlled by her fear of allowing herself to become dependent on men but doesn't know it. She is afraid of and angry at them. She fears being controlled and losing her identity to them.

On the one hand, she *seems like* the perfect woman; a woman you can feel safe with and trust. However, she drives men and herself crazy by getting involved then pulling back. She invites intense closeness, but then when men bite for that, she pulls away. After she has pushed the man away she feels safe again and resumes the relationship.

On a deeper level, she sees men as dangerous to the point where she cannot tolerate any dependency on them at all.

The Liberated Masochist

Julia, age twenty-six, is a beautiful and talented dancer, intelligent, "down to earth," politically aware and liberal. She has a thriving career as a dance coach and occasionally gives concerts of her own choreography.

She is idealistic, gifted, and strong but reveals her feminine core by choosing men who "master" and "use" her. She loses her strength and identity to them as they begin to make her decisions and allow her to assume more than her share of the financial responsibility.

This is the typical scenario with the "liberated masochist." She chooses men to whom she can give up control in order to assume a feminine role of putting herself second. Men attach to her for her success, her beauty and responsibility, and the fact that she signals that she can be controlled and manipulated and won't fight back.

Because she is so idealistic, she would never hurt the man she is involved with, so she winds up hurting herself. Part of her "liberation" involves understanding the struggle men have. She feels bad for them and sees them as far more oppressed than women. Therefore she expects little of them and gives everything.

While her "content" is humanistic and liberated in her insistence on taking full responsibility for everything that happens to her, her process is self-denying and traditional in its masochistic, "suffering" quality. She is an earth mother in disguise because in her relationships she actually does become the victim, but unlike the traditional feminine blamer, she blames herself and *takes* the abuse, rather than venting rage.

She is the genuine female victim. Even though she participates in setting it up, ironically she doesn't see herself as a victim at all. Rather, she blames herself. She operates self-destructively in the purest sense of the word because she is afraid of her own power and afraid of losing her femininity by becoming "too strong." Thus she allows herself to be taken advantage of and controlled.

Gradually, the liberated masochist takes on the man's value system, and, in all cases, there is a serious deterioration of her potential for strength and power and the development of her career and standing in the world.

The Intellectualizer

The Intellectualizer manifests her "liberation" by her high level of intellectual awareness of issues. Widely read, she dialogues and debates nondefensively and with great competence.

The fact that she is an earth mother in disguise is made evident whenever she enters into an enduring relationship with a man. Immediately she becomes suspicious and insecure that he might just be "using" her. When she feels slighted or in any way hurt, she gets cold, refuses to talk, and withholds sex. "You're just like every other man—shallow and exploitive," is something she has told several men with whom she became involved.

Her intellect and her deeper emotional responses are polarized. She is as liberated in her thinking as she is feminine in her process. Thus, men find her powerfully attractive when they first talk to her, but then become progressively discouraged about the involvement because her spontaneous reactions reveal her great fear and distrust of men. Like a traditional woman, she will punish them by her sexual withdrawal for their "crimes," and often they are not even aware of why, because she withdraws rather than fights it out. Once angered, there is no discussion, because she is convinced that she has been "nice" and "fair" and the man has been unfeeling and shallow. She tries to control her feminine core with her intellectual skills but is only successful at that at a safe distance.

The Liberated Seducer

Gwen, age twenty-three, is a policewoman. She is strong and athletic and projects a healthy, independent image. However, career, "gutsiness," and independence are hooks to attract men to take care of her. She wants a man who is stronger and more successful than she, but she knows that in today's society, dependency makes her unattractive to the kind of man she wants. She is an earth mother in disguise, however, in that she uses independence as a way of getting a man to take care of her. She knows that independence is the new thing that men want, so she projects that.

Once he is attracted and committed to a "liberated seducer," her deeper dependency needs emerge and she will gradually "give up" her work "for him" by becoming progressively more "hassled" by its demands. Her "priority," she tells him, is the relationship. However, she is "giving" something that is really for her—not for him or them. She signals her traditional core by the unreal extreme to which she carries her independent image at the start—a purity of self-reliance that cannot be real.

The Female Rescuer

Beverly is a thirty-nine-year-old administrative assistant for an elementary school district. She is very strong in her feminist stance and handles her fear of losing her autonomy to a man by picking men whose lives are in serious trouble. She can rescue and dominate them and, as they get stronger, they leave—which validates, in her mind, the notion that it is dangerous to get too close to or give anything to a man.

The "female rescuer" is strong, independent, and liberated on the surface, but continually winds up in these self-punishing situations, rescuing alcoholic men or men wounded from a broken relationship, who are lost, frightened, passive, and unstable. Her traditional feminine core is manifested by the low self-esteem she displays in relationships, which she handles by choosing to be with men who are in trouble. This gives her a temporary sense of importance and allows her to avoid dealing with her own anxieties.

Because of abandonment fear, she can't deal with the pressure and anxiety of being with a thriving man whom she can't control. Because she is the one who controls in her relationships, she winds up generating anger in men and being left, without knowing why. Or she leaves the relationship just about when the man is on the verge of becoming strong again, because she gets "bored."

She brings out in a man, very directly, the core of male dependency, which most women don't see. Eventually, he will leave her, if she doesn't leave him first, because to see himself as weak or dependent beyond a certain point is intolerable for most men. She is an earth mother in disguise because her great anxiety over "losing her strength" to a man unconsciously causes her to be attracted to defeated men who either end up feeling angry and controlled and leave, or pull themselves together, at which point she abandons them.

The Adorer

Adrienne, age thirty-four, and in her fourth marriage, recently received her license as a real estate broker and is brimming with her strategies for success. She has done well as an agent for three years and is excited over the prospect of running a real estate office of her own.

Her feminine core shows through, however, in that everything she does, even her career planning, is related to getting her latest husband's approval. One senses she is doing it all for him, rather than for herself. She is always seeking his approval, wanting reassurance that he is still "on her side." She tells him all the time how brilliant and gifted *he is,* even when he is only doing mundane household repairs.

This adoration is unconscious manipulation and a way of maintaining feminine control. The "adorer" *seems* to be a giver, but gives on her terms. She fears that acknowledging her power will drive a man away.

Adoring a man is a way of giving herself over to him but then she begins to hate him for not giving enough back—if he doesn't smile or say nice things in return. Unconsciously, she builds up anger because of her sense that she is "nobody" with him.

Eventually, she "has to leave" in order to regain her identity and "self-respect," so she begins the same process again with the next man: adoring, giving herself over to his approval, building up rage, leaving, and going on to a new partner. She insinuates her way into a man's identity and then blames him for the loss of hers and for his lack of appreciation for all she is giving.

The Liberated Self-Server

Cheryl, age forty-five, is an insurance company manager. She is known for her support of women in their quest to achieve economic independence and she prides herself on her competence and success in the business world. She is quick to reach for the check on a dinner date with a man and claims to enjoy sex thoroughly.

In her unconscious personal process, however, Cheryl is an example of someone who wants things both ways: the prerogatives of being liberated when it suits her and the emotional benefits of a traditional relationship. She would not allow herself to be passed over in promotions "because she is a woman," but expects to gain an advantage because she is. It is as if a woman runs for political office without the qualifications and gains her nomination because she is a woman, but then blames a "sexist power structure" for her failure to win the election.

The "self-server" unconsciously uses independence in the service of feminine needs; much as a macho in disguise would use sensitivity in the service of his motives, such as seduction. Feminism becomes a way to get it all. Traditional feminine blaming and guilt making are used to put others on the defensive and to gain advantage, but the "blaming" is done indirectly and in disguised ways—meaning an atmosphere is created in which the male feels he needs constantly to prove his "nonsexism." Any criticism or less-than-positive input is subtly or harshly construed and confronted as an attack on her *because she is a woman.*

The self-server, therefore, by being maximally manipulative, may manage to gain all traditional feminine prerogatives while taking on only those responsibilities she chooses to accept. This approach can operate in personal or business involvements and render the other person "powerless" by her indirect "intimidation" of implying chauvinism or sexism.

In a personal relationship with a man, she might say, when asked by him to do something she doesn't want to do, "Do it yourself, I'm not your mother. I'm not here to serve you." The man, who is unaware of what is going on, finds himself constantly explaining, defending, or apologizing. This gets him in even deeper, as she informs him that he really *must* be a sexist because he is so "defensive" and always needing to prove that he isn't.

If unchecked, she winds up indirectly controlling everything and he feels increasingly guilty asking her for anything or for not giving to her. Her feminism is a disguised weapon to achieve traditional earth mother goals, indirect power over men through guilt making, implied or overt blaming, and promoting of his tendency to feel responsible and self-hating.

The Complete-Liberation Crazy-Maker

Alice, age thirty-nine, is a corporate vice-president. Charming, quick, and geared to achievement and success in her own right, she has been able to travel widely and impresses men because she is well educated and sophisticated.

However, Alice is a "complete-liberation crazy-maker" because she embodies, in her process, the antithesis of her outward image. Her process is classically feminine, while her content is very liberated. She is strong, but becomes silent and withdrawn, and refuses to "argue" when there is a conflict. She is sexual, yet wary that men are "using" her. She is aggressive in her work as an administrator, yet allows men to be emotionally abusive to her and cries when she is angry. She is fiercely independent, yet completely "knows her man" and where he is and what he's doing all the time. The moment a man becomes dependent or displays his vulnerability, she backs off. When a man backs off, she accuses him of fearing commitment.

The "crazy-maker's" moods and responses confuse and disorient men because, once they get involved, they feel that her reactions are totally capricious and "impossible" to understand. That is, she seems to be changing constantly as the contradictory parts of her come out "randomly";

the core and the defensive reaction against that core cause her to react in opposite ways, seemingly from moment to moment.

Out of touch with the contradictory messages she gives off, she comes to the conclusion that men don't really like successful women, or that men can't stand to be out of control and she won't let herself be controlled for the sake of a relationship.

The Liberated Black Widow

With her "deep understanding" of men, the liberated black widow spins a web composed of old-fashioned ingredients of feminine power: total adoration, manipulation of his insatiable ego, and total satisfaction of his denied little-boy dependency. Thus she traps him in his bloated ego. He is the man who flaunts his women, his triumphs, his power and "toys," as well as his indulgences in alcohol and drugs, while she "selflessly" accepts even his most blatant macho behaviors in the name of being aware, liberated, and loving.

Like a martial arts master, the "liberated black widow" uses his energy to let him destroy himself while she plays adoring audience and devoted supporter to avoid confronting her own problems—the anxieties and conflicts she has over the maintenance and direct expression of her identity and power—along with the deep distrust and hostility she feels toward men.

The machos she draws to herself believe, in their grandiosity, that they have found the ultimate woman in her—someone who "understands" how to love a man and to let him be himself. Unbeknownst to either of them, she is providing the slack for him to hang himself. This process occurs indirectly and unconsciously. Her lack of self and resistance to his ways provides him no reality or boundaries to force him to recognize and acknowledge the macho-inflated stupor he lives in. Instead, he spirals farther out, his ego expanding geometrically until he self-destructs, whereupon his earth mother in disguise transforms and emerges calmly, coldly, and powerfully as a strong force who will take over the reins of the empire he created.

Perhaps she is the politician's wife, or perhaps the driven businessman's or the doctor's spouse—the big man's lady—attaching herself to men whose egos became too large to take in any one else's but their own. They were men who believed they could have it all, and never survived intact long enough to recognize their self-delusions. They are remembered for the potential they had and couldn't harness.

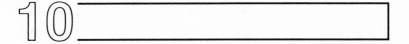

10

MACHOS IN DISGUISE

Xavier thought of himself as a liberated man. Very few others did, however—particularly the women he had been involved with, most of whom saw him as a "macho pig" in a liberated disguise.

His perception of himself came from the fact that he was never possessive of the women he dated; never asked them to do anything for him and was also always honest with his feelings, which generally amounted to him saying that he didn't feel comfortable getting too involved or being monogamous.

Their perception of him came from the fact that, at least indirectly, he made it clear that a relationship had to be his way or no way. Furthermore, while he saw it as "liberated" that he would make dinner at his house and never pick a woman up in his automobile, they saw it as macho arrogance. While he put no direct sexual pressure on them, the message was clear: "Either we go to bed and have fun or I'll be bored being with you just talking and will probably never see you again."

The fact that he never paid for dinner for the women he was with, when they did go to a restaurant, was seen by him as "respecting their autonomy." For the women, however, it came across as liberation opportunism. The choice was *his*—it was not mutual.

Elissa particularly was enraged by him when they stopped

171

seeing each other. "He's worse than my dad—who's an unabashed macho. Xavier makes it clear in a thousand ways that he doesn't need a particular woman in his life, that most women are interchangeable, and that any woman who wants to get close to him and says so is automatically, in his book, a clinger or a manipulator who wants to be taken care of."

When she confronted him with his controlling, macho ways, Xavier was bewildered. "I don't know what you mean—give me specifics." Elissa could only reply, "That's the point—you can't see it, and I'm not going to prove it to you. I just want you to know that I'm not ending this because I want a man to marry me. What I need is some continuity and emotional involvement, and you clearly don't want either. You may think that 'Whatever feels good!' and 'Whatever is honest is okay' is what being liberated is about. But it's old-fashioned male egocentrism with a liberated facade."

Authentic Versus Pseudo-Liberation

When a man changes by adopting a new philosophy, outlook, or attitude, he is altering the externals and not his process—and he thus becomes a macho in disguise, a man with an appealing, "enlightened," sensitive, angry, or egalitarian image—but with the deeper core unchanged.

The confusion between content and process, image and substance, real change and the appearance of change in society today is reinforced by certain equations, when it comes to men: "He's such a 'nice' guy, he's not macho," or "He's not a macho, he writes poetry and loves to cook," or "He's very gentle and loving and spends a lot of time with his kids—he's not a 'macho,' " or "He's a soft, sensitive, quiet guy who cries real easy—he's not macho." Or it may be said in reverse: "He's a real macho pig. He wants his wife to quit her job and put *her* career on hold to be home with their daughter," or "He's real macho. His favorite thing is to go drinking with his buddies."

The macho-in-disguise may reveal his macho core by the fact that he sees his "liberation" as a series of issues and sets about to remedy them with external solutions, by altering outward behaviors or habits. He is seeking *external* solutions to problems caused by his externalization. His "liberation" becomes a contradiction in terms as he blames the system, the politicians, the economy, the courts, women, a sexist society, big business, or social pressure. As a result, after an initial "high" that comes from the sense that he has found an answer and a target and may be doing something about it, the problem gets worse. This was the experience of many of the liberated men of the 1960s and 1970s, who changed their attitudes and orientation to women and other men externally and eventually found their personal lives in more of a shambles than ever. Their content change was "liberated," but the process used to get there was externalized, so while they *thought* they were changing, they had become instead more deeply and invisibly embedded in their macho process.

A macho in disguise can be recognized by the *how* and the *why* of his behavior. If his sensitivity to women emerges from an intellectual awareness of women's issues, the content may be "liberated," but the intellectualized, self-monitoring, "proving" way he goes about changing is the macho process.

He becomes a macho in disguise and a caricature of the very thing he consciously reviles. His ego is more massive than ever before. Now he has the *truth* and knows the way *everybody* should live and even how the world should be changed.

He becomes critical, self-righteous, and passively aggressive in his severe judgments of everybody who is *not* like him, even though he denies doing this. He is connected to his principles, philosophy, and abstractions and tries to con-

trol others with these. Often, he will even sacrifice relationships in favor of these principles. He will drop friends
who don't share his ideology. He may even expect or demand
"nonsexist" behavior from his children and thereby control them with his beliefs by obsessively monitoring the toys
they play with, the language they use, and the ideas they
express. The content of his "liberation" appears to be
enlightened. The process, however, is oppressively judgmental, controlling, critical, and authoritarian.

He will come to be disappointed, if not shocked, at the
ways these "best efforts" on his part backfire. Friends, children, and his wife or woman partner will come to resent
him, and he won't understand that it is not his ideas but his
process that produces rage in the way that any controlling
person elicits profound anger in those he unknowingly intimi-
dates and seeks to control; even if it is only with his well-
intentioned brand of the truth. He is alienating himself as
he is trying to "humanize" his life and others. He is more
out of touch than the machos he reviles and doesn't know
that his relationships are failing until after he has totally
isolated himself.

The macho in disguise *knows all the answers* but ultimately finds that he can't make them work. He becomes more
disconnected and isolated than the "sexist" men he is trying
not to be like. These men actually have more adhesion in
their personal lives than he does, and so he is finally left
hugging his principles as he drives everyone away.

Initially, he may get support by surrounding himself with
people who "agree" with him, but this bonding will prove
to be superficial and temporary because it is based on shared
abstractions and ideological self-consciousness. It is based
on mutually shared content, which produces a lifeless bond
that flakes off under very little pressure. Inevitably, one man
begins to see the other as hypocritical, flawed, "neurotic,"
or "hard to talk to."

The macho in disguise has not changed internally, he only

thinks he has. He is more enclosed, self-deluded, and disconnected than ever. He is trying to change by doing more of the same, only *harder* and with a different language. His enlightened image or veneer has given him a self-righteous sense of being *right* that is encompassing, self-obsessed, and impenetrable; even though now he talks the *language* of feelings, closeness, love, and openness beautifully.

The Intimacy Mechanic

Charles is an "intimacy mechanic." He abstracts intimacy. He knows and does all the appealing intimate behaviors. What he believes is coming from inside him, however, is actually intellectually monitored. He is *working at it and trying*. His "intimacy" is mechanical.

Specifically:

1. He talks *about* his feelings. Even when he "shows them," he knows what he is *doing* and can control them.

2. He makes an effective effort to listen. Mechanically, he *is* an excellent listener. But it is hard to know when he is or is not *really* interested because he *always* listens with the same degree of intensity, which indicates that his listening is disconnected from his feelings.

3. He touches to "be close" and to make contact and show that he cares. Again, the touching is defensive, because it is automatic. It is "mechanical touching." He always says, "It feels good!" but the "good feelings" don't really show. He *knows* that touching is "intimate" and is supposed to bring you closer, which is why he does it.

4. He takes seminars on fathering, relationships, caring, etc. He is acting out the "macho" fallacy of learning the "right way" to *do* these things; a "way" that exists *apart from* himself. Inevitably he will be accused by his partner and

his children of not really being intimate and he won't understand why the bonding he worked so hard at is so weak.

5. He is *always* compassionate, caring, and "understanding." That is, he seems incapable of saying, "I don't give a damn." Thus he is exhibiting a defensive reaction to his masculine core, which creates an opposing and extreme caricature of "intimacy" that even more traditional women cannot match.

6. He is always "being nice." So his attitudes and reactions are predictably rigid in their "niceness."

7. He studies and knows about the "right" places to touch a woman sexually. He asks solicitously if she had an orgasm and if sex was "okay for her." He works hard to learn about the "sensitive" places on her body to make her "feel good." He believes that such "magical" places do exist.

8. He *always* makes eye contact when he speaks or listens and always tries to care.

9. He uses the language of intimacy continuously. "I'm feeling very close to you right now," or "I missed you a lot," or "I want to share what's going on with me." To the sophisticated ear, these phrases emerge with a mechanical, emotionally hollow ring.

The "intimacy mechanic" has beautiful content but is profoundly disconnected from his "intimate" behaviors or else he could never maintain such a high level of consistent "intimacy" so automatically and instantly, especially in light of his early conditioning, which is in total opposition to what he is now. It's too good to be authentic.

The intimacy mechanic ends up frustrated and disappointed because his efforts at intimacy don't produce the closeness he strives for. While his women appreciate him, at some point when they feel safe or angry enough to do so, they tell him what he does feels unreal and mechanical and that they don't really feel close or connected to him. They are correct in their perception, because, in fact, after breaking up with one woman, he can move readily to the next and immediately be just as "intimate" and "loving" there, proving that the previous woman's sense that his connection to her was "profoundly shallow" was accurate.

The tell-tale signs of an intimacy mechanic are that he is never really out of control of his "intimate" behaviors and that there is no real energy behind his acts. They are monitored and automatic and therefore defensive.

Mr. Perfect

He's successful and powerful, "gentle" and "intimate." He expresses feelings but is still very much "a man" "where it counts"—protecting, making decisions, and helping "a woman in distress." He's a winner, but with liberated attitudes. He's the sensitive, understanding, and hardworking macho-in-disguise. He's the feminist woman's hero, the new image of Superman. He's "perfect," except for the woman or man who tries to get close or blocks him from doing it "his way." Then his undertow is revealed and the problems start.

"Mr. Perfect" is a macho-in-disguise because he needs to live out the image of total superiority and flawlessness, to "prove" himself, to avoid the great "guilt" he is prone to for being "macho" and less than perfect, to keep himself free of criticism and to avoid acknowledging and dealing with the anger and "not nice" feelings that unconsciously burn powerfully inside him.

Mr. Perfect is usually a loner and a compulsive achiever/performer who hides his need for total control by acting "gentle" and "sensitive." But he chooses women and male friends who will "adore" him and be awestruck enough to avoid getting in his way. Eventually, however, they all become unhappy because, as a "macho-in-disguise," he is never *really* emotionally available.

The further away people are emotionally, the better Mr. Perfect looks. The closer they get, the more pain they feel because he is so externalized he has little to nothing to give in a sustained and ongoing way. The "promise" that his image projects can never be fulfilled.

He is drained in the process by trying to be all things to all people and secretly builds up deep resentment over the pressure to perform he experiences. He really wants everyone to go away and leave him alone. His image and his guilt won't let him say so, however.

His woman tries to be "patient" and generally "blames" herself. She tells herself, as others do, too, "He's so thoughtful and nice. He tries *so* hard. It must be *me!*" But her depression and anger build regardless, because the reality is that their interaction is superficial and "unreal," and actually she gets next to nothing from it. It looks great. It feels painful. People don't understand when she seems so depressed. "You have everything," they tell her, which makes her feel even worse.

His children desperately try to please him also, in order to be part of his perfection. They become passive and lifeless as a result because they are children trying to be perfect adults to please a distant, "perfect" daddy.

His wife and children both exhibit various symptoms. Perhaps she eats too much, can't get her career going, or feels inexplicably sad. His children feel like failures much of the time because they can't match his perfection. They may give up trying altogether and become barely functional in their sense of hopelessness.

He tries to remedy all these problems like Superman, flying in and out of the trouble spots. *But there it breaks down.* These are not problems to be "cured" like an external problem. These problems are the end results of his underlying, distanced, defensive need to be "perfect" to which everybody else in his life falls victim. Finally, he must confront the "mess" that his defensive perfection has made and for which there is no quick "Superman" cure.

Everyone else now feels guilty because *they* let Mr. Perfect down, but it was *not* their fault, and until they see beyond the surface image, they will suffer guilt and self-hate.

If and when he "opens up" in a real way, the hidden agendas of his life surface, including very possibly the young girlfriend he has hidden away and with whom he can be playful and really "himself." At this point it can be recognized that "nobody really knew him." They only knew his image of perfection. They thought he was perfect, but he was hidden, manipulative, and distanced. No macho in disguise, not even Mr. Perfect, avoids paying the price of his denied "macho" process.

The Professional Understander

Kenneth was a well-known psychologist. He was highly esteemed and considered brilliant. As best he could, he applied his professional wisdom to his family, but with disastrous results. His three sons, to his dismay, never formed lasting relationships and were all extremely neurotic. His wife spent her free time shopping and playing cards. She "drove him crazy" with her "shallow concerns" and seemingly endless complaints and worries about the children, money and the future.

Try as he might, he was unable to "build his wife's esteem," as he put it, so that she would have a successful career of her own and have something "constructive" to do. Her lifestyle angered and bewildered him and he wondered if she was really the woman he had married.

He himself was so well analyzed he wondered where he had gone wrong. Simply put, he was the victim of a commonplace, seemingly obvious macho blind spot for his own process. This deeper process transformed the content of his understanding. No matter how much you know, the outcome of a relationship comes from its process, not its "wisdom," and he couldn't see it.

Be he a therapist, professor, minister, physician, or hairdresser, the "professional understander" listens compassionately and skillfully to the pain, frustration, and anger that build up in women inevitably as a result of their being involved in a polarized relationship with a traditional man.

He is the ultimate *fusion fantasy symbol,* the perfect "intimate relater" who will not hurt or disappoint the women so long as their involvement is controlled and limited and he remains a symbol, not a real person.

The professional understander gives women exactly what they want, which is the fantasy of a perfect, "intimate" relationship with complete understanding, acceptance, and "warmth." However, it is *perfect* only so long as it is confined to limited, controllable boundaries. Pushed beyond these limits, the professional understander becomes just like every other man, if not more so.

His practice is reserved for those, like his patients, employees, or congregants, to whom he can relate at a controlled distance and who reinforce his grandest ego fantasies of specialness by putting him on a pedestal. With them he is the wonderful "wise man" and the compassionate father figure.

He is, however, a macho in disguise, and his frustrated, angry wife and children will testify to that. He "knows everything" and always has the answers. He's too busy to be involved, to a point where he is vulnerable or not in control. At home he is distant. He seems open, but he isn't. He seems to be a great listener, but he's busy figuring out the answer or thinking of something else when others speak. He talks compassion, emotions, flexibility, and generosity, but they're abstractions he can live out only from a safe distance. In reality, he is quickly bored by everyone but himself.

Constantly he hears from his wife, "You always have time

and patience for everybody except your family. If they could only see you here, they'd never come to see you professionally again."

He, too, cannot see his process. He's too busy understanding, and so, like all other machos in disguise, he watches helplessly as his own personal life unravels and becomes the polar opposite of what his clients, patients, students, congregants, or followers would imagine he has. At home, things are as painful and "crazy" as they are positive and rational at the place where he is the "professional understander."

The New Age White Knight

Women are an abstraction, a category that the "New Age white knight" is rescuing. They appreciate him at a distance and as a symbol but not as a person—much in the way men appreciate a beautiful woman. He is a more disconnected, New Age variation of the traditional macho who rescues women one at a time. The New Age white knight is a macho "good guy," a modern Prince Charming who wants to rescue the whole female gender.

His clay feet are seen when he tries to "come close" and in the direction of a one-to-one relationship. The closer he gets, the more he reveals his inability to relate. He shines when he is on a rescue mission from a distance.

He is a variation on the minister who is out to save the world, while his wife is depressed and his children are delinquent and drug addicted. He can't "save" them. His "need to rescue" is self-serving: a defensive way he projects an image to "prove" something and to deny his own anger and the macho hostility toward women that macho men have traditionally reacted against by being compulsively protective.

The New Age white knight thrives and is dependent on the approval of women. He is the proverbial loner; the hard worker; the compulsive achiever and competitor. His driven, macho undertow and his isolation make him very needy of a woman's "love."

When he rescues one-on-one, he always seems to choose a woman "in distress" whom he is teaching how to fight and succeed in the outside world. He is kidding himself, however, as he discovers that she wants him permanently to take the role of her rescuer, and the mere fact of his presence means she will never become autonomously strong because the mutual interlocking needs that form the basis of the relationship will be lost. So she seems to be "trying" to learn what he is "trying" to teach her, but he invariably gives up and does it all for her.

The New Age white knight is the "nice guy" who is easily manipulated because of his strong unconscious "macho" guilt which he is not "in touch" with. Further, his defensiveness is revealed by his rigid inability to feel any negative feelings toward women. Women "love him" because he shares their perception of themselves as being victims of other macho men who are not "special" like the New Age white knight.

His macho core is revealed also by the fact that he always chooses pretty and sexy women to rescue; women who act very feminine and adoring around him and are quiet and passive in public with him. "Sexy" to his mind means they have beautiful breasts and pretty faces.

When he meets a strong and equal woman who does not need to be "rescued," he does not find her attractive. He is only turned on by the woman in distress. He "tries" to make the latter strong and independent, knowing he has a lifelong contract to satisfy his deeper "macho" needs because neither he nor she really wants to change the pattern of the relationship. He wants macho-validation and she, despite her career symbols, wants to be taken care of and pedestalized.

Once in the relationship, therefore, despite his best efforts, she becomes *more* dependent and childlike as she turns him progressively into a father figure. She tries to isolate him from friends or any other close relationships (even his children from a previous marriage of whom she is jealous), so that she can have him all to herself to solve problems and make decisions for her.

Until she gets him there, she will maximize her emotional, physical, and relationship-oriented distress to pull him into the rescuer role. Meanwhile, he unconsciously wants her to remain weak so that he can avoid being vulnerable or out of control with her. He may be "New Age," but he still believes a man should be "a man."

His stance vis-à-vis other men is traditionally critical, judgmental, competitive, and superior. He maintains his hero image by selecting women who seem to be "liberated" and "open," just as he seems to be, but who really aren't. He expresses ideas that are consistently liberated and humanistic. He seems very open to dialogue but unconsciously chooses situations where he can continue to prove himself superior to other men and be the white knight rescuer.

The Liberated Manipulator

Of all the machos in disguise, the "liberated manipulator" seems to come closest to having "the best of both worlds." As a liberated manipulator, Walter got all of the "rewards" traditional "machos" seek, only he got them faster and at far less expense. He intuitively "understood" women and their "liberation game" and unconsciously manipulated it to meet his needs by projecting an image of perfect liberation.

During courtship, he could avoid spending any money, making decisions, or taking responsibility, but he could expect sex by the first or second time together because if she was "really" liberated she couldn't say no. Walter would regularly benefit from the fact that the women were out to "prove" to him that their liberation was real, so they would even pay for *him*, initiate the dates, drive the car, and put *no* pressure on him for commitment, fidelity, or anything traditional.

With his "liberated" sensibility and "intimate" behavior, skillful eye contact, ability to tune in to a woman's needs, sensitive lovemaking, "compassion," "patience," "gentleness," and facility for the language of "closeness" and "sharing," in addition to his liberal and liberated attitudes, women could not resist him and would *expect* nothing from him, to prove to him that they did not want to be taken care of "like the others." If he wanted, he could *keep the "pressure to prove" on them* by telling them that most women don't show their true motives until they are secure in the relationship. Thus, women could be kept permanently on the defensive about showing their "needy," "dependent," "demanding," "weak," or "engulfing" sides.

Likewise, he could prove that he was not macho by "giving" them control and "letting" them make the decisions. His "giving" to them was designed to reinforce *his* image of being sensitive and "intimate" and freed him from the guilt of taking responsibility. It never took anything away from him. Rather, it *bolstered* his control to be sensitive, intimate, and caring.

This macho in disguise gets the rewards without being accused as machos traditionally are. He avoids commitment and gets the "benefits" of devoted female companionship. Behind the "liberated" veneer, he is the ultimate "selfish" male who gets everything but gives nothing in return, but he is not called on it. Through it all, he can remain disconnected and relate to the woman as an object—and even can accuse her of trying to manipulate him with guilt if she complains that he is in any way doing that. "If that's the way you feel, maybe we should stop seeing each other," he tells her. But she doesn't want him to leave, because he is so "special."

His "liberation," as is the case for all machos in disguise, is for the fulfillment of *his* macho needs. It validates his attractiveness and power and allows him to remain disconnected and in control.

However, there is a fly in the ointment, even for him. Invariably he gets "bored" because he is so totally in control that there is no challenge or stimulation. Thus he moves from one woman to another until he finds the one who challenges him and whom he cannot manipulate and control. Then he "falls in love" and experiences "excitement." At this point his manipulativeness and flawed capacity to relate make him the powerless one. At this point he embodies the psychological reality of the macho, which is that, while he craves control and power, he becomes "excited" only when he is challenged and powerless.

The Liberated Angry Man

This macho in disguise does a variation on the traditional feminine role. He sees himself as exploited and unfairly accused by women and it makes him angry, and he says so loudly. He tries to use his logic to show women how things "really are," and to prove them wrong, but by and large they can't relate to him.

He is a macho in disguise because he focuses on external issues. Like the feminists, he, too, blames and wants to change society, whatever or whoever that is. He sees himself as a victim of a sexist society that oppresses men.

Trying to be helpful to other men, particularly if he is a professional, he misleads as he "helps," because he places the focus of men's problems externally and targets as the cause the ways that society "abuses" men. Thus he unconsciously reinforces the very problems he would like to "cure." He develops his own "closed-system" logic to answer everything, much as defensive feminists are prone to do.

He has a "blind spot" that regularly gets him "in trouble." He is "issue-oriented" and translates behavior literally. If a woman goes to bed with him right away and pays for her own dinner, he concludes she must be "liberated" and therefore they have the potential for a good relationship. Likewise, because *he* asks nothing of her, he sees himself as relating to her in a "liberated" way. With women, therefore, he often confuses accommodation or manipulation with "being liberated." He doesn't see how clearly he signals exactly what he expects, and how this will draw to him the manipulative feminine accommodator, the very women who *will* come to blame him the most and reinforce his worst self-fulfilling prophecies.

Therefore, in his relationships to women, he is vulnerable to manipulation because he unknowingly is the proverbial "hurt little boy" looking for a "good mother" to "understand" and love him and make him less angry. Because his opinions and ideas are so militantly and aggressively obvious to see he attracts the manipulative accommodator, a woman willing to be what he wants because he will have it no other way. However, since he is a macho in disguise, he doesn't see the process and falls for the "ideal" content she gives him and creates the same illusions over and over. "She must be 'liberated' in the right way because she agrees with me or at least doesn't disagree," he reasons at the start.

However, tension in the relationship rapidly builds, since the basic, defensive distrust that underlies his anger causes him continually to keep her at arm's length, and she becomes increasingly angry and frustrated. "Can't you ever let go of your liberation speeches and your defensive, cynical attitudes?" she lectures. "I'm *not* like all those other women. I'm not out to get you, so lighten up," she protests. But indeed, she is becoming like "all other women," and his own "deluded" interpretations are a part of the polarization process that gets him into the same mess repeatedly.

The relationship falls apart as he interprets its problems ideologically by focusing on "issues" rather than process. He can't seem to move beyond that. He talks equality but he wants distance, control, and to be "right"; and because he "fights back," anger, frustration, and misunderstanding build rapidly on both sides.

In the end, she either leaves in anger or the relationship becomes a "stalemate," characterized primarily by angry, "ideological" arguments and no "loving" or sexual passion.

The Totalitarian Humanist

At a birthday party for his seven-year-old son, Benjamin, a humanistically minded high school counselor, dressed in his corduroy pants and tennis shoes, was unknowingly and rigidly enacting a caricature of his nonsexist, egalitarian, "fairness" principles with the children who were his son's invited guests. He and his wife, Beverly, a social worker and "healer," were both into "love" and "caring," as could be seen by the many quotations on signs decorating the walls of their home.

The party began with Pin-the-Tail-on-the-Donkey. To make sure everything was "fair," the blindfold was securely placed on the faces of the little children, who were then twirled to the point of disorientation. Regardless of their size or age, they were not given help in finding where the donkey was, even though some could barely even reach it. Other children were lined up waiting "quietly" for their turn. They really didn't want to play, but Benjamin and Beverly didn't notice.

Then came "hit-the-piñata" and get-the-candies time. Each child, no matter how big or small, was given exactly three hits at it. Their son missed all three shots and dissolved into tears. He wanted an extra chance since it was his birthday. As he cried hysterically and flailed on the ground in a tantrum, in front of his little friends, his mother lectured him, "Now, Sean, don't lose control over your emotions. You *know* what happens to you when you start getting like that."

The son started to run screaming toward his room. His father, now clearly on the verge of a rage himself, said in stern tones, "You didn't sleep enough last night. You're very tired." In a huddle, Dad said to Mom, "I can't reinforce this kind of spoiled behavior, and we can't let him have an extra turn," but then, with resentment and out of expediency, they let Sean have one more shot at the piñata. The party's atmosphere had now changed completely. Meanwhile, through all of this, the other children were lined up waiting to hit the piñata in the chilly outdoors. They stood quiet and lifeless, but "well behaved."

It was time for a juggler. The children were bored and distracted and wanted to be on their own to play. Dad said, "No, we planned it this way."

Dad's process was militaristic while his words were "enlightened." His wife, becoming increasingly upset through the chaos, turned to her angry husband to make the decisions. "What should *we* do next?" she asked repeatedly, and her pent-up husband became even angrier.

Perhaps the most obvious, and yet closed-off, unaware parody of traditional masculinity is this "totalitarian humanist." He is the "liberated" male brimming with his political, economic, and social philosophy, but his traditional macho process is telegraphed by the facts that:

1. He clearly believes he has *all* the answers.
2. He rejects outright all other unenlightened men who don't agree with him.
3. He reaches a level of righteous rage almost instantly when he is disagreed with.

4. He has all the answers, and no dialogue has ever altered his opinion on any issue; most of the time he won't even permit such a dialogue to continue.
5. If his secret fantasy were acknowledged, it would be to eliminate all those who had opposing views—the "nonhumanists."

He is saving the world: rescuing women, minorities, or the poor with macho process. He judges people based on the opinions they express and he "involves" himself only with those who agree with him. His "hot buttons" are many and powerful.

Invariably the woman he is with either agrees with him or is being "taught" the "truth," i.e., her consciousness is being raised by him. What he sees as open-mindedness in her often turns out to be old-fashioned feminine accommodation.

With a woman of equal conviction or strength, he seems to lack sexual or romantic passion because the dominance, control, and hero role he needs in order to get sexually turned on are not there, so he finds an accommodating, passive woman. If she finds he will not commit himself, or her rage grows too great as a result of being always powerfully and rigidly controlled, she leaves and abandons all the ideology and philosophies he worked so hard to indoctrinate her with.

The totalitarian humanist is a profound crazy-maker because of the contradiction between his content, which is idealistic, humane, and people-centered, and his process, which is judgmental, arrogant, "closed off," intellectualized, rigid, and critical. Consequently, he is surrounded, like the old-time macho he reviles, only by those who agree with him and by submissive women who seem to "adore" him for his "brilliance" and his convictions.

Like all machos, he makes no genuine personal contact. Communication with others is abstracted, and issue orient-

ed. There is no flow. Judgments and interpretation are superficially made, based on externals such as people's expressed
opinions and surface manifestations. For example, he sees
an alcoholic vagrant on the street and diagnoses the man a
victim of the economy. One "wrong" word and a person is
negatively labeled by him. The fact that he patronizes wom-
en by seeing them as downtrodden victims and relates to
them as such does not seem like sexism to him. Thus, his
personal life is consistently a shambles of explosive misunderstandings, withdrawal, recriminations, and accusations.
In these relationships, he finds himself in a burlesque of
the traditional male/female interaction because he unknowingly relates "logically" and in distanced, controlling ways
while she hungrily searches for reassurance and "love."

Out of touch with his impact, he generates a brittle, self-
conscious, mechanical interpersonal atmosphere, much like
that at a church gathering where all the conversation is on
the same "nice," "ideal" plane and no one disagrees with
the commonly held doctrine.

The massive macho ego of the "totalitarian humanist" is
revealed in that.

1. He *never* acknowledges the "legitimacy" of someone else's differing perception, is never heard to say,
   "I see your point."
2. His own interpretation and perception of people and
   events are black and white.
3. His feelings are not emotions, they are ideas: When
   he says, "I feel . . . ," he really means, "I think . . ."
4. He never stays involved with a woman who has different opinions from his and holds on to them.
5. He vigorously denies being "macho" at all because
   he interprets "macho" externally or mechanistically
   as meaning a certain set of expressed attitudes or
   opinions. Thus he is completely "closed off" to input
   regarding himself.

6. He appears to listen but hears or absorbs nothing that changes his mind. Unconsciously his "macho" ego has expanded to the maximum.

7. He perceives himself as humble but his impact is one of arrogant superiority, self-righteousness, and an absence of playfulness.

8. He knows *all* the answers.

9. His unspoken message to those who disagree with him is that "You don't deserve to be alive on this planet."

10. He is readily enraged or detaches from anybody who doesn't agree with him.

11. His relationships are based on shared ideology and are therefore brittle, self-conscious, intellectualized, and out of control.

12. He cannot tolerate "weakness" or "imperfection" in himself or others and he defines "needs" as weakness. Once involved with a woman, he may even promote her self-destructive behavior by pressuring her to respond based on principles as he would, e.g., he advises her to tell her employer off: "I don't think you should let your boss say or do that to you," without really understanding the full situation.

He is exasperated if his female partner is not "logical" enough, but fails to see how his own logic is his weapon of distance, control, and superiority. He never acknowledges that *his* logic is thus flawed by his process. He is "surprised," therefore, when his relationships deteriorate into a series of increasingly out-of-control, "irrational" encounters.

Overall he denies the "macho" attitude, while he embodies an extreme form of it. He is the classic macho egomaniac, deluded enough to see himself as having God and the Truth on his side.

Women and men alike will receive far more compassion, dialogue, openness, caring, and energy from the traditional macho with no pretenses than from the totalitarian humanist, who is a highly polarizing, toxic macho in disguise.

The Egalitarian Disconnector

Egalitarianism in a relationship is an abstraction and can only be maintained from a detached posture—and this disconnected process will undermine the "ideal" content.

Sheldon is an "egalitarian disconnector." Both he and his wife have strong careers. He is careful *never* to ask anything of her that would encumber her in any way. When they are together, he tends to be passive and nondecisive. He never raises his voice in anger, and never tries to control her overtly.

Unconsciously, Sheldon chose a woman who is too insecure ever to ask anything of him either. For him, being "egalitarian" is his unconscious way of remaining detached. He is a "macho-in-disguise" because he is distant and uninvolved emotionally and manipulates the relationship at a distance. Being equal is the line of least effort and least resistance, freeing him of involvement and guilt.

While the content of his manner is "egalitarian," the process says, "Leave me alone." He strategizes that if he doesn't ask anything of her, he won't be obligated and she won't be able to make him feel guilty, so he can remain uninvolved and keep his options open. Asking her for *anything* (for example, "Please go to the market for me") would constitute too much involvement and commitment, so he never does that. *His outward behavior appears "liberated" but is actually very macho.*

Egalitarian disconnectors involve themselves in relationships that are intellectualized, distanced, and highly controllable. Emotional involvement and sexual passion are absent. Both he and his partner are busy being "undemanding," "respectful," and "independent." Both become workaholics because the playful, spontaneous part of their interaction is dead. Instead, they spent large amounts of money for entertainment, such as dinners out, travel, theater, etc., which they schedule compulsively to disguise the lack of energy and involvement between them.

The egalitarian disconnector relates in a nonsexist way for these defensive reasons. Such "perfect" equality would be impossible in a nondefensive relationship where emotions and needs prohibit detached control.

The egalitarian disconnector fully reveals his true nature as he begins to look outside his relationship for the emotional involvement, energy, and sexual excitement he craves. Invariably he chooses the traditionally "adoring," "sexy," "feminine," and "dependent" woman to turn him on.

While he sees himself as liberated from the traditional way of relating to women, his approach is a socially approved disguise for disconnection. As a result, he builds up great tension, frustration, and anger because he craves the "adoration," "control," and "sexual passion" that come from being with the very "feminine" woman. However, he wants that *without* involvement and commitment, so he seeks it outside of his "committed" relationship.

The Self-Hater

Macho process produces guilt and self-hate because of the masculine man's conditioning to initiate, perform, and take responsibility. When things go wrong, therefore, he is filled by these feelings. This is an inevitable inner experience for all traditional men.

The liberated "self-hater," a macho in disguise, unknowingly acts out his self-hate by selecting as a woman-partner an angry, attacking, critical woman who uses the banner of feminism and liberation to flog him continuously.

He chooses her as a partner originally for her ideals and her seeming strength. Then he becomes her whipping boy, thereby atoning for his deeply rooted guilt.

He tries to satisfy her, support her, be intimate and sexual and all the other things she says she wants, and accuses men of withholding or being incapable of. However, he too is eventually found lacking and then becomes the man she criticizes and attacks the most.

With time, he becomes increasingly passive, resigned, and "understanding." He tells himself that her anger and attacks on him hide her pain and hurt and he will "heal" her wounds and show her that men can be trusted and loving; that there are exceptions and he is one of them. Instead of this happening, however, he finds the intensity of her anger building.

Because he is a macho in disguise, he interpreted and related to her literally and mechanistically. He could not see beyond the obvious, which is that her continuing outbursts of rage result from the fact that behind his "nice" content, he is just like all other men. His "mistake" however, is in denying this and falling into the trap of macho "omnipotence," believing that he can undo the "hurts" of her past, and be different from all the others.

Conclusion

No one person is actually exactly like any single type described. Many "liberated" people, in fact, embody characteristics of several of the types. However, all of the prototypes described are similarly illustrative and designed to reflect my perception and belief that the image of seeming "perfection" projected by many supposedly liberated people is psychologically defensive, unreal, and potentially misleading to others as well as to the persons themselves. The false belief and pursuit are promoted that content can be substituted for process and image for substance to create a new psychological reality. The undertow of gender cannot be transformed readily by altering externals, and yet we are and have been continually seduced into believing that it can. The impact of this notion is deleterious to many people on various levels of consciousness who are initially exhilarated and "liberated," then find themselves more trapped than ever before by the illusions they have created.

11

THE PAIN AND COMMUNICATION BREAKDOWN OF THE SEEMINGLY LIBERATED

Cynthia and Martin were both successful in their careers as attorneys. They were equally articulate regarding world affairs, competent in finances and child-care responsibilities with their seven-year-old son.

They jogged and skied together and belonged to a tennis club where they participated in mixed-doubles tournaments. When they entertained friends at their home, they projected an image of perfect liberation. Each prepared favorite recipes, served the guests, and washed the dishes without regard for what was supposedly a man's or woman's job.

Their personal interaction when alone, the unconscious process of their relationship, however, was more traditional even than their Old World parents, whose values and style of interaction they rejected as "sexist" and destructive. Specifically, Martin never went anywhere without telling Cynthia first, specifying when he would be back home and what he'd be doing while away. Even when they were home together and Martin would be in the basement with one of his many hobbies, he'd begin to feel guilty about neglecting Cynthia and he'd worry that she might be feeling hurt or angry over being "ignored." He would call to her to make sure everything was all right. Cynthia told him he didn't have to do that and that she wasn't feeling insecure at all, the way he thought.

Martin's father, whose conventional attitudes Martin rejected, regularly went on fishing and hunting trips alone or with his buddies when Martin was a boy, without "feeling guilty" over leaving Martin's mother and the children behind. Martin, however, never went anywhere, evenings or weekends, without Cynthia and couldn't imagine going for a vacation without her. By the end of their first year of marriage, Martin had stopped seeing his own friends entirely and had given up his favorite activities such as softball and touch football, because he couldn't share them with Cynthia. "She's my best friend," he rationalized, "and I want her with me."

Cynthia, who had rejected her mother's "old-fashioned" values, was in process even more traditional. She always knew where Martin was and remembered everything he ever told her. Whenever possible, she would accompany him, often waiting in the car when he ran his business errands. She had no interests or friends of her own and was "content" just to be with Martin. In truth, she had greatly eroded her own strong and separate identity since marrying.

The hidden conflicts in their relationship revealed themselves most clearly in bed. Cynthia had once complained that intercourse hurt her, so Martin almost entirely stopped pursuing her sexually. Instead, he masturbated regularly while Cynthia did with very little sexual contact. Though she secretly wished "to be taken" and resented Martin for his passivity and inhibition, she never mentioned it because she didn't want to make an issue of it.

Both rationalized, "liberation-style," that they didn't want to "pressure" the other and that "sex wasn't that important," though both had considerable hidden frustrations and anger over it. Although they thought they were more liberated than their "uptight" parents, they actually had less of a sex life than their parents. Cynthia would release her tensions by shopping for household furnishings, compulsively keeping the house immaculate, and "indulging" in chocolate binges, which afterward she'd feel guilty about. Martin "released" his tension through workaholism and preoccupation with money matters.

Periodically, some little thing would trigger an angry eruption. Cynthia's deeper resentment over Martin's "nice-guy" behavior and her feelings of boredom would come out. "We're like two old people," she'd complain. Martin would lash back that Cynthia was a "controlling bitch." Rather quickly, they'd apologize to each other and reaffirm their "love" and slide back into the old patterns.

The *content* of their relationship in terms of taking responsibility and role expectations based on gender was almost perfectly equal. However, their moment-to-moment process, which was more traditional than their parents', caused them pain, created a deadness, and generated pent-up anger that they needed to deny and cover over. Secretly both considered leaving the relationship and were bewildered and frustrated that something that seemed so "perfect" didn't feel good at all.

One New Year's Eve, Cynthia stumbled into their posh bathroom, partially drunk, and found Martin masturbating on the phone to a "dial-for-sex" conversation. Martin felt humiliated, but Cynthia responded positively and compassionately. "God, I know exactly how you feel," she said. This accidental encounter proved to be a turning point that launched a dramatic and positive shift toward relating to each other's real feelings.

Consider the case of thirty-seven-year-old Leonard, a maitre d' at a posh hotel restaurant, who left a fourteen-year marriage. "She didn't like the way I worked, played, related, or made love. I don't think that she liked anything about me." The final straw, which caused him to leave her, was when she told him that her analyst had told her that Leonard was causing her to have a nervous breakdown. "That weekend I left and I vowed to myself that I'd never get involved with an emotionally dependent, blaming woman again."

He began dating many different "independent, sexy, and strong" women until he met Donna, director of a nearby urban redevelopment agency, at the restaurant one night. He described her to himself as the "most grown-up woman I've ever met." The chemistry was powerful and mutual because Donna, too, had gotten fed up with the "little boys" she'd been involved with: "passive, 'liberated' 'nice-guys' " who, she said, "didn't really want an equal relationship, they wanted me to take care of them." In Leonard she felt she had found someone who had it all. He was successful, generous, open, individualistic, sensual, playful, and "doesn't want to control me, or have me take over for him."

The first few weeks of the relationship were idyllic until they had their first fight on a vacation in Las Vegas. Donna asked Leonard to lend her money for the slot machines since she had left her traveler's checks in the room. She won $100 and when Leonard, "as a matter of principle," asked for his $20 back, she got angry and reacted like a "hurt little girl." She said resentfully, "You carry the money. You carry the airline tickets and the credit cards. You control everything."

This "pressed" Leonard's "button" and he responded in anger. "Here's your goddamn airline ticket. Here's a credit card. I don't want that responsibility." They didn't speak again until the following day. The morning after, Leonard pushed for communication and "evidence" for Donna's contention that he controlled her. "You wouldn't understand," she said. "If you don't see how controlling you are and how you obviously resent and distrust women, I can't make you see it." When Leonard pushed for "proof" of what she was saying, Donna withdrew and refused to talk. "This doesn't make sense," he repeated several times to her. Once, because of Leonard's continuing demands for "facts," and accusations that she was trying to make him feel guilty, Donna began to cry and Leonard backed off, saying, "Okay, let's just drop it and enjoy the rest of our holiday." Leonard fell asleep by the Jacuzzi and Donna acted rejected and accused him of "tuning out" and "cutting me off." By now Leonard wasn't sure what to say or how to make sense of the rapid deterioration in their communication.

That evening, he decided to disclose to her his impatience with their sex. "You love oral sex but you tell me you can't do it for me because of your early experiences with men who treated you badly and took advantage of you and left you hung up on being 'submissive' to a man. Well, I can't buy that excuse anymore. You're not even trying to overcome it—and I don't want to be punished for what some other guy did to you." Leonard continued, "So far as I'm concerned, you're controlling me sexually because you know how much I want oral sex. You're acting just like my ex-wife."

Their final argument was over the possibility of living together. Leonard said they should find a place that was affordable on Donna's significantly smaller income so that they could share the rent and living expenses equally. "If we get a place I can afford," he said, "I'll wind up paying for most of it." When Donna retorted angrily, "In my career, I want to be independent, but in my personal life I want to be with a man who's not afraid to take care of me," Leonard found himself withdrawing completely. "I don't trust her," he thought. "I don't know where she's coming from."

Only six weeks after a euphoric coming together between two seemingly liberated people, Leonard and Donna were polarized into a noncommunicative, mutually blaming, and traditional interaction in which Donna saw Leonard as "selfish, controlling, and insensitive," and Leonard saw Donna as a "manipulating, blaming little girl." The process of dealing with conflict had become severely polarized as Leonard "attacked" with "cold, detached logic" and Donna withdrew and "punished" by withholding affection and sexuality. Once she withdrew, she wanted Leonard to pursue and court her back and he refused. "You're blaming all this on me? You tell me I've got problems; that I hate women and I have to work out my relationship with my mother. I'm not buying that!"

The "perfectly" equal relationship-promise of the beginning splintered to the point where they were not even capable of a brief phone conversation without tempers building intensely and one or the other hanging up in anger. The relationship ended with as much miscommunication as it had begun with perfect communication.

Their relationship broke down because, in fact, Leonard and Donna were only seemingly or defensively liberated; but were actually completely "traditional" in their defensiveness at the core. Their "liberation" was born of defensive anger and reaction against past experiences. Increased self-protection was hidden behind philosophies of egalitarian idealism. Leonard was still traditionally macho in his unconscious process, as Donna was feminine in hers. While they could see that clearly in the other person, they denied it and were unable to recognize or acknowledge it in themselves. Like most traditional couples, their relationship ended on a blaming note with no awareness of how each was very much the creator of the pain and communication breakdown. They blamed each other's "hypocrisy," "hangups" and "phoniness" instead.

Indeed, Leonard's "liberation" disguised his macho need to distance women, to distrust closeness, to maintain control and autonomy, and to use his logic and ideology as a weapon. During a conflict he would attack relentlessly with "reason," like an attorney breaking down a witness, and then would call Donna "irrational" and "crazy" when she responded in hurt and anger.

Donna's femininity was evidenced by her blaming and withdrawing, in her passive manipulation and her attempts to make Leonard feel guilty by crying and accusing him of intimidation and even potential violence. "You scare me with your anger. It's so intense. You're going to lose control of it." After each argument she would withhold affection, communication, and sex. Indeed, in these ways she was "just like" Leonard's ex-wife. As the relationship began to develop, her deeper desire to "be taken care of" also emerged strongly but she justified it as a romantic urge.

The Seemingly Liberated

The pain and communication breakdown of the "seemingly liberated" illustrates how relationship process impacts, transforms, and ultimately negates and destroys its "beautiful" content. The feelings in a relationship after the initial fantasy "high" that is present at the launching of a romance are created by its undertow, the unconscious gender core, and not the content or "what" of a relationship.

Progressively, the content basis of the initial attraction, the symbols, words, and images, is eroded by the unconscious process. The people who thought themselves liberated, open, and fair—and potentially a wonderful couple—are left feeling disappointed and embittered. They fall into the self-deluding trap of believing they could find fulfillment and relationship success through their ideals and attitudes. If they never see beyond this blind spot they will ultimately be led to false and defensive conclusions: "Relationships are hopeless," "I can't seem to find the right person," or "There are no good partners left."

While some people are better suited for each other than others, the "right person" is still largely a fantasy and an illusion. People seem "right" at a distance, when only the *content* is being related to, and the deeper gender process has not yet begun to transform it. To the degree that the deeper process is defensive, the relationship is impacted and altered rapidly. As a result, inevitably, all relationships begin to look the same.

Liberation movements, by their emphasis on content change as the key to equality, have not only distracted from but have also seriously damaged the potential for relationship growth by making it a "sin" to acknowledge one's traditional process. The "seemingly liberated" are defensively and rigidly deluded and develop a highly charged guardedness around their image of themselves that causes them to blame and withdraw from anyone who might threaten their idealistic and inflated beliefs about themselves. They become powerful crazy-makers, giving off conflicting and impossible double-bind messages because of the opposition between their liberated content and their traditional process. It is *that* split in themselves which leads them into "hopeless" relationship experiences and it is *that* which causes their repeated disappointment, which ultimately encloses them even further behind a defensive self-protection, even as their ideals become more purely liberated.

There are various forms of "false" or "seeming" liberation, all of which create the "pain and communication breakdown" of the "seemingly liberated." The content, which is attractive, sensible, and humanistic, is the seducer or the web that pulls others in. The process is the "poison" that distorts and then destroys the relationship. None are more lost, defensive, and deadened behind their images than the "seemingly liberated."

Male "Seeming Liberation" by Anger

He's been "burned" in a traditional marriage or relationship where all of his "best efforts" led to his being blamed for being controlling, critical, cold, and selfish. "There was no way to satisfy her. The more I tried, the more I failed," he might say. He comes to "liberation" with the cry of "Never Again!" Like the female feminist, he has felt abused and exploited and wants nothing more to do with "dependent" women. But he hasn't changed *who* he is. He has only changed his attitudes and expectations.

The relationship fantasy of this man who is "liberated" by his anger is of a strong, independent, self-supporting, reasonable, "grown-up" woman who will meet him halfway. Instead, because he hasn't really changed, he draws his polar opposite, a traditional woman with a "liberated" facade. Both are left feeling disillusioned as the relationship begins to resemble the ones from the past.

Male "liberation by anger" may also occur in a man who has been bound closely to an "engulfing" mother and never broken away psychologically. He still wants to be taken care of and therefore doesn't want to be "responsible" for someone else. Many such men have a macho appearance, unconsciously designed to allow them to deny and counteract their little-boy craving and attachment to mother. The external image is of a self-contained, seductive man.

In either case, this "seemingly liberated" man thinks that he doesn't want to "control" a woman. While his appearance is "liberated," he is actually *more* distanced, distrusting, closed off, and invulnerable than before. Behind his veneer, he is *more* macho, though he thinks the opposite is true. He is therefore continually surprised when his relationships not only polarize in the same old way, but do so with increasingly greater speed.

Female "Seeming Liberation" by Anger

She too emerges from a relationship history that left her feeling controlled, with her "intimacy needs" frustrated and her male partner perceived as noncommunicative and "cold." He "made me feel unneeded," she says.

She may become the militant feminist: a closed-system blamer who says, in countless different ways, "No man will ever dominate my life again." Because it is a "seeming liberation," a reaction born of anger, she is "closed off" and unable to see how her deeper defensive process drew and promoted the responses she got. So she never grows but instead becomes more traditional in her blaming and reactive process, all the while believing that she is liberating herself.

Male "Seeming Liberation" by Guilt

The traditional male who is highly dependent on the validation of an attractive woman for his masculine self-esteem and who is prone to high levels of unconscious guilt and responsibility in a relationship becomes "liberated" out of this powerful undertow of feeling guilty and responsible.

His "liberation" is projected by "being nice" to women, not being "chauvinistic," because that's "wrong" and "demeaning," and by "supporting" women in their perceptions of themselves as having been exploited victims of men and in their "struggles" to be free. While he thinks that makes him nonmacho, in fact he is more macho than before in his denial of his own needs, in his "rescuer" posture and his ready tendency to stand accused and feel guilty over his "sexist mistakes."

His idea of being "liberated" is that he does not ask of women any traditional role behavior and he lets them "teach him" all the many ways he has been a "chauvinist." Like the old-time macho, only more so, he does not express any needs of his own because he feels guilty for asking for anything. It might be interpreted as his being selfish, demanding, or controlling.

His liberation, however, is strictly "seeming": an intellectualized regression into a more rigid, macho posture that will leave him drained and manipulated. He will be bewildered when he gets the same response of anger and accusations of being distant once he is in a committed relationship again. He believes he is liberated but, because he is actually more rigidly macho than before, even though the facade is "nice," he will draw and bring out the "little girl" needs that can't be met, because he chooses unconsciously the woman who will "make him feel like a man." That is what he *really* wants.

Instead of succeeding in helping her in her struggles to be stronger, she will increasingly become the traditional feminine female in her moodiness, lack of energy, endless physical complaints, eating obsessions, sexual "frigidity," and passive aggression (such as procrastination, lateness, and "helplessness"). While he may be disappointed, he has created it because in his process he still treats her like a little-girl object. His mechanical orientation is disguised by "niceness." Therefore her frustration and rage will build in traditional fashion.

His motivation for liberation was self-deluded. It was really an accommodation based on *his* need for being seen as the ultimate chivalrous man validated by women for being

"wonderful" and protective. His concern is for his own grat-
ification and not really for *her* situation.

Female "Seeming Liberation" by Self-Denial

"Men are not responsible for my happiness, my orgasm,
or my fulfillment," she says when she is with a man. She
asks him frequently, "Are you *sure* that you're comfortable
with that?"

Just as the traditional male is "seemingly liberated" out
of an intense need for female approval, this "seemingly liberated" female is motivated by the very traditional feminine elements of low self-esteem, self-denial, and a fear of
rejection. She tries to please in a new way by being "liberated" and not putting "pressure" on men the way that
"other women do."

Her liberation involves taking complete responsibility for
herself. Unconsciously, she invites into her life the "same
old" "selfish," controlling male who doesn't appear to control her because he doesn't have to. That is, her inability to
ask anything of him and her guilt when she thinks she is
being demanding already make her totally controlled. She
pays her own way and often even pays for him. When she
gets no sexual satisfaction she blames herself and makes
sure his needs are taken care of. She doesn't put any pressure on him for marriage but still makes herself always available to him. She will initiate sexually, financially, etc., to
take responsibility, but her process is still self-denial.

Because her process is a variation on the old-time female
masochist, instead of getting appreciation she gets used and
related to like an object and a mothering figure. She really
does become the victim, as the kind of men she attracts
inevitably hurt and abandon her and wind up seeking "excitement" elsewhere. However, right to the end she never

blames the man, but feels guilty for being blaming or engulfing and therefore "driving him away." Because her core is so traditional, she draws the traditional polar-opposite and suffers as a result.

When the "Seemingly Liberated" Meet

Initially, they appreciate each other and are relieved to be in a "real" and equal relationship. As the deeper polarization begins to transform the relationship, they try talking about it—endlessly. However, despite their best efforts, it continues to deteriorate and they are surprised at how traditional their arguments become. He's asking for space; she's asking for closeness and commitment. He feels engulfed, she feels distanced. She is frequently angry while he is explaining and feeling guilty. They tell each other these responses are crazy and unnecessary, but in fact they are the logical and inevitable result of the polarized undertow which creates the real nature of their interaction.

The "seemingly liberated" are consistently misled by their accoutrements of liberation. Unless they can see beyond the surface, they will become progressively more polarized in self-defense as time goes on, while their outward behavior becomes more "purely liberated." They are being torn apart by these extreme opposites in themselves and it causes their relationships to become increasingly fragile, volatile, draining, and ultimately hopeless. Unconsciously, they make it impossible for anyone to come close. They have become victims of their own defensively liberated delusions and nothing else. Unfortunately, the worse it becomes the less they can see it because the outward feelings and ideas and the deeper process have become extreme and opposites and they choose to believe they are what they appear to themselves to be.

12

WHY WOMEN STILL WON'T ASK YOU TO DANCE

Gary, age twenty-eight, is an attractive, athletically built man who is very much involved in men's issues. His "male-liberation" focus began after a series of painful encounters with women on his midwestern college campus; it became an obsession after the "lynching" of a friend of his named David by the "feminist mob," as he called them.

David had a sexual encounter with a woman he met at a fraternity pledge party and found himself charged with attempted rape by the young woman he met that night. He drove her to her apartment on campus and after kissing passionately in the car, she invited him to her room. In a moment of drunken bravado, inside her apartment, he pulled down his pants and in a commanding voice said, "Suck it!" The woman started to scream and campus police broke into her room and arrested him.

After a highly publicized trial, he was thrown out of school and given a six-month jail sentence. In his defense, he stated they had been passionate in the car and had been "joking and talking 'sexy' " all the way home and that he had no intention to use physical force. "I guess I got carried away by her men-and-women-are-equal talk and the out-front way she talked about women's orgasms as a liberation issue. I know I was quite drunk, but when I pulled my pants down, I was playing with her mind—testing her to see if she could handle directness.

"All she would have had to do was to tell me to put my dick into my pants and, sheepishly, I would have. I never in my life expected her to yell like a frightened kitten. But tell that to a jury. A man is considered guilty whenever he takes the sexual initiative."

David's tragedy haunted and infuriated Gary. He could acknowledge that David's behavior was extremely offensive, stupid, and had the appearance of a potential assault, but he knew David well enough to say with assurance that David was harmless and that under no circumstances would he ever lift a finger to hurt a woman. In fact, David had been known for going out of his way to be chivalrously protective. Gary also knew that David was wrong and had acted, he thought, immaturely and irresponsibly, but the whole way the matter was interpreted by the feminists on campus seemed grossly unfair to him, and distorted by their need to prove men to be vile rapists.

"Where is the humanness in all this?" he thought. "That could have been me. I've come on strong occasionally. Someone has to or nothing happens. This kind of thing almost makes me wish that I was gay."

As part of his own liberation experiment, in an attempt to prove that feminist women are hypocrites, he and two friends decided to go to different singles bars and sit without initiating conversation with a woman. They would wait for a woman to make the first move—talk, offer to buy a drink, or ask for a dance. Over a three-evening period during a holiday weekend, they each waited a total of thirteen hours, dressed, groomed, and looking as "harmless" as they could. Not one of them was approached by a woman. "In fact," Gary narrated in a journalistic report, "several women looked at me like I was a creep for just sitting there and doing nothing."

The Distortion of Gender Issues

Men complain that in spite of fifteen years of liberation focus, women tend to behave traditionally in their dating and romantic involvements with them. Women still find it difficult to initiate a relationship or actively pursue a man, pay their share of the bill, make the decisions on a date, or ask a man to dance. Why?

The question is one that reveals the tendency to trivialize gender issues and the misleading, even harmful effect of women's and men's liberation. In politicizing gender issues, they have vastly oversimplified the complex process of growth and rebalance between the sexes. The illusion created is that change is a matter of desire and awareness. So he may say, "She wants to work and have a career just like a man. She wants independence and equal 'privilege,' so she should take on the same risks and responsibilities too." Or it may be stated that men just have to stop treating women as inferiors and objects and woman simply have to begin to access their power. *It seems so easy for a woman to ask a man to dance,* but it isn't—any more than it's "easy" for a man *not* to ask a woman to dance if he's attracted to her.

It *looks easy,* but emotionally it is very difficult. Yes, any woman can ask a man to dance, and many do. They will call a man up for a date or initiate a conversation—once. Then they'll expect the man to take over. Rarely will they continue the pattern of taking the initiative and the responsibility for following through.

There is a tendency then for men to say that women are hypocrites. They perceive them as deliberately hanging on to the particular traditional behavior that is comfortable for them or serves their purpose, but wanting to avoid the consequences of that pattern. They see women as aspiring to the privileges of "liberation" and at the same time clinging to their feminine prerogatives when it suits them.

Likewise, women can be heard to complain that men are rushing to enjoy the fruits of an additional paycheck in the family but avoiding or minimally taking on a fair share of the household responsibilities. Women and men alike minimize the difficulty of change in the opposite sex.

Judy and Allan are a couple in their mid-thirties who have been living together for six years. Judy was saying that she has always refused to do Allan's ironing. "I wouldn't mind doing it if it were just a little bit, but he goes overboard. Everything he wears has to be ironed—even his workshirts. Besides, I work just as hard as he does at my career. I do notice, though, that I seem to always get a little grouchy when he's doing his own ironing. I don't really say much, but I always have that feeling that he's doing it at the wrong time or in the wrong room. I really didn't think he minded doing it that much. In fact, sometimes I would think that he felt kind of good about being independent in that way. But the other evening he had the fireplace in the living room going and he wanted to do his ironing in there. When I saw him closing all the drapes, I asked him why—it was a full moon and it looked so pretty outside. He said, 'You think I'm going to leave them open and let the whole neighborhood see what I'm doing?' "

It's an alienating injustice for men or women to label members of the opposite sex "hypocritical" because of their liberation contradictions. It suggests that the freeing up process is merely a matter of altering certain externals. Judy and Allan have not truly changed. Allan is doing his own ironing and Judy has her career, but both are still traditional in their deeper response patterns. The growth that would have made these outward gestures congruent with inner flow has not yet occurred.

At this stage of male-female interaction in our society, when a woman asks a man to dance it is for most an external gesture, a symbol, rather than a fully integrated, "natural" response. She has to make the deliberate effort. Rarely does it have roots. Therefore, she can do it once, but, because it's a self-conscious effort, she won't do it again. It's a behavior she was able to push herself to do, but it's disconnected from her internal self. It's not deeply felt. She is working at being liberated and that's different from an integrated, spontaneous response that occurs when there is real growth. If it were authentically a part of her, she wouldn't have to make an effort and it would be easy to continue once she started. It would be a natural part of her ongoing repertoire, unnoticed even by her.

You can intimidate someone into changing externals, which is what liberation has amounted to for many people rather than being an authentic expansion or freeing of proscribed behavior. The deeper defenses can't be changed that easily.

A woman asking a man to dance is symbolic of a very difficult change process. The struggle women have overtly pursuing the man they are attracted to is equivalent to men's struggle to be passive and not want to make an approach when they are strongly interested.

It's no more easy for women to take control than it is for men to give up control. It is no simpler for women to transcend their fear than it is for men to acknowledge their fear. It is no easier for women to take full responsibility for their sexuality than it is for men to give up concern for their performance and sense of responsibility when sex is not "working." They can do it for brief periods of time only. Generally, however, because it is alien to their deeper, conditioned response, it has little momentum.

As hard as it is for a man to avoid staring at an attractive woman, it is equally difficult for a woman to look directly at a man in an elevator. Men say, "Why won't women ever look at me? Why is it when I walk over to my office elevator, women look up to the sky or down to the floor, move away toward the empty elevator, but they don't make eye contact?" It is very easy for men to look at women they don't know—to look them up and down—and it is just as difficult for a woman openly to do that to a man. Conversely, it is very hard for a man *not* to do so. He can make a deliberate effort not to look, but inside he is straining and going "crazy" because he wants to. And a woman can make a deliberate effort to look at a man, but inside she is struggling with her impulse to look away, no matter how attractive she may find him.

Indeed, whatever is irresistible for masculine men to do is very difficult for feminine women in the male/female interaction, and vice versa. In a nutshell, that is the agony of male-female, person-to-person communication. *What seems to be easy or obvious to one sex is actually foreign, painful, and even frightening for the other, and that awareness needs to be grasped at a deeper level by both sexes, although few seem to do it.*

When we leave the traditional romantic model and try to bond with the opposite sex in a different way from before, we enter a psychological wasteland of uncertainty, confusion, and anxiety. New behaviors we attempt that are disconnected from our gender conditioning "just don't feel right."

Asking a man to dance seems easy to men because men do it. They project, "I can ask you to dance; certainly you could ask me to." They feel that a woman's refusal or resistance is proof she is hypocritical or an example of "wanting it both ways." Women commit the same sort of error with men. Because they find it easy to be close and seek commitment, for example, they can't understand why a man resists so powerfully. So they come to the conclusion that it's male selfishness, chauvinism, and bad will. "I can be close, and you could too if you just wanted to and made it a priority. It's really easy if you let yourself," she tells him matter-of-factly. But it has the same impact as a man saying to a woman, "Just be casual about sex and relationships. Forget about commitment and getting close, and just enjoy!"

In fact, these changes are not easy and it's an error of projection to believe, "I can do it. What is wrong with you?" The reason one sex can do it easily is because it's congruent with their defenses. It is deeply embedded in one and absent in the other. The opposite sex has polar-opposite defenses. The sexes are diametrically opposed in their unconscious response patterns, particularly within the context of the traditional male-female relationship, because its stressful nature seems to maximize the differences.

Therefore, it's much harder for a woman to be as directly power-oriented as a man on a sustained, long-term basis. It grinds her down. It is harder for her to make the development and accumulation of overt control and autonomy her comfortably maintained primary focus. Her deeper self seeks connection, unless she has already reacted powerfully against herself. It is just as hard for the traditional male to accept being submissive and powerless.

In my private practice, I have worked with any number of highly educated career women who still want to be reactors to men's initiative in relationships and experience great anxiety over changing this.

When it comes to male-female relationships, the deeper undertow takes over, and even though it seems as if it should be a simple matter for such a woman to be assertive and comfortable in the way she interacts with men, rarely does it work that way. She can make deliberate efforts, but it is not a comfortable act for her. She may even acknowledge frankly that though her career is successful, in her personal life she wants a man who will "take care of her."

Additionally, there is a constant subliminal fear of change

on the part of men and women alike, and rightfully so. As much as growth and change appeal to us as abstract ideals, they are threatening and resisted because the very sense of ourselves as men and women stands to be lost. When a man, for example, begins to let go of his traditional masculine response patterns, he will begin also to lose the feelings of "being a 'real' man." On a deeper level, therefore, much more is at stake than is superficially apparent. Our focus on the symbols of liberation has obscured our awareness of how difficult—even terrifying—this "letting go" of one's gender self-definition actually is.

The relief that many "liberated" women seem to experience when they finally get into a relationship with a man who they say really makes them "feel like a woman" is indicative of how distressing it is to let go of or to change our sense of ourselves as men and women. Until these changes have truly been incorporated into our self-concept on the deepest level, there will be a powerful desire, albeit perhaps repressed for periods of time, to return to our old sense of ourselves as men and woman. We can see that happening today everywhere. The braless, makeup-free, flat-heeled, "natural" woman seems to have become, in most cases, a memory of the 1960s and 1970s. Even career women are reclaiming their old feminine ways, just as men are doing on their end; the gray suits and ties come out of the closet, the hair gets shorter, and the new macho superheros regain our adoration and admiration at the box office.

In spite of decades of liberation, most women still get excited by "winners" or successful men and turned off by "weakness" and "losers." The attractive man is still the one with an aura of mastery, strength, and independence. Men encourage strong, independent behavior in women but then fall in love with the sweet, "adoring," compliant, "feminine" woman. They can only tolerate a limited amount of aggressive, dominant behavior in women before they tend to back away. So women call men hypocrites, just as men do when they see attractive women adoring success symbols.

These proclivities are all telling us that the deeper responses have not really changed, but that is not a "liberation crime" and should not be used to promote guilt or self-hate. We accuse women of being hypocrites because they are attracted to men who are winners or obviously macho, and we accuse men of being sexist because they still pursue the soft, sweet-smiling women. But we are asking the impossible when we expect people, simply through an act of will, to transcend their deeper selves and their gender conditioning.

We have trivialized our deep self-security gender defenses by trying to eliminate them through making the sexes "aware." In order for men and women to bond, however, we still seem to need the romantic undertow that creates our excitement, that gives her the feeling of "being swept off her feet" and him the sense of "being a man." This can only occur when and to the extent that the polarization is there. This polarization creates a mutually reinforcing, unconscious pull that works against real change. Indeed, most of the social and economic structures of our society are rooted in the motivations of gender polarization—the desire of men to be "manly" and women to be "feminine." Losing weight still seems to excite most women, as making money or "winning" excites men.

When we overlook the deeper struggle and resistances, and when we oversimplify them, we create a crazy-making situation based on intimidation. First, we accuse the opposite sex of bad will for not changing, implying they could change very easily if they only wanted to. That forces them into hiding their true selves and changing outward behaviors, and this makes the process of transparency and growth we are seeking all the more difficult, if not impossible, to achieve.

The roots of gender behavior are unconscious and self-protective. Thus we need to recognize the enormous resistance to deeper change and accept the contradictions and regressions of the sexes with generosity. Indeed, *we* can get to know about ourselves by observing the struggle and inconsistencies of our partners because they will reflect back to us our own "dark side." Because romantic attraction is based on polarization, men and women unwittingly promote the extremes in each other's behavior against which they protest mightily.

One thing clearly more destructive than the traditionally defensive response is a pseudo- or defensively liberated response. This confuses the external symbols of change with the deeper issues and makes a fulfilling relationship much harder to achieve, if indeed the parties involved have not destroyed their capacity for real bonding altogether as a result of the double layers of defensiveness, the new layered on top of "old" defensiveness, creating a whipsaw effect that is impossible to get through.

The best most of us can hope for at this point is a recognition on each person's part of our process and resistance to change and a willingness to take responsibility for our part in it. It is most important to read the map correctly, to know what it is we are struggling with, and not, as a result of a new defensive self-righteousness, to blame others for not changing in ways that we think they should, because we supposedly have.

We can try to build in, wherever possible, safeguards that allow some room for playing out these deeper traditional parts that we cannot easily alter; we can prevent some of the destructive end points by recognizing our own gender process and saying, "I know that I'm setting myself up for this and repeating an old pattern that never worked before. Nevertheless, I can't help it, but I'm aware of what is going to happen here and I'll only blame myself."

In other words, we may not be able to make great changes immediately, but we can recognize the cherished patterns we find so hard to alter and be consciously prepared for the inevitable end points or price we will have to pay, and blame *no one* for them. You cannot have a romantic bonding, for example, without an eventual, underlying experience of guilt in the male over feeling responsible; or pressure for commitment together with anger and confusion in the female over feeling controlled or fearing loss of herself. Communication breakdowns inevitably lurk ahead. It is a major step forward to begin to see the responses and feelings that we have in these situations as being the inevitable products of this mutually polarized and chosen connection rather than as something that is being done to us, caused by the other person, or the result of a "mistake."

Those who can acknowledge and respect the limitations, paradoxes, and contradictions of change that we all experience will be the least disappointed and embittered and the most capable, in the long run, of creating enduring and satisfying relationships. It will create a stronger feeling of respect and patience for one's partner, as well as a greater sense of self-respect and comfort with our own limitations.

Then men and women can gently lead and patiently support one another as we all try to work our way into a new understanding and responsiveness, free of blaming, guilt, and displaced rage and full of understanding, tolerance, and generosity.

PART FOUR

WITH HIMSELF

13

FEELINGS: WHEN ARE THEY REAL AND WHEN CAN YOU TRUST THEM?

Milton and Sally were both convinced that they were in touch with their feelings. The trouble was that instead of bringing them closer together, their frankness with each other seemed to drive them farther apart.

Sally would say, "I feel as if you're always pushing me away. It makes me so angry and frustrated." Milton would reply, "I feel so frustrated, too, as if nothing I do is ever enough or satisfying to you."

Other times, Sally would say, "I need you to hold me now. I need a hug," seemingly at times when Milton was least in the mood, and, although he would accommodate her, he would feel irritated and sometimes say so, which hurt Sally to the point that she wouldn't speak to him all day.

Some evenings Milton would say, "I need to be alone. I think I'll sleep in the other room tonight. It has nothing to do with you. It's my feeling—it's just me." Still, it would make Sally feel rejected, and sometimes she would cry about it. Milton would see this and begin to feel guilty, as if he had hurt Sally. When he would tell her this, she would respond, "You and your darn guilt. I just feel abandoned by you, that's all, but I'm not trying to make you feel guilty.

223

Can't I even tell you that? I don't want your guilt. Guilt only means you're angry." Milton, in frustration, would respond, "Well, I'm only telling you what *I'm* feeling too. I thought that's what you wanted me to do." In turn, Sally said, "God, I feel so bad for what I do to you," to which Milton would respond, "I don't *want* you to feel bad for me. I'm not suffering. I'm just struggling and trying to tell you what I go through." Instead of feeling comforted by these open exchanges, they would come to feel more alienated from each other.

Sally, in an effort to bridge the gap one time during these dialogues, said, "Why don't we just stop talking and go to bed and make love." Milton responded as if he were attacked, "I feel like you don't even know me when you say that. You know that's the last thing I want to do when I'm feeling like this." "What's happened to us?" Sally asked. Milton responded, "I don't know. I've worked so hard at growing and sharing, but it only seems to get worse. I tell you what I feel and instead of it bringing us closer together, it only seems to drive us farther apart."

After the sharing of feelings, Milton became convinced that Sally really didn't want him to express his feelings, and Sally became more frustrated because Milton's "sharing" felt to her like a disguised attack or one more way of pushing her away, rather than making himself more vulnerable and close.

The "Freedom" to Feel

A prevailing notion about men in particular, because men traditionally stifled their emotions, is that their growth will mean the freedom and ability to express feelings. This sanctification of emotions obscures an important issue, namely that the communication of defensive feelings can be worse than the expression of none at all.

When women first experienced their liberation, they began articulating what they felt. What emerged was anger and blaming rage, defensive outbursts emerging from the repressions produced by feminine conditioning. Were her oppressors really men or was it her conditioning that destroyed her ability to take control and power because of the anxiety that created in her? After all, most men have experienced the frustration of being with a woman who resisted or seemed unable to make a decision, even when implored to.

Men, once they begin to "get in touch with their feelings," often find themselves with the same potential for expressing defensive, self-righteous emotions that, instead of "freeing" them as people, will only push them further into distrust, isolation, and self-protection.

Did society or women pressure men to take the masculine-provider role or force them to be under sexual pressure to perform or prevent them from expressing vulnerability, developing friendships with other men, acknowledging fears and needs? Or was this a by-product of their masculine conditioning, part of the training that made a male feel like a man?

Indeed, what is a genuine or nondefensive feeling that can be trusted and that facilitates communication and the life process? When does the expression of feelings merely entrap and alienate one still more? When we speak of men getting in touch with their feelings, what do we really mean?

A man says to his wife, "I feel engulfed and manipulated by you and it makes me angry. You are always trying to make me feel guilty. I haven't acknowledged or respected my own feelings but I'm not going to let *you* or anyone else stop me from feeling what I feel and being real anymore." What he is doing is describing the by-products of his own defensiveness, something created largely by his socialization, not something that is being *done to him by her*. While unconsciously he may have chosen a partner who reinforces these tendencies, she did not create his propensity.

The man who expresses great love and passion toward a woman who is not interested in him at all and tells her he has never felt such depth of emotion before may actually be feeling not love or passion but the fantasy excitement of desiring a "female object" he cannot have. Is it enough, therefore, to feel comfortable expressing his vulnerability and emotions, particularly since he doesn't respond positively or lovingly to those who *are* in his life and who *do* care for and love him, except that they don't "excite" him, so he doesn't feel great "love" in return? Is "feeling sad" and saying so, because he "loves" a woman who is rejecting him, what being free to express your feelings is really all about?

When a man is experiencing intense anger because his control is threatened and this expression of feeling is a way to create further distance and regain control, is it enough for him to justify himself by saying he has a right to express his feelings?

Traditionally conditioned men, when they first "get in touch with" and express feelings, often turn out to be narcissistic feelers, meaning their emotions have little to do with the objective reality of their lives. Their feelings are "disconnected" and defensive. Thus "getting in touch" with and expressing them is worse than not expressing feelings at all, because expressing them further alienates and isolates a man and sabotages what he really needs, which is connection and nondefensive, authentic relating and closeness. For example, he may conclude falsely, after expressing these feelings, that women "don't really want to know what a man feels," which enrages him and alienates him still more and exacerbates his distrustful defensiveness.

A feeling must be nondefensive if it is to produce connection and "humanization" or "personalization." If the feeling emerges from polarized and defensive masculine needs, it corners him worse than before because now he has "proven" to himself others don't want him to be human.

Clearly, the notion of "getting in touch with" and express-ing feelings needs to be explored.

Feelings Not to Be Trusted

Polarized Emotions

Men's conditioning results in the repression of certain needs, responses, and feelings that in sum total produce his sense of manliness, along with a tendency either to overreact defensively or not respond at all.

Defensive Autonomy

A man thinks, "Nobody really cares about my needs or what I feel." The more traditionally masculine he is, the more his dependency needs are repressed, which is respon-sible for producing this feeling. Acknowledgment of his need for others, the desire to be taken care of, feelings of helplessness, weakness, or fear are responses that tend to be denied and blocked and not consciously experienced.

The repression of dependency needs gives the macho his loner, "self-made" orientation, which produces the de-fensive projection that "nobody really cares about my needs," or "nobody knows who I am or what I feel." His perception of others as not caring for or knowing him is a self-fulfilling prophecy—the inevitable end point of this re-pression. Indeed, the people he has chosen to surround himself with and the way he relates to them may actually result in or produce this. They may *not* be interested in what he needs, but that's why he chose them. They relate to him for his performance, his image and "strength," and what he can do for them, but he chose them because they reinforced the role he needed to play in order to validate himself as a man. *They do not do it to him. His process created it and they feed into it.*

"Getting in touch with his feelings" may result in a self-pitying, self-righteous justification of his resentment and rage and produce still more isolation and disconnection if he does not see beyond the immediate experience toward a total perspective. So *these* feelings cannot be trusted and will only trap him further by confirming his already negative belief that people use each other and that "the world is a jungle." The common masculine experience of feeling smothered and engulfed in a relationship exists in proportion to his defensive self-containment or autonomy, which creates in him a progressive intolerance for *any* closeness.

The repression of dependency generates a powerful move away from connection, in addition to a desire to disconnect from all personal relationships on which he is dependent, particularly under conditions of stress. The defensive sense of "I don't need you or anybody" results when he feels hurt. The need to have "space"—to be autonomous and avoid closeness—also expands progressively as a result of this repression, and anybody he can't control and distance will cause him to feel engulfed.

Defensive Rationality

His masculine conditioning causes him to experience and interpret his life in distanced, unemotional, or mechanical ways that he perceives as being "rational" or "logical." However, his "logic" is a part of his defensive self-protection and therefore becomes a weapon he uses to aggress, dominate, and distance himself.

He creates "safe," "logical," mechanistic answers to explain complex personal interactions and processes. He doesn't see this "rationality" as a private or autistic logic designed to isolate himself from personal involvement. Others feel put off, misunderstood, exasperated, and attacked by his reasoning or "logic," which may be superficially correct but only because he perceives his human interactions mechanically and selectively, not personally. He lectures his children for "their own good," without realizing that they don't even "hear him," and feel alienated by his insensitive communications. He is talking to himself while he believes he is talking to them.

His rigidly defensive use of rationality and his style of "being sensible" cause him to be impatient with and overreact to what he sees as the "irrationality," "unreasonableness," or "craziness" of others, who don't accept his ready supply of answers, advice, and solutions to every problem instantly. This leads him to feel irritated and despairing over the "hopelessness" of communicating with the many "irrational" people in his life, i.e., his children, his wife, or others to whom he relates in this rigidly literal way.

Furthermore, the repression of his own emotions will cause him to have distrustful feelings about the emotional responses of others. When his wife cries or his children act fearful or upset, he may tend to discount or disbelieve their responses and see them as manipulative. One middle-aged client of mine, the father of five children, had totally alienated himself from them by consistently doubting and minimizing their emotional concerns. They would describe a personal problem and he would insist that it really wasn't that bad—or that they were making it up entirely.

In relationships, his logic is meaningless, alienating, and "irrational," even though he can "prove" his point and be "right." That is, his "logic" may make sense to him but is actually "crazy" in its superficial or one-dimensional quality and its inappropriate short-circuiting of the relationship process. It betrays the fact that he is not "tuned-in" to those who are in his life, and in that sense doesn't know who they are. Moreover, he will not be able to see how his cold logic is, in part, responsible for promoting the overly emotional, desperate, or "crazy" responses of others who feel frustrated, attacked, and pushed away by his detached rationality. This confirms to him that "everybody is crazy"—except himself.

In defensive masculine process, the intellect is a weapon and intellectualization is a protection against feelings. He abstracts and "thinks" in order to distance personal parts of himself. This creates an obsession with "truth," correctness, and a belief that discovering "answers" is the way to improve his life, convince others, and "change the world."

Defensive Aggression

Masculine conditioning causes men to defensively deny and "fear their fear" or vulnerability and to block or transform fear into bravado, defensive counteraction, or total denial of reality. This produces a self-destructive overreaction to situations that challenge or threaten his defensive need to prove, "I am not afraid," "I am not a coward," "I am not a sissy," and "I *am* a man." It is sad to think of the many rigidly defensive young men who either permanently damaged or even lost their lives at a young age because of the need to prove fearlessness ("I'm not chicken!").

This defensive need to prove himself and to deny fear supersedes and triumphs over his instincts for survival and creates impulsive self-destructive tendencies and defensive displays of "courage" and "fearlessness." This may express itself blatantly in involvement in violent encounters for essentially meaningless reasons where nothing but image or "need to prove" is at stake, or it may take the form of inappropriate risk taking, such as accepting a dangerous physical challenge. It may also cause him to engage in defensive, reckless acts and habits in which he is acting on his distorted sense of invulnerability or fearlessness.

He pushes on when he should pull back, directly in the form of senseless, physical confrontations or indirectly through a hyperaggressive goal-driven style, characterized by relentless, insatiable ambition and the endless need to compete and be better than others.

The defensive aggressiveness exists in proportion to his denied or repressed fear, and, because he projects it outside of himself and sees it in others, it causes him to perceive that "life is dangerous," "people will hurt and take advantage of you if they can" and "the world is a jungle."

Defensive Assertion

The defensive need to control that characterizes masculinity is in part a reaction against deeper passivity and submission that he fears and denies in himself. The more powerful the defensiveness, the more instantaneous and encompassing his negative response to anything or anyone he believes will control him or take control away from him. In proportion to his masculinity, the need for control is insatiable and expands progressively.

Unconsciously, he lives in a polarized world of "control or be controlled." He traps *himself* as his life space narrows and constricts to include only those who will tolerate his control. Progressively, he is surrounded by people who, because of their fears and insecurities, can accept being dominated, although it generates intense invisible anger in them toward him. On some level he senses this, and it further fuels his distrust and need to control others.

Defensive assertion also means that he will impose his ego (ideas, opinions, and decisions) in increasing degrees and become intolerant of or unable to hear or absorb the input of others. His ego inflates limitlessly until no one else can "get in." Being an "egomaniac" is a characteristic of masculinity and is present in proportion to masculine defensiveness.

Defensive Sexuality

In proportion to his masculine defensiveness, he is sexually obsessed and sensually repressed. Paradoxically, he is preoccupied with sex but fearful of and resistant to intimate touching unless the latter is instrumental and will lead to intercourse.

This repressed sensuality is in part responsible for producing a great need for space and a strong tendency to feel crowded and smothered by others, particularly when he is being touched, caressed, or hugged.

His urgent preoccupation with sex, *because it is defensive,* does not diminish when it is satisfied. The obsession builds continuously. However, the need is not really for sex per se, but for the reduction of tensions created by his isolation, for contact and control, and the reassurance of his "manliness."

Extreme and Opposite-Extreme Feelings

A common by-product of masculine conditioning is a cycle of extreme emotional highs and lows. These are "roller coaster" feelings, or extreme reactions men experience, none of which are to be trusted or should be acted upon. The more externalized a man is, the more pronounced are the swings in his self-perception, from arrogant superiority ("I am the greatest") to depressive self-contempt ("I am nothing").

Romantic highs and lows are a form of this roller coaster phenomenon. When fantasies are being satisfied and a man feels safe and validated, he experiences a "high." When reality sets in or problems start that threaten him, his romantic feelings dissolve and he has intense opposing reactions of rage and distrust.

These roller coaster feelings are *never* to be trusted as guides to reality or decision making, because inevitably they are short-lived and will turn into their opposite. Acting on them is comparable to making important decisions when you're drunk.

Interlocking Feelings

How we create and promote the responses we get while blaming others is part of the phenomenon of gender-derived interlocking feelings: emotions that are defensive and therefore also not to be trusted.

The feminine woman complains, "You don't open up, and it makes me feel rejected," but she is unable to see how her way of communicating helps to shut the man down. The slightest negative response by him is defensively construed by her as an attack or criticism, which she reacts to by crying, withdrawing, or accusing, thereby progressively "closing him up." Or she complains that he doesn't talk to her enough and doesn't seem truly happy when he's with her, without seeing how her tendency to *react* and not initiate or make choices and decisions creates an atmosphere that is "boring" to him because he is getting no input or stimulation.

Conversely, he *blames her* for not knowing what she wants, when he tends to make decisions instantly and inwardly resents participating or cooperating with her when he has to do something *she* wants. Similarly, he criticizes her for shopping too much, when his tendency to be "always working" promotes her tendency to respond to frustration materialistically.

These interlocking feelings are mutually blaming responses that do not take into consideration how one's own process has, in part, created and promoted the very response one reacts to negatively.

Anger Toward Women

The conditioning of men in relation to women to initiate and take responsibility for "making things happen" inevitably produces feelings of guilt when things go wrong. Once "in touch with his feelings," it is only a short distance from masculine guilt and feeling responsible to feelings of resentment toward women, whom he sees as blaming and manipulating him.

It is not enough to say in defensive anger, "I'm not going to let any woman blame, manipulate, and use me again." His masculine defense process has in part invited and created that experience because he could only relate object to object, and if the defensive process is not changed, the pattern will continue to repeat itself over and over again. Until he sees how his process creates the emotional reality he experiences, he will want to push all women away in anger except, perhaps, those he believes are completely independent in their own right, in which case a new set of problems will arise out of this distorted fantasy perception of the existence of a "perfect," self-reliant woman.

Women have not manipulated, blamed, or engulfed men beyond men's own need to choose women who are adoring and submissive and easy to "control." Until this process that helps to create his experience is changed, defensive anger toward women entraps and isolates him and makes things worse. Therefore, these feelings are not to be trusted because they will make him increasingly wary in his relationships with women.

Distorted Overreactions to the Opposite Sex

Polarized conditioning produces defensive distortions in the perception of the opposite sex and feelings that should not be trusted.

Women's urgent and bottomless need for closeness stemming from feminine internalization causes them to perceive men as withholding and much more closed off and distant than they potentially are, just as his "fear of closeness" causes him to see women as much more needy, engulfing, and pressuring than they potentially are. To the extent that a woman is defensively feminine, his externalization is partly creating the "vacuum" that heightens and promotes her "neediness."

For him to see her as engulfing, or for her to see him as distancing, without each of them recognizing how their own process exaggerates the response they are getting, is a misleading and self-entrapping defensiveness.

In general, the polarized defensiveness of each sex produces the following effects: Her repressed aggression causes her to see men as more dangerous, hostile, and angry than they are, just as his repressed fear and exaggerated aggressiveness cause him to see her as more fragile than she is, causing him to be defensively protective of her and to fight her battles when she could easily do that for herself and really doesn't want him to. Further, it causes him to resist showing her his "true feelings" for fear that he will "crush her"; this too stems from the exaggerated perception of her as unduly vulnerable and fragile.

Her repressed sexuality causes her to blame him for being sexually obsessed and out of control sexually, just as his repressed sensuality causes him to react in irritation to her "demands for holding and touching."

His repressed autonomy causes her to see him as much more unneeding than he is, just as it causes him to overreact to her desire to be close. He will view her need as infantile.

Her repressed assertion and his repressed submission cause her to feel, "He always wants to control me," while he comes to feel resentful that he always has to make the decisions.

Through all of this, mutually self-fulfilling prophecies are created and reinforced. Each sex generates and promotes the very response they resent and fear, and then blames the other; this leads to an inevitable and unfortunate end point of alienation and hostility between the sexes.

Disguised Self-Serving Feelings Between the Sexes

Disguised self-serving emotions cause both men and women to feel something, obtensibly for the other person, but actually in the service of their own self-image needs.

A woman feels compassion and caring and a desire to nurture him, often when that is not what he wants from her. She is giving him something he is not asking for but is seeing herself as doing it for him. Then she is angry and hurt because he does not respond positively or with appreciation to something he didn't want and is even repelled by.

The kinds of compassion and understanding feelings he really wants, which is to have his "not-nice" feelings such as anger, boredom, or sexual feelings for other women accepted compassionately, she won't give him. She wants to give him compassion when it suits her needs and not his.

Likewise, he has protective feelings of wanting to "help" and "be there for her," which he believes are for her but are really for his own defensive purposes. Then he feels hurt by her negative reaction to them. In fact, she may have wanted the exact opposite, but he couldn't hear her desire because it did not serve his needs.

She spends hours preparing a meal that he didn't want her to prepare and then only feels pressured to eat and enjoy. In turn, he works hard and long "for her" when she would rather he be home more. Or he does things to "turn her on" sexually that only make her feel pressured to respond and are for his satisfaction, not hers.

Traditional gender conditioning causes men and women to want to give to each other that which is not wanted and to not hear correctly and not give that which is wanted. Narcissistic feelings are disguised as "caring" ones. Feelings of wanting to do for the other that have not been asked for or checked out should not be trusted. They are defensively self-serving and therefore lead to hurt and a spiral of misunderstanding.

In summary, "getting the feelings out" is not enough and easily can be destructive. It is not appropriate to say, "It's my feeling and I'm entitled to it." Simply to get feelings out is, in the long run, more harmful than anything else if the feelings "gotten out" are the by-products of gender defensiveness.

14

WE CAN SEND A MAN TO THE MOON BUT WE STILL CAN'T HANDLE RELATIONSHIPS: EXPLORING A MISLEADING CLICHE

Dr. Ford is a proponent of making meaningful relationships the number one priority in order to transform the quality of life in society. This is in spite of the fact that she herself is a veteran of two bitter divorces from men she refuses even to mention by name, and a series of young lovers from whom she pulls away the moment they become dependent or possessive ("Why can't I live with the prerogatives of a man? Good sex, total control, and no commitment pressures," she confided to a best friend.)

Dr. Ford gave the following emotionally charged lecture to a group of seven hundred members of a midwestern Unitarian church:

"If we spent one-tenth of the energy, and two percent of the money that's involved in space research and weapons development on the business of relationships—communication, closeness, and caring—we could re-create the Garden of Eden in our world today. I get furious thinking about all the money and time wasted on the negative in our society, war, drugs, disease, crime, while a thirty-thousand-dollar grant proposal to the government to research the psychological components of love or a proposition to budget money for marriage and parenting training for all prospective newlyweds gets either mocked or just ignored. I go up the wall. What will it take to make those paranoid, cynical politicians see that if you want the positive you've got to put the focus there. Life can be anything we choose to make it. And I think that it's time to choose warmth and human commitment, rather than technology and power. If we can send a man to the moon, we can certainly learn to manage and enhance the experience of personal relationships."

The cliche complaint, expressed in many different variations on the theme that we can send a man to the moon therefore we should be able to handle relationships, embodies the commonly held, pseudo-psychological notion that relationships turn on the simple mechanics of emphasis and effort. The underlying idea is that if we are so brilliant and can make inroads on the mysteries of the universe by conquering space, surely by applying equal energy and will on the personal side of life, we can dramatically improve the male-female relationship.

The statement can also be seen as one made against the "priorities" of men. Which sex is traditionally seem as mechanical and resistant to focusing on relationships? Males. Therefore, what is really being said is, "If only *men really* wanted to, they could dedicate themselves to improving marriage and family, and the world would be a significantly better place."

This is a seductively misleading notion. It unknowingly overlooks the underlying dynamics of masculinity involved in the conditioning of men that makes putting a man on the moon possible. That is, the same defensive process that makes it possible for men to have a focus on and genius for technology unconsciously disconnects them from the personal side of life and human relationships and makes them "incompetent" there.

Further, it is a misleading cliche because it suggests that relationships and their success are a matter of conscious desire and effort. We often hear it expressed that all there is in this world is people, so why don't we make people the priority? The classically misleading inference is that it is a sad commentary on the human race that "objects have become more important than people."

But men do not choose to make mechanical objects a priority. Nor do they choose to make work a priority, even though it might seem that way on the surface.

The deeper psychological reality for men and masculinity is that relating in personal ways is unconsciously threatening, frustrating, and unsatisfying, and in the polarized male/female relationship and within the traditional family dynamic a man *can't* be different by a simple act of will, even if he wanted to, which most men *do*.

Furthermore, to the extent that he is not able to perform "as a man," capable, so to speak, of technological, goal-oriented achievements, he would not feel good about himself, nor would he be attractive to the woman. The very basis of the attraction between a polarized or traditionally male/female couple is that he embodies the masculine capacities and she the feminine. A man cannot maintain a relationship if he is filled with self-hate or if he is experienced as a failure and a loser by himself and his wife, which happens as men fall short of being masculine.

Sending a man to the moon is actually a symbol of the embodiment of the masculine pursuit of externalized goals, which is what validates men among each other and makes them attractive in the eyes of women. But the defensive conditioning that makes him goal-focused and achievement-oriented is the very process that also weakens or eliminates entirely his capacity for personal relating. The masculine conditioning externalizes and disconnects him, making the personal side of his life one that is fraught with anxiety and discomfort, while whenever he focuses on "impersonal" objects, goals, and abstractions outside of himself, he experiences an anxiety reduction, satisfaction, and sense of *being a man*.

The elements of masculinity that make him attractive "romantically" initially to a woman and that define him as masculine (ambitious, productive, aggressive, decisive, logical, autonomous, etc.) develop *at the price of his internalization or the capacity to relate person to person*. In other words, the more masculine he is, the less he *can* relate personally, regardless of whether or not he *wants* to. Macho men who *try* to relate to each other in personal ways and inevitably come up against the defensive barriers are keenly aware of this impossibility.

In proportion to his masculine conditioning, unconsciously he does not experience people as people. Feminists have informed us that men don't experience women as people, but rather as objects for need satisfaction. This is true because in proportion to his masculine conditioning, a man relates to people generally, male or female, in externalized, mechanical ways because he is cut off from his inner self, which has been repressed through his conditioning. To reconnect with that part of himself is to face losing his sense of "being a man," so he unconsciously avoids it.

Women are objects or possessions whom he unknowingly uses (he *thinks* he *is* relating and being loving), and who, in return, manipulate him. Other men are competitors or allies in his goal pursuits. Children, if they are his own, are object extensions of his ego. He needs contact with people because of the buildup of great isolation and loneliness tension resulting from his externalization, but he can't relate even to his family in a genuinely personal way. It is object to object. He can do with and for them, but is incapable of *being* with them, in proportion to the existence of his masculine defenses, or the unconscious processes that produce the experience of "feeling like a man."

The feminine woman does not experience the man *as a person* either. She is no more capable of authentic caring for him than he is of her, because to the extent of her femininity, she is fearful of, and resists, externalization, and looks to him to counterbalance her fears. He becomes an object of *her* need satisfaction, and to the degree that he is unable to provide that and does not want to "take care of her," she will become uninterested or angry with him.

She believes she wants love, closeness, contact, and communication, but she is "using" him just as he is "using" her. Furthermore, she is trying to get intimacy from a man who, to the extent of his masculine externalization, has no capacity to give it to her.

The relationship between the feminine woman and the masculine man is not a relationship between two people at all, which is what makes it fragile, volatile, and readily destroyed. Therefore, when she says to him, "You put all this energy into your work and into your selfish goals, and you're so good at all of that; you can certainly put a little bit of energy into our relationship and improve that," it is misleading and "crazy-making" because he really *can't*. It is comparable to his saying to her, "You're so good at relationships, why don't you learn to run a business or design a new piece of sophisticated mechanical equipment by making that a priority." To the extent of her "femininity" and internalization, she will defensively resist.

Similarly, it is commonplace for doctors' wives to say to their husbands, "You care about your patients and are so dedicated to them. Why can't you be that way with your family?" The illusion is that if he can do one, he can choose to do the other.

Unconsciously, however, his patients are not people. They are objects or extensions of his ego. They are controllable, like objects, and in reality that is how he relates to them, his "niceness" notwithstanding. If they become "uncontrollable" he can discontinue working with them, or they will go away on their own out of frustration if they need to relate to him in ways that he resists. Patients do not make demands for closeness on physicians. In the eyes of the patient, the doctor is an object and a symbol about whom they may have fantasies, but whose reality they rarely, if ever, get to see. Indeed, if they did they would probably be disillusioned and threatened by the gap between his image and his personal reality.

In his personal life, demands are made on him to relate in ways he *seems* to be capable of because his professional behavior makes him seem capable of such personal caring, involvement, and dedication. However, this is an illusion. Professional attributes are qualitatively different from what is required in genuinely personal connection. Indeed, that which motivates and makes it possible for a doctor to become the great surgeon, for example, externalizes him to the point that he is mechanical in personal interaction. He can relate intellectually or by doing and providing but not in the ways that women mean when they speak of being "intimate," "open," and "close." This frustrates and finally enrages his formerly "devoted," "adoring" partner, who believes he is deliberately and selfishly withholding. She chose him in the first place for his symbols rather than his reality but builds up tremendous intimacy or fusion frustration because of her internalization, and he *cannot* satisfy her. Physicians' wives are known for the rage and pain they build up in their marriages.

Similarly, in conversation between a clergyman and his wife, she may say to him, "You love humanity and you love people. Why are you so cold and disinterested at home with your family?" He is the great communicator from the pulpit and with his congregation, but seems to her unable to be really personal and patient in the same way with his own wife and children in the way his family believes he can, if he only *really* wanted to.

The inability of these men to be close and personal and involved with their own families, while *seeming* to be so with "everyone else," is not ill will or lack of priorities. Psychologically, the two are qualitatively different and opposing. No matter how personal a man may *seem* to be, when he is working the people he interacts with are actually controllable objects that can be distanced to his comfort level. He functions safely from behind his role and not from his person, even though it may not appear so because he *seems to be* connected.

There are many "great men"—poets, scientists, professors, humanistic thinkers, missionaries, and doctors—whose work has been impressively and powerfully humanistic, while their personal lives have been a shambles, with wives having emotional breakdowns and attempting suicide and children disturbed to various degrees, perhaps drug-addicted or simply not productive.

In fact, more than likely there is an inverse correlation between a man's competence and success in his work life and his competence and success at home. Hard as he may try, and indeed, he really *does* until he begins to "give up" the impossible quest, there is an invisible wall that prevents him from being effective in the "personal" arena. He cannot cross this wall. Similarly, a woman's feminine conditioning allows her to be intensely and deeply tied into the personal aspects of her life but dwarfs and destroys her capacity for sustained, goal-focused, impersonal productivity, abstracted relating, and external power games.

Because the process of creating a good relationship is largely an intangible matter, it often seems simply to be a matter of goodwill, time, and effort—something that *should be* easily within the reach of everybody who "really" wants it and is willing to work to make it happen. Compared to sending a man to the moon, creating a "good" relationship would seem to be a simple matter for any healthy person.

The "Best of Both Worlds" Fantasy

What is *really* meant when we talk of the need for men to make relationships a priority is that we would like to have the best of both worlds by preserving the qualities that make the young man a creative and dedicated technological person, while superimposing on that an equal competence in relationships. *In fact, the psychological undertow that makes one possible, to the same degree makes the other impossible.*

The technological sophistication that emerges from masculinity is related to the male's unconscious disconnection from the personal world. Typically, the dedicated male scientist or creative engineer, for example, is someone who can spend days or weeks comfortably pursuing his work in the laboratory or behind a computer with no pain or frustration (though he might feel guilt). He works to achieve his research goals with no gnawing hunger for personal, "intimate" contact, beyond, perhaps, a release of sexual tension or a need to know that his wife or family is still there waiting for him. In fact, he is more comfortable being "left alone." *Unconsciously, his capacity to be externally goal-focused in an impersonal setting exists to the degree that personal interaction makes him uncomfortable and unconsciously he seeks to avoid it.*

A graphic example of the unconscious disconnection of masculinity was illustrated on a recent nighttime news documentary about robots. The scientist being interviewed casually made the incredible and revealing statement: "Robots are our children." It said everything about his unconscious, because, indeed, on a deeper level, that is *exactly* how he experiences his mechanical creations—as being alive and an extension of him. It is a variation on the way many men become passionately attached to and involved with their cars, boats, and computers but impatient and uncomfortable when "forced" into personal conversation or interaction with their family. Robots, for that scientist, probably are preferable to real children because they are controllable and personally nonpressuring.

The best-of-both-worlds fantasy—the belief that you can reap all the rewards of externalization (material wealth, power and success symbols, etc.) together with having a personal world that emphasizes humanity, ecology, etc.—is perhaps the greatest and most misleading and disastrous of contemporary illusions. It is probably most distressing to women and men who are perfectionistic and believe the fantasy can work if they only try hard enough. They drain, destroy, and embitter themselves trying.

In fact, many "liberated" women today are experiencing the pain and price of that illusion. They have made successes of their careers but their personal lives are in painful disarray. They are caught in the illusion that it is just a question of conscious choice and that their priorities have become distorted. In fact, the defensive process that externalized them and allowed them to develop, like men, successful careers has made their personal experiences and relationships as brittle, fragile, painful, and conflicted as they have always been for masculine men.

Many men trying to play the new superman role, successful in the work world and great husbands and fathers at home, are equally the victims of this fantasy of "the best of both worlds" and are drained and torn apart trying to accomplish it. *Achieving the ultimate in externalization and internalization at the same time is a psychological impossibility, because one exists to the degree that the other doesn't. You can't have the best of both worlds. You can only manipulate matters enough to give the temporary appearance of having the best of both worlds.*

As we become increasingly externalized, the capacities for mechanical invention become awesome, but at a price. In modern medicine, for example, disconnection and externalization are exemplified by the recent invention of mechanical hearts and highly sophisticated technological medical treatments that encourage, again, the fantasy of the best of both worlds. It is a fantasy because the same process that allows us to create those mechanical parts has disconnected us from our own bodies and crippled our capacity to respond naturally and instinctively to our physical selves. This creates the disease that mechanical inventions then are invented to cure. *The process that creates the "cures" is the same process that creates the illness.* Therefore, the "promise" always eludes us.

The technological wizardry of our time has a dark downside, made up of a whole myriad of physical and emotional problems that emerge directly from the disconnection that makes it possible. Women indirectly contribute to this to the degree that their internalized femininity unconsciously demands that men be goal-driven and externalized. *Women and men in tandem, not just men, promote the fragility of the human connection.*

From the masculine unconscious there emerges an obsession with work that has little to do with purposeful productivity. It is work in the service of anxiety reduction, personal distancing, validation of the masculine ego, but *not* in the service of *life*. The achievement-driven male is caught up in a production/achievement obsession. Work is not work per se. It is an escape from internalization and a validation of ego.

Likewise, the feminine capacity and preoccupation with "love" and relationships has nothing to do with love either. It is "love" in the service of internalization and fear and resistance to the external. It is relationship in the service of anxiety reduction and defensive need satisfaction. *Her*

relationship focus is as defensively motivated as is his pro-
ductivity obsession.

The more externalized he is, the more object-oriented,
work- and goal-obsessed he is, the easier success in the ex-
ternal world becomes, and the more impossible personal
relationship becomes. Likewise, the more internalized she
becomes as a result of her feminine conditioning, the more
her relationship focus is compulsive and out of control. She
defensively "overloves," and her external functioning is
impaired.

Is her defensive obsession with "love" any better than
his lack of capacity for personal connection, when her obsession with the personal causes her to overrelate and over-
elaborate in her nurturing role, while she makes herself sick
with a buildup of rage toward the man she perceives as insensitive to and frustrating of her needs?

At this stage, we don't even know what a good relationship is. Conscious attempts to produce them have not been
successful. Certainly nobody has made relationships more
of a priority than psychologists, psychoanalysts, and thera-
pists in general. Yet their track record for successful marriages and families is certainly no better than the population
generally. Many mental health professionals have dedicated themselves to relationships, learning how to keep an open
flow between themselves and their partners, and it has not
been enough. *We know what the image or ideal of what a*
good relationship is, but we do not know its reality.

Relationships are not a matter of conscious decision. You
can't decide, with a simple intellectual alteration of opinion and understanding, to make relationships a priority.
However, you *can,* perhaps, decide to work on the rebalancing process that will make men and women less defensively masculine or feminine. *This is the challenge and*
the hope.

Telling a man "If you can do those mechanical things so
wonderfully, you could put more time and effort into your

relationships" therefore needs to be recognized as a haunt-
ing, misleading illusion that will drive him "crazy" if he
believes it and "tries." He will come to hate himself more
when his best efforts are unsuccessful. *His underlying process and degree of masculine defensiveness determine the limits of his capacity to relate personally, and not his intentions
or his "priorities."*

15

MASCULINE SELF-DESTRUCTION: A CONTINUING TRAGEDY

Jim Tyrer was one of the best in the world at what he did. His job was to lead the way for his team's running backs and protect his quarterback. Jim did this for more than a decade as the all-pro offensive tackle for the Kansas City Chiefs. "If you could pick a prototype out of a Sears Roebuck catalogue, Jim Tyrer would be it," said his longtime coach.

After his football career ended, Jim Tyrer remained a highly motivated worker and a solid citizen in his community. However, a number of his business ventures failed and left him heavily in debt.

"How's it going, Jim?" the secretary for the Chiefs' coaches asked Tyrer the day before this father of four killed his wife and then committed suicide. "Fine," he answered smiling, after having just watched, with his younger son, Jason, the Kansas City team play Seattle.

Sometime that night, the forty-one-year-old Jim Tyrer "decided" that he could not cope with his failures and that his life was "not worth living." The bodies were found in an upstairs bedroom of the Tyrer house.[1]

James Peres "acted out" the self-destructive, self-hating core of the masculinity in pure form. In 1980 he entered an

Ultimate Urban Cowboy contest and was one of five final-
ists in this casino-sponsored duel with a mechanical buck-
ing horse. His girlfriend was watching as he lost the contest.
He reportedly told her after the winner was announced,
"You don't love me anymore because I didn't win." He killed
himself.[2]

And there was Ronald Miller, an ex-marine and a construction worker, who paid the full price of such masculine
denial at the young age of twenty-three. He died of head
injuries suffered during the First Annual Central Pennsyl-
vania Tough Man Contest because he fought a 250-pounder,
although he himself weighed only 167 pounds.[3]

Vic Ayvazian, too, was a victim of self-destructive macho
toughness. In LaVerne, California, he fought a heftier
patron in a Toughest Cowboy contest at the Last Chance
Saloon. Forty-seven days after being battered, he died, without regaining consciousness, at the County-USC Medical
Center.[4]

On the extreme ends of the gender-defensive continuum,
a self-destructive "psychotic" and explosive potential exists
in the masculine unconscious. These are moments of intense, irrational destructiveness. The feared undertow of
masculinity threatens to be exposed by a triggering event,
creating a "blindspot" and producing an "out-of-control,"
insane outburst. Given proper and sufficient stressors, this
psychotic potential exists in all traditional masculine men.
It is particularly strong, however, among men who ordinarily
are most out of touch and unaware of their deeper unconscious process.

Because the defensive processes underlying gender conditioning are "invisible" and so much a part of a man that
they are taken for granted because they create the sensations of feeling "manly," the "insanity" of the behavior is
rarely highlighted or explored. We feel sorry for men such
as Jim Tyrer and James Peres and assume these are just
extreme cases. However, these experiences of direct "acting

out" of the deeper process that exists in traditional men have much to teach us about the "undertow" that is a permanent, underlying part of all men conditioned in the masculine mode.

These episodes of "temporary insanity" keep out of conscious awareness the inner-forbidden and permit a man to avoid dealing with feelings and impulses such as fear, failure, unacceptable sexual desires, weakness, feminine "feelings," impulses to submit, or intense neediness. An event triggers one or more of these buried feelings or desires and "pushes the button," causing the destructive episode or counter-reaction.

All of the accounts in this chapter were reported in the mass media. Each event highlights an aspect of masculine self-destructive potential.

Masculine Omnipotence and the Fear of Acknowledging Fear

In the Air

There is an *unconscious* equation operating in men between "backing off," acknowledging "ignorance" or uncertainty, and unmanliness. The crew members of PSA flight 182, whose crash claimed 144 lives in the nation's worst air disaster up to that time, according to the *Los Angeles Times*'s front-page account, never told air traffic controllers that they had lost sight of a Cessna they had been warned was just ahead of them. According to the account, they told air traffic personnel that *they thought they knew* where the Cessna was when, in fact, all five men in the cockpit were intently searching for it just moments before the two planes collided. The PSA pilot reported to the controllers that he had "traffic in sight" and would maintain visual separation. At that point the primary responsibility for maintaining a safe distance from the Cessna shifted from the controllers to the PSA pilot himself. The Lindbergh tower controller received an imprecise and uncertain response from the pilot as the distance between the two planes narrowed, less than a minute before the planes collided; the pilot seemed uncertain as to where the Cessna was. The controller, however, was not prompted to pin the pilot down. "He wasn't concerned," he said of the pilot.[5]

Similarly, the recorded conversation between the captain and the first officer of the fatal Air Florida jet crash into the Potomac near Washington International Airport was revealing and chilling in its demonstration of unconscious defensiveness. A half hour before Flight 90 became a tragic statistic, the first officer expressed sensible caution. "Want me to tell ground control that we're 'temporarily indisposed'?" he asked. The plane had been deiced but had again become "very heavy." The tape is silent for twenty-five seconds and then the first officer, possibly embarrassed at seeming to be too nervous, backed away from his concern. "It's twenty-five [degrees]. It's not too cold, really." The captain concurred, "It's not really that cold." Were they mutually engaging in "feigned nonchalance"?

The tape continues, and we hear the first officer commenting on another jet that had just come in for landing. "Look how the ice is just hanging on his back, back there. See that?"

The captain saw the potential for problems. Twenty minutes before takeoff he mentioned "going over to the hangar and getting 'deiced.'" The first officer agreed with him, but then a stewardess entered the cockpit. Apparently she provided a diversion, because they changed the subject and chatted casually. She said, "I love it out here. . . . The neat way the tire tracks form in the snow." The first officer responded, "It's fun." But he couldn't have meant it, because only two minutes before he had been cursing the terrible snow.

Fifteen minutes later the pilot noted the thickening layer of ice again. He commented, "Boy, this is a losing battle here. I'm trying to deice these things. . . . I hate to blast outa here with carburetor ice all over me."

The control tower told him to taxi into position and hold. It still was not too late, as the first officer said to the captain, "Slushy runway. Do you want me to do anything special for this or just go for it?" The captain asked what he meant and the pilot described how he would lift the nose wheel early and "let it fly." "I'll pull it back to about 1.5, supposed to be about 1.6—depending how scared we are." And they laughed.

It was their last laugh. At 3:50 P.M. the plane took off. The gamble they never should have taken ended at 4:01 P.M.[6]

On Land

In the nine hundred accidents in the Los Angeles area studied by a professor of safety at the University of Southern California, 78 percent of the motorcyclists killed wore no helmets. Research in the beginning of 1980 showed that fatalities from motorcycle accidents increased 46 percent after individual states repealed mandatory helmet laws.

In spite of the fact that motorcyclists triple their chances of being killed by failing to wear helmets, and suffer two to four times as many head injuries, freeways continue to be filled with young men who fly down these roads in an omnipotent stupor without a helmet on their heads. They are only a moment away from death that would most assuredly result from an encounter with a car, oil spill, a moment of carelessness, or the sadistic impulse of an automobile driver. These realities don't seem to have much impact on the many "machos" who continue to go without protection.[7]

Desperate Machos

Whose lack of self-awareness interfered with the good judgment that was so badly needed in the case of Dorothy Stratten, *Playboy*'s Playmate of the Year in 1980? Her manipulating, desperate husband initiated and directly played out the tragedy by "using" her while being in seeming complete control of her. He began as "master" and ended up desperately dependent on her and out of control of himself to the point where death became preferable to living without his "subject" or "possession" and with his battered macho ego.

Then there was Dorothy's sophisticated and talented director, Peter Bogdanovich. His brilliance, however, was not enough to inform and warn him of the lethal dangers of one man involving himself with the young and beautiful wife of a possessive, dependent, controlling, and desperate macho husband whose ego was totally tied up with his child-woman-wife. Macho omnipotence must have interfered with his judgment when, while she was still a married woman during the making of the film *They All Laughed,* Dorothy Stratten was invited by Bogdanovich to move into his hotel suite in New York, while her threatened and jealous husband was barred from the set.

Hugh Hefner's magazine is a conduit for masculine fantasies, even though Hefner himself is a romantic idealist and a seeming innocent about the meaning and impact of his product, which promotes and feeds on the cravings and fantasies of the masculine psyche for the distant, perfect "sex object" who is perceived as the way to achieving heaven on earth. He sees himself as a philosopher and cultural liberator. The defensive distortion that *Playboy* magazine feeds on prevents men from growing toward a nondefensive experience of sex that might be less "exciting" but would facilitate a realistic perspective and an elimination of dangerous blind spots in the pursuit of frustrating and self-destructive illusions.

In this tragic scenario, Hefner seemingly functioned with honor. He had played it clean with Stratten and apparently handled her paternally, within the arms of the *Playboy* family. Nevertheless, the irrational cravings and self-destructive tendencies of the men who made up the undertow of the scenario went unrecognized until the dreadful end point.[8]

A similar scenario involving Howard "Buddy" Jacobson, Melanie Cain, and John Tupper played itself out in the "glamorous" world of fashion in New York. Melanie Cain was only five years out of high school when, as an aspiring model, she began her romance with Jacobson, a well-known racetrack figure. He set her up as head of her own modeling agency. Soon her picture was in *Vogue, McCall's,* and *Redbook.*

Then she left Jacobson to move in with her new lover, John Tupper, thirty-four, who lived right down the hall. Shortly thereafter, the beaten, burned, and murdered body of Tupper was found in a crate in a Cadillac, with Jacobson at the wheel. Once again the controller became the controlled and a supposedly powerful, independent, and invulnerable was driven by desperate cravings into irrational violence.

Whose psyche was more disturbed? Was it the lover who omnipotently moved in with Melanie Cain, in the same building as Jacobson, and continued the affair even though he was aware of Jacobson's obsession with her and the fact that Jacobson was continually watching them from his terrace? Or was it Jacobson himself, whose power, fame, and fortune were not enough to buffer him from the agony of loss, and the jealousy that engulfed and destroyed his own sense of judgment and produced his defensive outburst of rage?[9]

Another form of such destructive explosiveness occurred in November 1980, when Ronald Crumpley, a preacher's son, former transit policeman, and the father of three was jailed after a machine gun attack on two homosexual bars in Greenwich Village. The attack left two men dead and six hospitalized. Crumpley's unconscious demons triumphed over his rationality. His father, the Reverend G. Grant Crumpley of New Rochelle, told the press, "He's told me that he hates homosexuals. He was obsessed with it."[10]

Choosing Self-Destruction Over Self-Exposure and Vulnerability

Police are symbols of courage and strength. They epitomize the fantasies of ultimate masculinity. A high percentage of series on television are cop fantasies.

In December 1983, Police Chief Willie Jordan, forty-one, shot and killed himself while playing Russian roulette. Out of "respect" for the dead chief, the coroner had previously said that the gun went off accidentally. However, according to a fellow officer in whose trailer home the game had been played, Jordan "was upset about something" and insisted on playing. The coroner didn't say what the man was upset about.[11]

Unbearable and unexpressed pain and self-hate also caused Highway Patrolman Paul Garrett to take his life in May, 1983. Clearly, death seemed to him a better alternative than the self-exposure, humiliation, and vulnerability that he believed faced him as a result of child-molestation charges. There was deep shame over tarnishing the image of the California Highway Patrol and the fear that he had lost the respect of his father, whom Garrett had spent his life trying to please.

His sister, Nancy, said, "I don't know what my brother did, but I know that he adored children. From the time that he was thirteen, he always had kids around him. . . . Paul never had a childhood. He had to behave like a man at all times. He couldn't cry. He couldn't act weak. . . ." The one thing he did that pleased his father was to become an officer. His sister went on, "It was the loss of respect he couldn't live with." Public Affairs Officer Merle Poppen added, "He was so much highway patrolman, so much blue and gold, that he could not handle it [the arrest] in his own mind, even though he knew the whole office was his friend."[12]

Johnnie Howe, fifty-two, was not a policeman but a construction worker and explosives expert from a small town north of San Francisco. He was distraught over the breakup of his marriage. He responded in pathetic macho fashion to his great pain. One morning in October 1980, in view of his wife on a downtown street, he blew himself up, along with his fourteen-year-old daughter.[13]

Edward Leonard, thirty-nine, was also shattered by the breakup of his marriage. In response, he constructed a San Quentin-style gas chamber in the bathroom of his house. Laying on a cot on a summer day in 1984, he inhaled a deadly combination of cyanide and acid. His was not an impulsive act. In an elaborate scheme, he had rigged a timer to a bathroom light fixture and run an electric cord from the timer to a tiny plastic basket that contained the cyanide pills.

He set off the timer, lay on his cot, and at the designated time, the electric current melted the plastic handle on the pill box, which fell into a small bucket of acid, producing the deadly gas that is similar to that used in the execution of criminals.[14]

Other Variations on the Tragic Theme

A fifty-four-year-old Brooklyn man was shot to death in a Bedford-Stuyvesant luncheonette because he refused to kneel. He was a victim of the deeper macho tendency to resist automatically when feeling "humiliated" by a demand to submit. He was one of six customers at Jimmy's when three young men entered to rob the store. He was among several customers who were ordered to get down on their knees by one of the young robbers. "I don't kneel for any-one," he said, and those were his last words. One young robber responded to this resistance by firing a shot and killing him.[15]

A thirty-two-year-old millionaire investment broker was convicted in October 1984 in New York of shooting a motor-cyclist. The unconscious compulsion to defend masculine ego symbols motivated him. The precipitating element in Granni's murder was that the cyclist had dented his rented Ferrari. They had an argument over the accident in which the seventy-thousand-dollar car was damaged. The jury convicted the millionaire on one count of second-degree murder and accused him of "depraved indifference to human life."[16]

A seventy-two-year-old former New York City fire cap-tain pleaded guilty to murdering his wife. The insatiabili-ty and fragility of the masculine ego was in operation again. At the time of his guilty plea, he told the judge that he had strangled his wife of two days after she made some dispar-aging remarks about his sexual prowess. She had compared him unfavorably with one of her two former husbands.[17]

The Distortion of Close Bonding

Anxiety and resistance to feelings of love and affection among young men are intense. Masculine defensiveness causes men to fear and distort their desire for closeness and affection. In the process of getting their needs for loving met in acceptable "macho" ways, they exhibit pathetic and destructive behaviors.

In order to be able to "love" a woman, they must first make her unreal and put her on a pedestal and romance their fantasy. When they try to get close to other men, often they distort their need in the opposite direction, by degrading and insulting them instead.

When Dr. Donald King, dean for student affairs at Alfred University, telephoned Mrs. Eileen Stevens, it was to tell her of the death of her son, Chuck, who died in the trunk of a car. He had not been deliberately murdered. Rather, he had been the victim of a distorted process of friendship and closeness.

As part of the ritual of proving oneself worthy of the affection and acceptance of fraternity members, Chuck was given a pint of bourbon, a bottle of wine, and a six-pack of beer. With two other pledges, he was stuffed into the trunk of a car. The three were told they wouldn't be let out until they had drunk all the liquor.

When the trunk was opened, almost an hour later, Chuck was unconscious, while his two fellow pledges were having difficulty breathing. Before Chuck could be taken to a hospital, he died.[18]

Chuck Stevens joined a sizable list of young men whose desire to be in a bonded, caring relationship with other young men cost them their lives. For example, Thomas Fitzgerald was nineteen when he was killed by the accidental stab of a knife, plunged through the main artery of his heart during a hazing ritual. William Flowers, nineteen, smothered in a grave he had been forced to dig for himself at a beach during a fraternity ritual at Monmouth College. Bruce Wiseman was struck by a car while walking blindfolded across a highway during fraternity rites, and Fred Bonner was abandoned in the mountains by his Pierce College brothers and fell five hundred feet to his death.[19]

Mark Seeburger, an attractive, athletic eighteen-year-old,

pledged the Phi Kappa Psi fraternity after enrolling at the University of Texas. To gain their friendship, his fraternity brothers forced him to drink more than half a bottle of rum. He died in his sleep in his dorm room from alcohol poisoning.

Not long before that, at the University of Texas, twenty-one pledges to the Alpha Tau Omega fraternity were locked in a room and pelted with raw eggs—almost ten thousand of them—for three days.

At Texas A & M, in 1985, three students admitted they forced freshman Bruce Goodrich to participate in hours of calisthenics during a cadet-corps hazing that caused his death from heat exhaustion.[20]

Senior Steve Ryckman was smarter about it. He lost interest in joining the Delta Sigma Phi house after he developed a burn on his nose from being forced to rub it along a carpet. "They wanted to see how much they could humiliate you. It was degrading," he said.[21]

Notes

1. D. Anderson, "The Tragedy of Jim Tyrer," *The New York Times,* September 18, 1980, p. 17.

2. "Cowboy Suicide," *Seattle Post-Intelligencer,* August 14, 1980, p. A-8.

3. L. Langway, et al., "The Tough Guy Bars," *Newsweek,* April 6, 1981, p. 66.

4. "Man Injured in Saloon Boxing Match Dies," *Los Angeles Times,* April 27, 1981, Part 1, p. 4.

5. "PSA Jetliner Crash: Analysis of Tapes; Impending Disaster," *Los Angeles Times,* October 25, 1978, Part 1, pp. 1, 26–28.

6. P. Battelle, "A Study in Machismo: The Last Moments of Doomed Flight 90," *Los Angeles Herald Examiner,* February 17, 1981, p. A-19.

7. P. Girard, "Rise in Cycle Deaths Linked to Repeal of Helmet Laws," *Los Angeles Times,* April 11, 1980, Part 1, pp. 18–19.

8. T. Carpenter, "Death of a Playmate," *The Village Voice,* November 5–11, 1980, pp. 1, 12–17.

9. "The Adventures of Melanie Cain," *Time,* August 21, 1978, p. 19; A. Haden-Guest, "Love and Death on the Upper East Side," *New York,* September 11, 1978, pp. 42–49.

10. "2 Die in Machine-Gun Attack on Homosexual Bars," *Los Angeles Times,* November 21, 1980, Part 1, p. 4.

11. "Police Chief Killed in Russian Roulette Game," *Los Angeles Times,* December 12, 1980, Part 1, p. 2.

12. T. Barnard, "Death of 'Good Cop, Nice Guy' Leaves a Tragic Puzzle," *Los Angeles Times-View,* May 18, 1983, Part 5, pp. 1, 6–7.

13. "Bomb Expert Kills Self and Daughter," *Los Angeles Times,* October 6, 1980, p. 1.

14. J. A. Cohen, "Suicide in his Homemade Gas Chamber," *Los Angeles Herald Examiner,* June 7, 1984, p. A2.

15. "A Killer Slays Man Too Proud to Kneel," *New York Post,* September 25, 1979, p. 1.

16. "Millionaire Guilty of Killing Motorist Who Dented Ferrari," *Los Angeles Times,* October 5, 1984, Part 1, p. 30.

17. "Probation for Man, 72, Who Killed His Wife," *New York Post,* August 20, 1980.

18. P. Burstein, "Her Son's Pointless Death Spurs an Angry Mother's War Against Fraternity Hazing," *People,* February 12, 1979, pp. 31–35.

19. "Death of a Fraternity Pledge," *Time,* November 22, 1976, p. 61.

20. C. O'Connor, with F. Gibney, Jr., "Death Among the Greeks," *Newsweek,* November 10, 1986, p. 32.

21. "Death of a Fraternity Pledge," p. 61.

PART FIVE

WITH THE FUTURE

16

PURSUING THE ILLUSION OF "HOW TO"

Jonathan, a wealthy man in his late forties, was obsessed with trying "to figure out" why he was depressed; why he couldn't find a suitable, "exciting" woman who also could be trusted enough to make a commitment to her; and why he was alienated from his children and his sisters. Like many highly successful, wealthy men, he was unconsciously controlling, demanding that things be done his way, distrustful, and negative (though he would deny that emphatically because he was convinced that he was generous and good to people and they really liked him). Further, he was compulsively goal-oriented and critical of anyone, including his children, who did not behave the way he believed they should, though he thought of himself as being warm and accepting. His demeanor was cold and preoccupied, though once again he would deny it. He believed that he was caring and involved and no one would tell him otherwise.

He wanted to know why he found the women he dated and who liked him to be boring; why his relationship with his children and ex-wife had broken down and they seemed to be ungrateful and unconcerned; and why he felt depressed and deadened. He wanted "how to" answers that would change all of that and grew impatient when encouraged to spend time exploring these relationships in greater depth. He felt righteously mistreated and not responsible for creating those things that happened to him. He came for counseling to learn techniques to change what troubled him.

Like many other highly successful men, he had become so because in addition to being smart and having a money-making focus, he had masculine defenses to the extreme and was rewarded, therefore, with great material wealth. These rewards made him behave rigidly. He was thus unwilling and unable to even examine, let alone set about to change, himself because he had been greatly rewarded for being who he was.

When clear, practical answers were not quickly forthcoming, he became impatient and angry. His masculine process was preventing him from solving the problems it had created. He couldn't tolerate being out of control, and the absence of clear-cut answers that would solve his problems made him feel that way, so he became resentful of the slowness and "vagueness" of the approach. Thus he terminated therapy.

Jonathan was typical of the traditional man in a relationship. When things go wrong, such a man tries to solve the problem by "doing something" such as bringing a gift, spending more time with his complaining female partner, or taking a vacation. His focus is on logical content solutions that solve the problems for a short time; that is, until the deeper process that caused them in the first place transforms the new content and re-creates the problem. When he spends a few extra hours with his wife or buys her a gift, it satisfies his urgent need to "do something," and there is "hope" and a distraction from the deeper issues, resulting in a temporary easing of tension. This affirms his belief that, indeed, "there are answers" and "more answers."

The paradox here is that the need for a "how to" solution is strongest in the very people whose masculine process is the most severe and who most need to change the process and stop thinking in terms of "how to." In other words, the ones who need to recognize their process the most are the most rigid and therefore the least able to do it. The defensive process that got them in trouble makes it impossible for them to "solve the problem." The compulsion to control, the distraction, and short attention span for others that comes from an intense goal-orientation, the intellectualization, the externalization, and the disconnection that are his defensive hallmarks, create an approach to change that is intellectualized and impatient, competitive and controlling. He comes to believe that more of the same will change things because that approach "works" in the external world. He wants mechanical solutions that will calm his anxiety and lift his mood, while not at all touching the elements of his personality that created the problem and define his masculinity and create the self-validating feelings of "being a man." The dilemma, simply put, is that the "sicker" and more rigid his defensiveness, the less likely he is to recognize the source of his problem or be willing to confront and alter the process that seems to "protect" him.

His problems seem to him to be external and therefore he wants an external answer or "cure"—the demand for which, unfortunately, is part of his problem or "illness": in effect, what got him into the mess in the first place. Typically and continuously he asks, "What should I do about that?" or "What do you think about this?" He is unconsciously blocked from the ability to focus on and see how he is creating the experiences, relationship states, and problems of his personal life. It is "how" he relates and experiences his life and not really what he *does* that is ruining him. In his eyes, however, he has *problems* to *solve* and he wants logical answers. In my work as a psychotherapist I have repeatedly seen a direct correlation between the degree and intensity of masculine defensiveness and the demand for "answers." Conversely, there is an intolerance for process, meaning the capacity to see one's "being" and not just one's "doing" as causing "the problem"; a recognition that the issue is not just "ignorance" or "lack of information"; and a willingness to focus on the "self-awareness" aspects through a gradual unfolding of deeper feelings and inner experience.

The degree of this defensiveness seems to be correlated with the speed and intensity of a man's developing resistance to an approach that he perceives as "not going anywhere"—meaning no concrete advice, no practical answers, and no "how to" with which to solve the problem. In the face of this approach, which focuses on process, he becomes impatient, guarded, and angry. In his mind he is wasting his time.

Whether or not, objectively, therapy "works" is less an issue than the fact that comfort in participating in therapy is a reflection of the capacity for internalization and loosening of rigid masculine defenses. This involves a capacity to let go of control, to suspend a goal-oriented, intellectualized approach and explore inwardly: in a word, to alter his process. Instead, most men until they experience a crisis deny that there are any problems ("Everything's great!") and after a shattering crisis demand a quick, external solution.

When I work with such men I always have a sense that they have one foot out the door and that our relationship is fragile. I can feel the pressure of discomfort, the anger and the distrust.

The masculine male, in effect, pursuing the illusion of "how to's," wants a mechanical solution to a nonmechanical problem. Relationships and other personal problems can't be repaired like automobiles.

When we say that something is "unscientific" or nonobjective, it is equated in our society with "unmanly." It is "tender-minded." Psychology, to the extent that it focuses on the personal and the internal, is experienced as feminine, and therefore unscientific and useless.

An approach that is not scientific is not necessarily unscientific, and that differentiation needs to be understood in order to make sense of the dilemma of masculinity. "Unscientific" implies something irrational, illogical, and invalid. However, there are problems of the life experience where logic and rational understanding are useless, so they don't yield to the scientific approach for examination. Relationship problems, sexual dysfunction, family crises, and other personal problems are all examples of this. The urgency for mechanical solutions, if given in to, promotes *more* externalization.

There is a significant difference between the constructive use of intelligence and the defensive process of intellectualizing. There is a major difference between the rational search for answers and the distanced, mechanical, externalized, and "cut off" orientations of the masculine process where the intellect is used as a protection against internalization. Intelligence can be used to solve a content problem, but the logical approach is ineffective with process. Rather, it is a form of avoidance. "Knowing the answer" is worse than useless. Abstractions serve the defensive purpose of creating distance from feelings and personal connection.

The male, in proportion to his masculine defensiveness, is "out of touch" with process. He is "surprised" by sudden and unexpected turns in personal events because his externalization creates a personal superficiality and an inability to "feel" his experience or even see when he is being manipulated in a personal relationship. He is comfortable with ideas and abstractions, not emotions. He relates in staccato fashion, with no "flow." He is the opposite of the femininely defensive woman who can talk for long stretches of time about her feelings and can probe her experience incessantly but is bored by discussions about mechanical problems or abstract issues.

His personal problems are created as a result of his externalization. The "how to" approach to solve them, therefore, is a manifestation of the defensiveness that trapped him in the first place.

Why the Resistance?

The alternatives to solving his problems are perceived by him in black-and-white terms: Either "I control or I am controlled." Situations are perceived in terms of opposites: "If I'm not masculine, I become feminine. If I'm not logical, I become irrational."

The medical mechanical approach to his problems, for example, is attractive to him because it does provide external, clear-cut, and instant answers. It is "how to" and answer-oriented, with the solutions always seeming to be rational and logical. He would sooner die that way than risk living another way. He can "forgive" medicine every blunder and atrocity, but he cannot forgive an approach that is "unscientific" even the slightest error. Thousands may die in surgery or as a result of their medical treatment, and that is somehow rationalized as acceptable. But if someone is "harmed" by an alternative, healing approach, accusations are instantly forthcoming of quackery and charlatanism that need to be punished.

Becoming aware of process, however, does not mean "getting in touch with feelings," which men are so often encouraged to do and which, upon examination, often proves to be an absurd notion. Only defensive feelings are there if his masculine externalization is very strong. It is no wonder, therefore, that he reacts with suspicion and resistance to the approach that "pressures him" to open up and explore his feelings. Asking the defensively rational man to express his feelings therefore is comparable to telling a feminine woman who is crying hysterically to be rational and then her problems can be solved. Traveling the path back to nondefensive feelings and the inner experience is a slow and fragile journey that will be met with the same degree of resistance as exists in all defensive emotional problems.

Solving the Problem

"Well, what is the answer? Or are you going to give me the typical therapy reply that '*You* have to find the answer,' or 'There is no answer'?" he says impatiently and with irritation. To answer him that the problem is *him*—who he is and not his ignorance or lack of answers—sounds to him like psychobabble. However, for him to ask "how to" is an unconscious form of avoidance and his way of saying, "I don't really want to solve the problem at all. I want a solution that won't touch or change who I am."

The notion of an external "how to" answer that will solve personal problems is one of the great contemporary cultural seducers—what I call the fantasy of "the magic key." This illusion has created a long history of contradictory "how to" books and approaches created in order to feed this need to solve problems externally. In child rearing, for example, the "solutions" vary from "spare the rod, spoil the child" to permissiveness, to a magical combination of both, and then, in frustration, back to strict discipline again. Each new "how to" approach always seems to be the answer for a while, but then it stops "working" for some "unknown" reason and it is time to try something else. Meanwhile, the personal problems become progressively more unmanageable and "hopeless." "How to" panders. It does not alter process, and process is the "invisible" element creating the "problem" or effect.

Women understand the delusion of "how to" most clearly. When a man says, "What do you want me to do?" in times of relationship breakdown, she knows that there is nothing he can *do* because who he *is* and how he relates—and not "what he does"—is the problem. It is comparable to telling the parents of a disturbed child "how to" handle the child when the problems of the child are, in effect, caused by who the parents *are* and how that impacts on the child, and not what the parents are *doing*. If "how to" were the answer to personal problems, *knowing* would produce emotionally healthy children and the psychiatrists, analysts, and psychologists, who "know" the most answers, would be producing the best of them.

"How to" solutions can be valid when they are congruent with inner experience and when the problem results from a lack of information. Otherwise, a "how to" answer may increase the damage, breaking down healthy resistance. "Curing" sexual dysfunction, for example, with "how to" denies the validity of the "symptom" as a statement or reflection of a deeper dynamic to be interpreted and understood and not simply gotten rid of.

Therefore, the "how to" answer that "works" will ultimately worsen the problem by providing a way of running away from a healthy resistance, thereby short-circuiting the potential for personal growth.

It is the interaction and the undertow, and not ignorance, that create the effect or "problem." The urgency for "how to" solutions exists, therefore, in proportion to the degree of one's defensiveness and need to deny one's resistance and inner experience and one's fear of acknowledging and exploring it.

When a problem threatens to expose deeper realities about one's self, the defensive inclination is to search for an external answer. The overweight person or the "failure" wants to know "how to" rather than "who am I and how am I creating this?" Consequently, problems that are reflective of the deeper self often come to be treated as mechanical problems to the degree that there is resistance to self-exploration. "How to" becomes the safe, nonthreatening, "legitimate" avoidance and reassures the person that he or she is "really trying."

The alcoholic who would deny his problem will ask, for example, "How can I control my drinking? Shall I drink more slowly? Shall I change the kind of liquor I am drinking? Shall I start drinking later in the day?"

"How to" solutions are almost always a path away from confrontation with the defensive self and therefore move one further into the pseudo-security of "mechanical" solutions that unconsciously reinforce the problem. They provide false hope that placates temporarily and then defeats. *Each "how to" that ultimately must fail brings a man closer to depression and despair out of a growing belief that "there just is no answer," which produces a sense of hopelessness and of being defeated.*

Because confronting and altering the power and the rigidity of gender defenses—since it is the process that motivates us—is so threatening, we continually search for new mechanical solutions that then create new problems. So, in spite of our "information explosion," we live in an era when drugs are harder, religions and cults are more extreme, personal relationships are more fragile, the breakdown in bonding capacity between the sexes is more severe, personal attention span for one another is shorter, escape through distracting entertainments is more prevalent, and "how to" fads come and go more rapidly than ever.

The man who is embarking on a course or quest for change will have to be aware of and patient with the resistances he is likely to experience inside himself and the intense hunger to escape, to disconnect, to find immediate "how to" answers and to be suspicious of anything that does not provide clear solutions. He will need to nourish in himself a gradual acceptance that unconsciously he creates his personal experience. Change will involve a threat to his image and sense of himself "as a man." Trying to have it both ways, however—change with no threat to the self-image—is the basis for buying into the further creation of "how to" solutions, which ultimately will isolate and rigidify him even more.

17

FINDING THE MIDDLE ZONE

What would the experience of life and relationships be like if unconscious gender processes did not distort and control us and if we were not driven by the defensive motivations that exist on the extreme ends of this polarized continuum?

What would the experience of life be like without the "excitement" created by the pursuit and achievement of gender-validating goals that give us motivation, "hope" and energy, and the sense of having structure, meaning, and progress, even as these ultimately mislead us by creating a nonachievable fulfillment and frustrating end point?

What would the experience of life and relationships be like without the "highs" and "triumphs" that sustain and reinforce us along the way and promote the illusions and longer-range fantasies that we pass on to the younger generation, who then pay the price by experiencing in more pure form the drain and difficulty of achieving still more disconnected, unfulfilling quests?

What would the experience of life and relationships be like without the pursuit of abstract truth in the external world or of great love in personal relationships; goals that progressively are revealing themselves to be elusive and often deluded. The "truths" and achievements of science move us deeper into personal disconnection and environmental and global destruction, even as they give us hope and exhilaration and excite our imaginations along the way. The romantic fantasies of love created by defensive polarizations that shape the course of our relationship life bring us closer to a complete breakdown of communications and capacity for sustained connecting between the sexes.

Clearly, the price has become too great to remain in the "far zones" that move us deeper into the effects and power of disconnection and the intense personal frustrations and pain that derive from fusion craving. The pursuit of these, because they are products of defensive, unconscious motivations where deeper process ultimately transforms and reduces content to a similar experience, has generated goals that are based on distorted experiences of oneself and of external reality. The farther out we are on the gender polarization continuum, the more the course of our lives is controlled by the uncontrollable "drivenness" of these far zones—creating a content of great "highs" and "lows"; anticipation followed by disappointment, with an increasing sense that things are not what they seem to be or were supposed to be. Paradoxically, the farther out we are in these far zones, the greater the resistance, fear, and seeming impossibility of finding our way into the "middle zone": reality undistorted by gender defensive perceptions, needs, and motivations.

We are witnessing the results of extreme polarization in our lives today, but the same defensiveness that created them prevents us from seeing the process within ourselves that created them.

Content changes that are not integrated with process change will prove to be disillusioning, misleading, and a temporary distraction from the progression toward further disconnection and its counterpart: more intense fusion-cravings and relationship breakdown.

When process is not altered and attempts to "solve" the problem are based on changing content, we are in the same hopeless quest and quandary as that experienced by an overweight, compulsive eater seeking "the answer" in yet another diet; the hostile, alienated male/female couple trying to "solve" their problems by altering externals rather than *who* they are and *how* they relate to each other; society trying to eliminate the drug or alcohol problem by lecturing about its "evils" without addressing the undertow that produces this *obviously* damaging craving; medicine attempting to "cure" diseases without altering personal process that creates the illness; government attempting to reverse the destruction of the environment without altering the undertow that generates the socially approved, insatiable need for the "production/consumption" cycle of artificial products; or leaders working to bring about world peace and disarmament without acknowledging and changing the unconscious roots of war, which include, among others, the externalized distrust, fear of connection, and buildup of disconnection tension that creates a craving for oblivion ("excitement"). The "unstoppable" war mentality is a phenomenon that is only a variation of the drug addict's headlong self-destructive compulsions in spite of "knowing better." For a defensively externalized society, a life that does *not* permit escape through disconnection, goal pursuits, and other ways of distancing and escaping from the "terror" and "deadness" of internalization is unbearable. For it, self-destruction becomes a preferable alternative, though the inevitable consequences of that path are defensively repressed and rationalized to the very end, thereby resembling the course and progression of any denied addiction.

Obstacles to Moving Toward the Middle Zone

Transforming the unconscious gender undertow is an elusive and threatening quest because of the reinforcing and self-protective feelings defensive gender-motivated goals provide. Furthermore, its by-products are socially approved and generally not recognized for their pathological nature.

Specifically:

1. Altering process requires a "working through" of defensiveness, which is resisted in proportion to the latter's intensity. An unconscious "terror of change" exists that makes the status quo—even when highly distressing—more appealing than its alternative, much like in any addiction.

2. Social reinforcement is greatest for those who have successfully polarized the most: the goal-driven, disconnected but successul man or the beautiful, manipulative and "powerful" female "sex object," both of whom are heavily rewarded for the results of their defensiveness.

3. Rationalizations and justifications to deny or interpret the growing effects of the defensiveness become entrenched in the form of scientific theories and religious or philosophical belief systems that soothe and placate as they generate false hope, comfort, and optimism. They deflect continuously from the distress of the experience until the painful end.

4. The ego-investment in the self-images created by masculine and feminine defenses is powerful in proportion to the intensity of these defenses. The "pure form" masculine ego is so defensively inflated that it cannot absorb anything but self-reinforcing input. Externalized, mechanistic thinking constricts the boundaries of his perception. Its counterpart, the feminine ego, resists input that will build her own power, aggression, identity, and sexuality because of the anxiety over losing her defensive-self, which gives her a reactive sense of control over her life by being "feminine." Furthermore, her beliefs are progres-

sively committed to the "nonrational"—such as the mystical, spiritual, religious, which become impossible to penetrate, or a commitment to defensive beliefs about "love," "niceness," and the "positive," which blocks out contrary realities.

5. Fear and distrust powerfully underlay the masculine self, which anticipates annihilation upon the loosening of self-protective strategies and beliefs.

6. In proportion to unconscious polarization there is a dread and avoidance of the "boredom" and "deadness" of a life without the defensively created excitement, structure, and ego-validation of polarized goals and motivations.

7. In proportion to masculine externalization, there is a fear and terror of unmanliness that makes his loss of masculinity the most feared alternative. Likewise, a loss of her femininity and the fulfillment of her relationship and "intimacy" pursuits are the traditionally conditioned woman's most feared alternative.

8. "Energy," "purpose," and "meaning" derive from the defensively generated motives. They are powerfully alluring and anxiety-reducing.

9. The confusion between content and process continually seduces us into believing we can alter our experience by replacing or adjusting "content." Because of the invisible nature of process, which defines our sense of self, it is only in short-term, periodic "breakthrough" moments that we are able to see how our process generates our experience of reality. Those moments tend to dissipate before permanent process change can be made.

10. Gender polarization generates, in proportion to its existence, a buildup of tension that compels these damaging behaviors to provide relief from them, much as the buildup of tension in a drug addict that is responsible for the uncontrollable craving.

This "middle zone" is not an entity or a new arena but is an undistorted reality experienced when there is a dissolving of defensive process. This reality is not controlled by the gender defenses that produce insatiable motives and rigidly predictable responses.

Decompression or diminishing of polarized defensiveness, I call "movement into the middle zone," where a reality experience, undistorted by polarization, with motives that are conscious and controllable and produce that which we intend, becomes possible. The middle zone makes it possible to have relationship bondings based on clarity and reality; biological process undistorted by the defensive motivations that create self-destructive habits that emerge to temporarily eliminate the tension buildup of defensive needs and frustrations; a body consciousness rooted in nature as well as in socialization; and a nondefensive synthesis of self and undistorted reality that makes life "controllable" in the best sense of the word.

Because the gender undertow is composed of unconscious, polarized defenses, the process of moving into the middle zone resembles, in kind, the struggle of a neurotic or even a psychotic who is faced with having to give up self-destructive responses that are experienced as self-protective and life-preserving in order to regain "control" in an undistorted reality.

Movement into the middle zone cannot be achieved through intellectualized intentions, because they are simply a form of content change. Nor is it something that can be effected rapidly or at will. Rather, it is contingent upon the acknowledgment and ability to observe one's process, the invisible undertow that is readily seen in others but rarely in oneself.

The middle zone would produce a life experience radically transformed, because there would be no gender-created addictive cravings, compulsions, extreme reactions, or insatiable motivations. Nor would there be the defensive "highs" and "lows" resulting from illusory pursuits and seduction by content and image, because of an irresistible attraction to what "looks good."

The "terror" of that middle zone is that, in spite of the repeated and constricting "dead ends" it produces, we are validated by the fantasies, romance, and "triumphs" that periodically occur to reinforce us. The success-driven man pursues more money and power *even as* he becomes increasingly rigid and unhappy, just as the romance-hungry female repeatedly hits up against the same unfortunate end points but continues to try and achieve the longed-for fulfillment by changing the externals (a "new man").

The middle zone seems, to the polarized, to be at best unexciting and at worst a life not worth living. It is much like the child who shuns fresh orange juice, which is experienced as "boring," in favor of the "excitement" of a soda pop, or would rather eat a pastry than a sweet plum.

The race is on between the addiction created by the polarized extremes and the reality created by lessened defensiveness, which generates, initially, sensations of "unreality" or of "something wrong," much like the alcoholic's experience of reality when sober.

Look at the macho male and the feminine earth mother female and see them as they are, driven by their compulsions and rigidly predictable and stereotyped in their responses, preferences, and habit patterns. Now imagine these free of the damaging undertow that drives them and able to fulfill their potential as people rather than living their lives as defensively driven caricatures. As a male, he would be no longer driven by an insatiable need to prove himself by producing, performing, and achieving. As a female, she would no longer be driven by defensive insecurities regarding her physical appearance, cravings for the fulfillment of unfillable needs for "closeness" and romance; she would be free of her fears of the external world and the countless physical symptoms and ailments that emerge predictably in proportion to the repressions caused by her feminine defensiveness.

Observe the polarized male/female relationship—angry, tense, and conflicted because of the couple's inability to grasp each other's reality. Then imagine them able to see and hear each other accurately and able to relate to each other unselfconsciously and nondefensively. You are picturing the "middle zone."

Imagine a world:

> Without the insatiable, expanding production/consumption cycle, which is replaced by a cycle that satisfies real and nondefensive needs instead;

> In which male/female bonding was based on friendship, not romantic fantasy;

> In which pleasure derived through interaction and not by escape and distraction from reality;

> In which biological function is used for biological necessity and not as a vehicle for reducing defensively derived tension and frustration, nor for "fun" to sublimate the masculine unconscious attraction to oblivion and the feminine craving for fusion;

> In which men and women experience reality in the same way and are able genuinely to communicate without defensively negative (masculine) or defensively positive (feminine) interpretations of reality;

> In which nothing was produced that was harmful to the human organism, not because of righteous morality but because of a renewed capacity to experience an unadorned "instinct" for survival and the human organism's inherent capacity to reject and be repulsed by that which is damaging to it;

In which fathers and mothers equally participated in parenting, and children were not "used" to enhance the parents' ego, or compensate for their frustrations;

In which work was not the way people defined their identity or structured their life experience and where people were able to relate person to person and not role to role or object to object;

In which work and love stemmed from real needs and not defensively compulsive, self-defeating, insatiable polarized motives;

In which science and spirituality were tools to enhance life experience rather than filters of reality used defensively to ward off anxieties;

In which nature was not perceived as a challenge or a threat but as the optimal support system for the biological human animal;

In which male/female bonding was free of the cycles of romantic euphoria followed by disappointment, alienation, and anger.

Put in another way, the middle zone would mean:

Work for work and not for ego or defensive escape;

Biological expression for biological purpose and not tension release;

Love as un-self-conscious connection and caring and not for defensive self-validation or retreat and escape from deeper parts of ourselves;

Science as a tool for understanding the mechanical world and not as a pathway to "truth" about personal experience;

Religious activity as an expression of the mystery and awesome nature of life and not for "salvation," consolation, fear, or anxiety-reduction or retreat from defensive reality;

Parenting that is not composed of overelaborated mothering or disconnected, underelaborated fathering;

Healing as self-awareness and not as an art or series of technical skills by practitioners.

The natural world as a supportive environment and not as a phenomenon perceived as an enemy, challenge, or mystery to fear, conquer, understand, or avoid;

Rationality and intellectualism for understanding and not for distancing through abstractions or the pursuit of "truth" to enhance ego or rationalize the compulsion to disconnect.

Getting There

The Feminine Unconscious Would Move From

1. *Repressed aggression,* which creates a victim consciousness manifested by defensive "niceness," avoidance of conflict and denial of anger and aggression, and a distortedly positive vision of the world.

It would move toward a nondefensive experience of aggression, which would free women from a sense of being "brutalized" in their unconscious quest of the polarized fantasy of an "all-loving" experience.

2. *Repressed assertion,* which destroys the sense of self and self-esteem and paralyzes women in matters of defining their boundaries, limits, and preferences and their ca-

pacity to initiate and pursue separately and comfortably whatever they wish. Thus they would avoid the internal experience of feeling controlled, the defensive need to be related to "sensitively," and the tendency to bond with men toward whom they will react rather than act, and therefore experience a loss of self and sense of rage because of the control.

It would move toward the development of a clear sense of self that is neither defensively rigid nor overblown in counter self-defense nor constantly in danger of dissolving. There would be a sense of being a chooser and creator and not a victim; a person free from feelings of being discounted, negated, controlled, or victimized.

3. *Repressed autonomy,* which creates an exaggerated, defensive need for closeness or "intimacy" in relationships; frustrated cravings for fusion that are defensively sublimated into overmothering, obsession with the religious, "spiritual," or mystical, frustration expressed through eating fixations; longing for the fulfillment of romantic fantasy; and anger over feeling one is taken for granted and treated as a child.

It would move toward a nondefensive autonomy that frees women from the need to romanticize their experience and would facilitate the achievement of a founded, positive sense of separate self and mastery of life.

4. *Repressed externalization* and a *tendency to overemotionalize* her experience under stress and to be engulfed by powerful and painful feelings.

It would move toward a balanced expressiveness.

5. *Repressed sexuality,* which creates a need to associate sex with intimacy and love.

It would move toward an experience of sexuality that is comfortably expressed and "in control" and is neither feared, denied, pedestalized, nor used for nonsexual motivations.

The Masculine Unconscious Would Move From

1. *Defensive aggression,* which as a young man makes him prone to self-destructive acts in the need to deny fear or "unmanliness" and produces a rigidly competitive, hyperaggressive state that makes him self-hating when he loses, alienates him from all other men who are seen as competitors and threats, makes him compulsively vigilant and self-protective toward a world he experiences as a dangerous jungle. It also makes him prone to self-destructive anger when frustrated and unable to resist challenges without feeling self-hating. Further, he is prone to physiological disorders emerging from a chronic self-protective vigilance; an aggression sublimated into a destructive intellectualism, an "attack" orientation toward nature and the environment; and a compulsive, driven productivity for its own defensive sake.

It would move toward a nondefensive experience of the world and others, and a decompression of defensive aggression, which would enable him to move away from chronic vigilance and self-protection. Aggression would be balanced with an equal capacity for unselfconscious interaction and playfulness, a comfortable responsiveness to fear when appropriate, an ability both to tolerate challenges and threats without feeling compelled to respond and to interact without competitive or chronically self-protective feelings.

2. *Defensive assertion,* which creates an insatiable need to control and to avoid everything where control is not possible; and creates a boundless ego and the compulsive need to impose *self* on everything, along with an inability to "hear" and "take in" other people's reality or share one's psychological space with them, in addition to a rigid resis-

tance to submission and an intolerance of ambiguity, vulnerabiity, and indecisiveness.

It would move toward an experience of life where ego protection and validation are not motivators, where the need to be controlling and to impose ego on others or withdraw does not exist, with the self not controlled by a need for defensive validation.

3. *Defensive autonomy,* which produces a craving for self-containment, "distance," and "space"; an intolerance and denial of inner needs and weakness; a compulsion to become totally unneeding; an inability to ask for help; and a movement toward progressive isolation and away from personal connection and the ability to bond closely with anyone, unless it is based on "using" or the fulfillment of an obligation; and a defensively adultlike self-conscious interaction and absence of playfulness.

It would move toward a capacity to freely attach, interact, expose, need, and be playful.

4. *Defensive rationality,* resulting in the use of logic as a weapon, detached coldness, a disdain and distrust of anything "not objective," a propensity to relate to and experience life mechanically, an inability to "sense" and experience life and oneself in nonmechanical ways; an attachment to objects in preference to people; an obsession with abstract truths and information as a pathway to understanding, while disconnecting from the personal and emotional, because it cannot be controlled by the intellect.

It would move toward a use of the rational mind to nondefensively handle the objective world as a useful tool and not as a weapon for self-protection and disconnection, while at the same time being able to experience, intuit, and feel.

5. *Defensive sexuality,* which produces compulsive behaviors and obsessive preoccupation with sex, which is then used in the service of avoiding connection and as a major way of feeling "alive" and achieving tension-release in a "per-

sonal" way, leading to the defensive equation between good sex and a good relationship with a woman.

It would move toward a capacity to experience sex undriven and undistorted by the need for tension release, self-validation or sublimation of the craving for personal connection.

6. Finally, the masculine unconscious would move from a *compulsive and insatiable need for self-validation of manliness,* designed to deny the powerful unconscious female imprint within.

It would move toward an ability to respond fluidly, self-caringly, and based on how things are and not how they fulfill masculine image concern, all of which would free him from the tight, potentially explosive and self-destructively rigid responses of *a defensive man.*

In the process of moving toward the "middle zone," he would move away from:

A craving for excitement that produces a false sense of being alive and compensates for an inability to feel;

An inability to "be" without a function or role;

Impersonal relating;

Unconscious self-identification as a mechanical object;

Defensively abstracted perceptions of life;

The insatiable quest for and belief in external solutions as answers to all problems to a nondefensively connected, noncompulsive, self-caring, and fully conscious state.

18

MAPPING THE TERRITORY: THE PSYCHOLOGICAL EVOLUTION OF THE MALE

The Journey

I mentioned to a friend that I was writing a book on "the new hazards of being male." He is a person I admire for his openness and ability to stay rooted and successful in the "real world" while still remaining in touch with and true to his deeper sensibilities and feelings. I am comforted by the way he laughs at the seemingly endless contradictions and paradoxes involved in the business of *being a man,* which often distress me, and by the way he expresses with an easy self-acceptance his sensitivity as well as his crass macho and ego-centered side. "A decade has passed since the original 'Hazards,' " I said, "and the issues that seemed so straightforward then, now seem so much more deeply rooted and elusive."

His response, I felt, eloquently captured the experience of many men who have made the matter of exploring and changing their experience as men a central focus in their lives.

Looking at my own life over those ten years, and my struggle to break away from the rigid and deadening patterns I observed in older men and many of my peers, and also to avoid the endless and compelling illusions and images that are the bait for most of us, has given me a keen appreciation of the phrase "the razor's edge' '—because that's exactly where I feel I've lived much of that time.

Working to make sure that my personal and inner life is as fully alive and important as the outer one, I often wondered whether I was deluding myself; just trying to be different, superior, or one step ahead—which is classic macho motivation—or if I was unknowingly trying to distance and disconnect, and set myself apart from others.

When I felt I was taking risks and pushing at the traditional boundaries and pressures, I had moments when I wondered whether I was going to go over the edge and do my own brand of macho self-destruction, New Age style. Each time I'd worry that my intuitive sense would fail me, even though it *never* did. Things would always fall into place in a healthier way, though I rarely had the perspective on that until months or more passed by.

Sometimes I'd feel exhilarated and vindicated for trusting that deeper part of myself that pushed me along in spite of the negativity I'd get from some people—and even from myself. There were regularly times too, when I'd feel defeated, disillusioned, and deeply exhausted— and I'd have to be by myself for a while, and shut out the outside input to get the energy going again.

Then there were those times when, like an ex-alcoholic longing to get bombed, I'd want to give in to all the old conditioning—the macho stuff. It seemed simpler to be controlling and dominating, to treat women like sex objects, to hide what I thought and felt, to be tough on my kids Marine Corps-style to get them "ready for life" without worrying about showing compassion or understanding, and generally just play the game of life for the symbols and wins, and not give a damn about the means, or the how's.

Those were the times I felt it would be so much easier to go with the flow and stop messing with the deeper forces of society that move relentlessly on, no matter what any of us thinks or does about them.

Besides, I've also come to know that I'm not that strong. I can't really go too far away from the traditional stuff without getting real tense and scared. In my gut I'm the same as every other man and I try not to forget that I need the games men play just as much as the next guy. I know I'd get bored to death if most men started acting New Age and sensitive. Part of me gets a little ill at the thought.

Even though I know it's dead end and often destructive, part of me loves those macho attitudes—you know, "playing to win," "I'm right, you're wrong," "the truth is out there, let's find it," "money and power are reality— and will make you happy," "look at my expensive new toy," "let's talk about getting laid," "we're the good guys and they're the bad guys," etc. Those games have been going on a long time and so they must be needed—who knows—or maybe they're like training wheels needed temporarily to get us ready for the next stage, whatever *that* is.

Those are my dark moments—but at other times the opening up and letting go of the tight grip makes everything feel so alive and rich, I'd catch glimpses in those times of how it could be in my life.

The hardest thing for me still is to avoid getting caught up in believing that I'm on a mission or a quest for truth or righteousness and that there's an answer somewhere out there to discover that'll make everything fall in place, or that there's a *right way* for men to be and live. I know I'm way off target when it begins to feel like religious preaching.

As a practicing psychotherapist for twenty-five years and as a male who has been on a quest for growth and for discovering the deeper psychological realities and undertow that pulls us along, I am keenly aware of the resistances, fear, and self-deception that are part of the process of personal growth and change. In particular, I see the paradox in my profession of psychotherapy where those who are the most defensive, who need help and freeing the most, are the most vehement and combative in resisting and denying that fact. The healthiest, or least defensive, are those who seem most eagerly and earnestly to expose themselves to the process of therapy and self-exploration.

This paradox operates just as powerfully and poignantly in the matters of the gender issues that I write about in this book. The men and women most deeply embedded in polarized defensiveness seem rigidly to deny it and resist almost *any* input that might produce self-awareness. The extreme macho, in particular, unconsciously often prefers death to self-exploration and change. The extremely feminine woman "seems to" want help ardently, but in her way she too resists powerfully and undermines any change that might diminish the security and power her internalized feminine defenses provide her with, even if she knows how her patterns repeatedly trap her in self-defeating behaviors.

True change, among groups of individuals, therefore tends to begin with those who are already the most open, who perhaps "need it" the least, and then filters slowly toward the more defensive. We live in a complex time when the forces of growth and change and those that operate counter to it seem to be racing neck and neck. We are not as innocent and open as we used to be, but we are also more realistic in our expectations, and we have to acknowledge the profound complexity and subtlety of the problems we face.

Mapping the Structure and Shape of Change

The psychological growth and evolution of the male ultimately will not be founded in external changes or the discovery of more answers, but rather will involve a lessening of the rigid externalized defensiveness that filters and distorts his internal experience and propels him toward disconnection. Change will mean greater flexibility of response and openness to experience—inner and outer, and social change will come from that. As men loosen up, the rigid self-destructive compulsions that are an expression and by-product of the tensions of externalization and disconnection will diminish. Men will reconnect with themselves and others, and *this process* of lessened defensiveness will transform the external reality.

As rebalancing and internalization occur, there will be a decrease in the need and use of biology for tension reduction, such as drinking, compulsive exercise, disconnected sex, and harmful eating habits that compel him by giving him momentary "excitement" or release. Nor will the need for sleep and the expression of passivity be repressed and remain unfelt in the service of defensive masculine over-activity. The passion and excitement of parental bonding will emerge, and men will be highly involved fathers not because they should be but because of the profound fulfillment it brings.

Furthermore, internalization will diminish the work compulsion (work to escape tension) and the use of TV sports and such to disconnect from personal tension. As the work and achievement compulsion diminish, the capacity to find pleasure and satisfaction in a simpler, more personalized lifestyle will develop; this lifestyle will be less dependent on mechanical toys or high levels of external stimulation for pleasure and escape from boredom.

As men and women rebalance and become capable of relating to each other as people and friends rather than polarized genders, the need to escape from each other through ritualized, "serious" interaction with a focus on tension-relating distractions (such as ritualized eating, drinking, shopping, television, and "going out") will disappear. Instead, there will be greater capacity for pleasure in playfulness and interaction between them.

Overall, the *experience* of an undistorted reality will once again motivate the nonpolarized male. How things feel, not how they look or how they allow one to escape internal tension, will be the standard for making choices.

Specifically, in Summary

1. The psychological evolution of the male is not a return to traditional role playing in the nostalgic belief that things were better then; nor is it a New Age fantasy of total male sensitivity, love, and gentleness and an idealistic ideology, Utopian vision, or pursuit of abstract truths.

Rather, it is a movement away from the defensive, rigid, insatiable conditioning that perhaps was once functional for men but now only serves to press them relentlessly into narrow, rigid patterns of behavior that produce their psychological or inner death in the service of a pursuit of an externalized fulfillment and satisfaction that can *never* happen.

2. *What* a man does, does not define him as "macho"; rather, the degree of the unconscious defensiveness that produces his disconnection defines him. A poet or humanist is as likely to be "macho" as a football player or policeman—only with a different surface manifestation or outward disguise.

It is this underlying, polarized defensiveness that ultimately makes the personal experience of all externalized men the same—be they workaholic, alcoholic, abstraction-fixated intellectuals, crusading "house-husbands," brilliant scientists or physicians, or successful businessmen.

3. The lessened defensiveness of the male would connect him to his *experience* of life and make him less vulnerable to engaging in defensive, destructive pursuits that are superficially designed to validate him as a man but in deeper ways serve only to reduce the constant buildup of tension that occurs as the distance from the personal and internal increases.

The lessened defensiveness will diminish the power of the images and symbols of masculinity as motivators of his behavior.

4. As relationships between men and women become person to person, rather than polarized object to polarized object, it will become possible to see how the sexes equally generate and reinforce the behaviors in each other that they resent and feel vicitimized by.

Furthermore, as defensive polarization diminishes between the sexes, romantic attraction as a basis for entering relationships will lose its power—in fact will become anathema. Simply put, romance won't feel good because to be with one's polar opposite, once its reality is undistortedly experienced, will be unattractive if not repulsive. The roller coaster of romantically founded relationships, from romantic euphoria to boredom and then rage, will fade.

5. The lure of "excitement" that produces a lemminglike attraction in men for self-destruction and oblivion (the oblivion of drunkenness, disconnected sex, physical violence, attraction to symbolic experiences, the "thrill" of danger, etc.) because of the urgent and unconscious need to reduce the tension of internalization will diminish. Self-awareness and self-care in the positive sense of creating conscious con-

trol by allowing men to experience themselves without distortion will increase.

In the past, when disconnection approximated totalness, the hunger for excitement (distraction and tension release) in relationship and life-choices increased, as did the tendency to feel bored and numbed when the craving for release and stimulation was temporarily blocked. This unconsciously pushed men into their unstoppable self-destructive patterns.

6. The psychological evolution of the male will alter the traditional way men relate to each other—guarded, self-protective, and distrustful. As masculine defensiveness declines, the distortions and projections produced by defensively externalized aggression and autonomy, which cause him to be distrustful and chronically "on guard," will diminish. It will become possible to separate out real danger from the projected danger that has motivated most men and that is a self-created, self-fulfilling prophecy.

7. Finally, it will become possible to avoid the "web of paradox" that characterizes the lives of traditionally conditioned men, such that the more they fulfill masculine expectations, the farther away the supposed rewards seem to be. Feelings of failure, disillusionment, and a sense of being defeated by the "lies of society," which constitute the inner experience of even the most successful of men who are out-of-touch with their defensive process, will diminish. Fulfillment and satisfaction will become controllable by-products, not wished-for elusive quests.

It is my hope that the "map" I have drawn in this book will make it possible for both men and women to see more clearly the way they participate in generating the distressing experiences of their lives. While the map is not the territory, perhaps it will be useful for taking the steps to enter and negotiate the territory successfully.